MW00686409

Nutrilicious

Food for Thought and Whole Health

EDITH ROTHSCHILD

THIS BOOK IS IN NO WAY INTENDED TO BE MEDICAL ADVICE. ANYONE SUFFERING FROM ILL OR DISEASE SYMPTOMS NEEDS TO CONSULT A COMPETENT HEALTH PROFESSIONAL BEFORE CHANGING ANY DIETARY HABITS.

AUTHOR'S WARNING!

THE AUTHOR ASSUMES NO RESPONSIBILITY FOR THE SIDE EFFECTS THAT MAY OCCUR WHEN EMBARKING ON A HEALTHIER LIFESTYLE, SUCH AS:

- A feeling of buoyancy.
- A sense of being in control of your life.
- A balance between your physical, mental, emotional, and spiritual being, allowing you to become more centered, intuitive and tranquil.
- Every day feeling stronger, more joyful and more grateful to God for being alive.

THE AUTHOR TAKES NO RESPONSIBILITY FOR THE KOSHER CERTIFICATION OF THE PRODUCTS MENTIONED IN THIS BOOK.

ISBN 978-1-58330-300-9
Copyright © 2007 by Edith Rothschild

www.nutriliciousforlife.com

All rights reserved.
No part of this publication may be translated, reproduced, stored in a retrieval system or transmitted, in any form or by any means, electronic, mechanical, photocopying, recording or otherwise, without prior permission in writing from the copyright holder.

Written by: Edith Rothschild
Edited by: Michael Rothschild
Editorial advisor: Tikka Smiley
Designed by: Rivki Bakst

Published by: The Nutcracker Press

Distributed by:
Feldheim Publishers
POB 43163, Jerusalem, Israel 91431
208 Airport Executive Park, Nanuet, NY 10954
www.feldheim.com

Printed by:
Old City Press
Jerusalem, Israel

OTHER TITLES I WANTED FOR THIS BOOK

Cooking Fast in the Slow Lane

Not By Bread Alone...

Stop Pigging Out the Kosher Way!

We Don't Catch Disease - We Eat It!

From *Narrishkeiten* to *Nourishkeiten*
(From Foolish Things to Nourishing Things)

"Tell me what you eat, and I will tell you what you are."

-Jean Anthelme Brillat-Savarin

"If we eat wrongly, no doctor can cure us,
if we eat rightly no doctor is needed."

-Victor G. Rocine

"There is absolutely no nutrient, no protein, no vitamin, no mineral
that can't be obtained from plant-based foods."

- Michael Klaper, MD

This book is dedicated to my beloved granddaughters:

Chani
Shuli
Ruchi
Nechami
Deena
Elisheva
Miri
Elisheva
Michalle
Sheera
Shifra
Shira
Tzipporah

And to my beloved great-granddaughters:

Ayala
Rachie
Shira
Michalle
Shana
Chaya
Rusi
Michal
Gili
Michalle
Noa
Kayla

With the fervent wish that someday, *B'ezras Hashem*, they will pass down their tattered copies of my book to their granddaughters and great-granddaughters.

FOREWORD

We are very familiar with the Torah placement of human life as utmost primacy. It even overrides 610 of the 613 *Mitzvot* (Commandments). However, we are less familiar with the primacy of 'prevention of life threatening situations'. On deeper research, we will discover a wealth of Torah responses on this subject. The obligation of a parent to teach their child to swim is indeed a fulfillment of the principle of preparing ourselves for a life-threatening situation. Prevention always wins over not being prepared. Maimonides offers almost a complete chapter in his legal rulings devoted to the subject of maintenance of excellent health as well as the prevention of illness (Hilchos Deot. Ch. #4). So high is the value of caring for our body that Maimonides placed this Mitzvah in the middle of his description of how a Jew should fulfill it in order to emulate his Creator. Maimonides describes the great importance of under-eating, good digestion and daily exercise. In his recommendations to physicians (Hanhagot HaBriut , Ch. #2, par. 21 & 22) he suggests that foods with medicinal properties should be offered to the patient before selecting medications as a remedy.

This book is about trying to live a life of excellent health and vitality, depending on what choices we make in our eating. It is about the basic idea that almost everything our body needs is found in whole and wholesome food; it is about prevention. The recipes contained in this book can become part of your plan to make better eating choices. In today's complex world, there is no better time than now to make such an investment and commitment, and the first pay-off will be high energy. Basically, our entire health profile revolves around the food we eat and how we eat it. As Maimonides, who himself was a medical physician, has clearly maintained some 800 years ago, that health is largely a choice of life style.

I commend the author for sharing her soul and her experiences, and for not holding back her addition of humor to her recipes. Get ready to savour the mouth-watering experience of G-d-given whole and wholesome food. L'Chaim! To Life!

Rabbi Jonathan Rietti, Senior Lecturer, Gateways

ACKNOWLEDGMENTS

My thanks and appreciation go forever and a day:

To my husband, Kurt, whose love, generosity and unstinting support all through our "stages" and "ages" has made this book a reality.

To my mother, Joanna Hertz, *Zichrona Livrocho*, who instilled in me at a very young age the love of nature and all things green. She was way ahead of her time and never missed a lecture by Dr. Bircher-Benner, the world-renowned Swiss pioneer of a raw food diet. She fed us muesli made with raw oat flakes, ground hazelnuts, shredded coconut, anise seeds, raisins and pure sugar from grapes.

To my son, Lenny, whose knowledge of printing was of invaluable help to me, and who graciously and patiently kept supplying me with truckloads of paper to feed my ferocious printer.

To my son, Michael, whose inspiration and steady encouragement kept me going to the finish line through many days of discouragement.

To the laptop brigade, who early on transferred my first and feeble attempts at writing about 'culinaria' from my technophobic 20th century brain to my dumb computer, which has absolutely no sophistication or discernment: Malka Hollinger, Elisa Usher, Ariella Nagel, and Rochelle Rutman.

To Angela Roberge, another vegan to come my way, who bravely kept commuting for a while from Aurora to Toronto, through sunshine and snow drifts. Her spirited and adventurous nature made working together real fun.

To Ora-Lea Tewel, without whom the last part of this project would have been unthinkable, and whose quiet and steady demeanor, intelligence and boundless energy has made it a pleasure to reach the home stretch.

To Tikka Smiley, who meticulously proof-read the manuscript and applied her excellent editing skills throughout, and who was an all-around invaluable support to me. With her comic personality and vegan lifestyle, we spent many hours working together on fun, food, and its function.

To Rivki Bakst, the graphic designer, who quietly and with steady determination has given this book its professional look and visual flavour and, thus, beautifully captured the whimsical spirit it represents without jeopardizing its profound messages.

To Sandra Temes, who herself wrote and published two cookbooks and, with her loving mother-like devotion and down-to-earth approach, kept me focused on the real stuff and wouldn't let me fly off into the yonder world of culinary imagination. How can I ever thank her for having voluntarily arranged the entire index to this book!

To Elke Pelt, the quiet, efficient and popular secretary to my husband, who's readiness to be of assistance to me anytime as well, goes far beyond the call of duty.

To Noreen Gilletz, for so generously sharing her keen knowledge as a most successful and popular cookbook writer.

To Yaffa Fordsham, whose freely-given professional advice is matched only by her lasting friendship.

To Ariella Samson, gourmet cook and cookbook collector extraordinaire, for her kind advice.

To Adelia, my kitchen right and left hand, who so diligently and faithfully helped me with most of the recipes over and over and over again.

To Daryl Vernon, who brings every Thursday the best and most beautiful organic produce to my door, including all my groceries (organic) and all with a hechsher (kosher certification).

To Uriella Sagiv, my charming Jerusalem friend, formerly with Simon and Schuster, who in her very cozy kitchen in the "Old City" gave me many great editorial ideas.

To Shoshana Hayman, founder of "The Life Centre for Parent Education" in Israel, for being so generous and supportive with her sage advice as a most successful and innovative publisher.

To Sarah Shapiro, an accomplished and popular writer of many books herself, who encouraged me at an early stage to share my book with the world. Incidentally, her father, the late Norman Cousins - long-time editor of the Saturday Review of Literature - and who later switched to becoming a famous whole health aficionado, was a most inspiring guide to me in the beginning of my own journey towards whole health.

To Chana Bracha Siegelbaum who, with her love of the Holy Land and all its natural bounty, e-mailed me spiritual sustenance all the way from the Judean Hills of Gush Etzion - Bat Ayin.

To Dr. Richard Schwartz, president of Jewish Vegetarians of North America and the Society of Ethical and Religious Vegetarians, whose friendly and enthusiastic e-mails gave me tremendous moral support.

To Dr. Edward Bach, M.D. (1886-1936), a great doctor and a greater humanitarian, whose natural system of Flower Remedies keeps me emotionally balanced when things get too hectic.

To Dr. W.H. Schuessler, M.D. (1821-1898), who with his biochemic system of medicine founded a healing modality consisting of twelve tissue cell salts (all present in our bodies) to cure minor ailments and imbalances and major painful symptoms. I am forever grateful to have these two self-healing modalities at my disposal whenever I need them, so that I can get on with the "good life".

To all our Friday night guests (and they know who they are) who over the years graced our *Shabbos* (Sabbath) table, helping us to celebrate the special aura of *Shabbos*. It is they who gave me the incentive to stay on my toes with my culinary creations and who gave me the opportunity to concoct new and, sometimes, fantasmagoric combos, and who seem to go home happy and well-fed vegetarians, if only for one night.

To all my friends and acquaintances, who never tired of asking: "So when is your book coming out?" and who never gave up on me.

And finally, with never enough words of gratitude to Hakodosh Boruch Hu (God) who, with His infinite Grace, Blessings and Assistance, has steadily held my hand from day to day to make my dream come true.

CONTENTS

INTRODUCTION

I am not really a health nut, but I am nuts about health. Health nuts are disciplined; I'm not. Health nuts have fixed ideas; mine evolve constantly. I am always amazed when I find out that most people I meet do not make the connection between healthy eating, good lifestyle habits and good health. In this book, I will share with you, besides the recipes, my knowledge and my personal experiences on the subject. Sometimes I think I know more about it than is good for my health. The emphasis throughout the book is on several ideas: 1) To inform how to achieve a healthier lifestyle, thus possibly circumventing the debilitating chronic diseases and premature deaths so prevalent in modern society today; the buzzword is "Prevention". 2) To de-mystify "health food", thereby making life in the kitchen less stressful while maximizing the use of the time spent there. 3) To share the notion that depending on what kind of food we eat and how we eat it can elevate us to a higher level of awareness, beyond satisfying our hunger, desires, cravings, and epicurean excesses. To put it another way; a side effect of healthful eating can add a spiritual dimension to every-day-living which, in turn, could keep one ageing gracefully with whole health (aside from getting a good seat in heaven).

Having suffered pain as a frequent occurrence for untold years, I also want to share what I have learned on the road to a more pain-free existence with God's incredible and consistent second-to-second help. Pain is always and only a symptom; it is not a disease. We need to treat the "causes" of our pains and not the effects.

What we eat can be our first line of defense. Food is a conductor of energy, and the kind of food we ingest not only influences our physical state of health but is also a factor in how balanced and integrated as human beings we can become in order to enable us to maximize our individual potential. Our bodies, being organically programmed for health and survival, need live food with live enzymes and other nutrients to survive with health into old age. I am not suggesting that all pains and illnesses can thus be alleviated. Food, in and of itself, does not make us well; our bodies heal themselves. The idea is to eat a diet that does not hurt us, while at the same time providing all the nutritional requirements for growth, health and successful aging. (Please read **A Brief Autobiography**, on page 12!)

As the book's title suggests, the recipes are made up of only pure and natural ingredients. All the products in the recipes have kosher certification. Living in a metropolitan city, I am fortunate to have available all kosher health food products; however, those living in smaller areas can perhaps avail themselves of these products through company websites and reputable health food stores.

Most of the recipes are geared to easy, quick and simple preparations. But at the same time, clear instructions are given as to how a number of the recipes can be taken to various levels of creativity, sophistication and elegance. Knowing how difficult it is to change one's eating habits, I have tried to take the middle road, away from the extremes of some of the diet gurus that are considered so trendy in today's society. There's a lot of stuff out there today that is more NEWtritious than NUtritious. It is my fervent hope that this book will enable all those interested to get the most benefits for a healthier lifestyle for themselves and their families in the least amount of time and effort in the kitchen.

Against the backdrop of the atrocious North American foodie scene, I have offset the novelty and discipline of dealing with only 'whole food for whole health' in my recipes with occasional dollops of humour, as this is as important an ingredient to sound health as the ones in the recipes. At the same time, I have tried in my aphorisms to couple timeless and profound truths with my own brand of fun and pun, hoping that some of the resulting irony will make for delicious fare for the reader. Whenever and wherever I break out into spells of rhyming, I humbly admit that this is a severe case of having been a frustrated poet all my life.

From the moment we are born, food is a basic and unavoidable reality in our life. Our attitudes towards food have many physical, psychological, emotional, cultural, and social overtones. A problem arises only if and when we cannot differentiate between what we need, what we want, and what we crave. In our modern culture, it is not easy to maintain sound health into old age, since anyone on the standard American diet is overfed on animal protein and undernourished on whole natural food. Over the years it has been well documented that the low fibre, high fat, high cholesterol and high protein diet of most North Americans and Westerners is largely responsible for the high incidence of chronic and degenerative diseases, leading to premature disability and death. Cancer, heart disease and strokes, osteoporosis and arthritis, diabetes, irritable bowel syndrome, dementia, and more, are to a great extent the direct or indirect result of the SAD (Standard American Diet). This diet is modified and refined by being commercially processed with chemicals and synthetic additives, such as: colourings, preservatives, stabilizers, hormones, antibiotics and more. It can also be genetically modified in this era of Corporate Bio-technology, and furthermore zapped with irradiation. Such a nutrient-depleting, devitalizing, toxin-leaden diet robs the food of its intrinsic and natural wholesomeness and cannot promote sound health and longevity because it is not life-supporting. It is well documented by countless scientific studies done over many years that consistently ingesting such a toxic diet has long term deleterious effects. (Please read **A Trip To The Supermarket, or The Seductive Evils of Processed Food, or Why Bad Food Tastes so Good**, on page 14!) For further reading on this major concern of mine, please check the bibliography for the books by: Dr. Joel Fuhrman, M.D., Dr. John A. McDougall, M.D., and others. Dr. Fuhrman puts it in a nutshell when he writes: "Stop being brainwashed by the false notion that only animal food contains adequate protein."

This book has no particular eating plan or diet program. In it you will find all the recipes you need to embark on a better lifestyle. The ingredients contain all the necessary nutrients, enzymes, fibre and low calories that are missing in a conventional diet. Following a more natural and whole diet may possibly, and always with the gracious help of God and perhaps a few good 'designer genes' thrown in, prevent one from falling prey to the aforementioned degenerative diseases. Just listen to your body - it knows best! Last but not the least, eating this way is the safest, most successful and painless way to an all-time-automatic-weight-control-system, where the more you eat of the "right stuff" the more you can lose in weight.

Ideally, all our food should come from the middle range of the food spectrum. The diagram below will acquaint you with this theory and its underlying principles, so that you may understand the premise of this book.

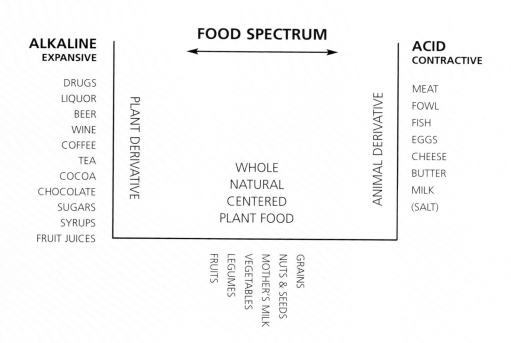

FOOD SPECTRUM

ALKALINE
EXPANSIVE

ACID
CONTRACTIVE

DRUGS
LIQUOR
BEER
WINE
COFFEE
TEA
COCOA
CHOCOLATE
SUGARS
SYRUPS
FRUIT JUICES

PLANT DERIVATIVE

WHOLE
NATURAL
CENTERED
PLANT FOOD

ANIMAL DERIVATIVE

MEAT
FOWL
FISH
EGGS
CHEESE
BUTTER
MILK
(SALT)

FRUITS
LEGUMES
VEGETABLES
MOTHER'S MILK
NUTS & SEEDS
GRAINS

In the middle range is the food closest to the earth, most natural, whole and pure. The more we branch out in our eating habits to the right or to left of center, the more we unbalance the acid-alkaline scale in our bodies. Without wanting to become too technical, I want to share with you the dynamics of this equation because therein lies the secret of eating "right" in order to build and maintain sound health and longevity.

For our bodies to operate and function optimally, the acid-alkaline level in our blood and other body fluids has to maintain a good balance, otherwise free radicals will develop internally which will jeopardize out health and make us age faster. Free radicals are the guys that attack and weaken the good soldiers in our blood and immune system. Sorry to be so blunt, but they can be likened to any other terrorist group, where one never knows when and where they will strike; and they do their work silently and methodically. As we become saturated with the food from the right or left side of the spectrum or both, there is neither appetite nor desire to partake adequately from the "good" healthy stuff in the middle range of the food spectrum. Therefore, in order to maintain our health into old age, we should be eating a diet that is more alkalinizing (fruits and vegetables) than acidifying, and that is the food from the middle range.

Unfortunately, the SAD (Standard American Diet) has totally reversed this process, with the consequence of creating harmful internal radical oxidation (free radicals) for anyone regularly on this diet. This, more than anything else, has led statistically to the chronic conditions mentioned before. The further we move away from the middle range of the food spectrum, the more we will eventually jeopardize our health, where neither physical well-being nor emotionally balanced behaviour can be maintained in the long run. The more we eat from the middle range, the more centered and balanced will be our bodies, our thoughts, our feelings and our behaviour. The food from the middle range of the spectrum will supply all our nutritional needs. Plant-based diets tend to be low in fat and high in fibre. Eating this way will furnish our bodies with the highest quality fuel available to us for potential maximum health. Thus we become less vulnerable to environmental, genetic and other internal and external influences. Many people pay more attention to the fuel they put into their cars than what they put into their bodies.

Fruits and vegetables, being high on the totem pole of a whole-health diet, contain a large variety of vitamins, minerals, enzymes, proteins and phtyochemicals that synergistically protect against cancer and other "modern" diseases. Scientific studies are continually uncovering new data as to the general and specific healing powers of fruits and vegetables and how they can reduce the ravages of eating a commercially processed diet. Whole foods have all their nutrients in the right proportions and need no ingredient list. They are cultivated by the Master Grower who needs neither glossy packaging nor T.V. commercials to promote his products. On His diet plan there is no need to study elaborate and impressive-looking labels, called "NUTRITION FACTS". Isn't life complicated enough without having to figure out how many percentages you have left to eat each day of: total fat, cholesterol, calcium, sodium, carbohydrates, dietary fibre, sugars, protein, blah, blah, blah? You can't beat the self-employed Master Nutritionist who created His computerized dietary program thousands of years ago without having to be sponsored by any one of the conglomerate giants of the food industry. Since food is a conductor of energy, it is incumbent on us to choose "live" foods with live enzymes as much as possible. The best food in terms of building and maintaining health is always fresh food using the purest and highest quality ingredients, and the best results will always be accomplished with the simplest ways of preparation, where less can be more.

It is a basic value in Jewish ethics and a positive Torah commandment that we guard our health in order to be able to fulfill as many God-given commandments as we can. The more balanced we can remain physically, the more will we be able to grow spiritually - **and that's what food is all about**. A diseased and painful body will have great difficulty supporting a physically, mentally, emotionally and spiritually healthy integrated being. There are many references in our scriptures as to the sacredness of food. Since food is God-given and alive, and we make a *bracha* (blessing) over it before we eat and when we finish, I maintain that wasting any of it therefore is sacrilegious and contrary to Torah values. I respect the food and the time and effort I invested in preparing it, and I don't want it to end up in my garbage bin.

One of our greatest sages, Maimonides, who practiced medicine in the 12th century, has put down specific guidelines for us as to what, when, how and how much we should eat in order to maintain our health, and trust me! triple-decker cheese sandwiches and pizza were not part of his dietary recommendations. Anyone versed in Torah and Talmudic studies will find many references by our sages, throughout the centuries, teaching rules about the importance of physical health and healing as it relates to cleanliness, physical fitness and food. To read some of this ancient literature today would have you believe that it was dropped in your mailbox or appeared in your Internet Hotmail Inbox as a promotional ad from a diet workshop. These health recommendations by our sages were not meant to teach about body image, the merits of walking to nowhere on the 'Dreadmill', building muscles, keeping the body "young" to go with that new facelift, or getting from a size 16 to a size 8. They were meant purely as a stepping stone towards the attainment of spiritual fulfillment in the service of God.

Come to think of it, the Children of Israel in those days had it much better than us 21st century frenetic, cell phone-toting, unanswered e-mail-drowning, microwaved-eating humanoids. It is true, they did not have all the choices that we have today, neither in terms of what to eat nor where to eat it. They never had the temptation to go to a Deli for a hot pastrami sandwich or a hot roast beef sandwich, or for a plate of chopped liver with oil oozing all over it. Or, come Motzei Pesach (at the end of the Passover holiday), to stand in line for a fresh hot pizza. Or, come Sunday-Brunch-Time, to overeat on bagels, lox and cream cheese in some noisy, overcrowded Dairy Restaurant, while the kids are happily spilling their chocolate milk or Coke all over the table, and dunking their limp cold fries in blue ketchup.

Instead, the Children of Israel were commanded by their prophets to: "…*put in the wheat in rows and the barley in the appointed places and the spelt in the border thereof…*" and "*Take though also unto thee wheat and barley and beans and lentils and millet and spelt and put them in one vessel and make thee bread thereof*". That was very *avant-garde*, considering the dreadful invention of sliced white bread a few thousand years later.

When we eat mostly whole and natural food there needs to be no waste whatsoever. Every scrap of food can be recycled by adding it to the next day's soup, grain dish, stew, stir-fry or pasta, or thrown into a salad to add new interest. Leftovers can be the stuff that patties are made of, and they make particularly good and attractive appetizers. I am a real klutz when it comes to painting and drawing, but I love to paint miniature pictures with my food. Of course my food ethics may not coincide with that of the "younger" generation, as I grew up with the dictum: "Waste not want not"; and I seem to be stuck with it. It gives me every time such a great feeling - 'like, I think it's so cool'- to use up all my leftover bits 'n' pieces and scraps in one delicious, attractive and creative way or another, and not to have to waste them.

I fully realize what a challenge the above 'way of life' represents to today's multi-tasking super-power women; those that pursue outside careers besides homemaking, as well as those who choose home-making as their sole careers. But when all is said and done, there is no better life insurance for ourselves and our families than to pursue the most natural lifestyle we can handle. However, this takes knowledge, motivation and commitment. Health is never guaranteed or permanent, but God gave us the tools to prevent illness in many or most cases and to heal naturally when we have unbalanced the divinely-given scale. Building health is a life-long, never-ending process and there is no cookie cutter solution. Each person has to find their individual health program according to their particular constitution, situation, needs and life goals. The human condition makes life always a stressful experience; but our life could and should be more than only a pain-free existence. When we give due respect to our foods, use them to maintain our health for as many years as we are given, we have the potential to grow every day in body, mind and soul. With God's help, we will have the strength, the patience, the tranquility and the joy to keep cooking fast in the slow lane until '120'.

I realize this introduction is rather heavy-handed, and may even be scary to some. But now that I've had my say and you read it to the end, or so I wish to presume, I will reward you with a more light-hearted ending.

Come listen to my story
And listen to it well
About the book you're holding
It is I want to tell.
Too bad you had to wait so long
It seemed like endless years
Of slave labour in my kitchen
With testing, tasting and tears.
It's all about good cooking
But in it you'll find much more
With bits 'n bites 'n tidbits
And sayings and stories galore.
There's something here for everyone
For body, soul or mind
You can use it in the kitchen
Or a bedtime story find.
The recipes aren't sinfully rich
In this healthy, gourmet cuisine
Instead of fats and sugars
You'll feast on veggies and the bean.
It's elegant, fast and simple
The preparations are quite plain
But you'll get lots of energy
'Cause it's fuelled with high octane.
The main thing is from the cooking
And the eating you'll get pleasure;
Don't shelve it with your other cookbooks
Use this one to full measure!
And if you really don't want to cook
Or feel you are not able
Just take this book and display it
On your kitchen or coffee table!

A BRIEF AUTOBIOGRAPHY

My preoccupation with holistic health is simply a matter of survival. For 25 years I suffered from dislocated disks, resulting in severe joint inflammations and chronic back pain, which in medical jargon is labeled as osteoarthritis. Being a rather independent person, the fact that at times I could not dress or feed myself was hard for me to bear. I tried the medical route, but that proved to be a (not so) merry-go-round. Consultations with various top specialists left me with a discouraging assortment of medical opinions, diagnoses, and prognoses. I was told that eventually I would need surgery and that on a good day I might be able to shuffle out of bed long enough to make supper for my husband. (No doctor ever asked who would prepare my meals). I was started on a course of medications, such as muscle relaxants, anti-inflammatory pills, and painkillers. While they looked attractive in their rainbow colours, two-tone pastels and easy-to-swallow shapes, my stomach did not like them.

It was then that I came to several conclusions. Number one: God did not put me into this world to be a semi-invalid. Number two: Since I had many joints in my body, but only one stomach, I would have to find "alternative" means to overcome my physical problems. Number three: Only by taking charge of my own health could I hope to gain some control over the quality of my life. My choice to forego the allopathic (doctor-prescribed) drug scene, withstand the social and medical pressures to stay with it and turn to God's natural drugstore to allow the healing powers He built into me to take over, turned out to be one of the daily, innumerous, heaven-sent blessings in my life.

My explorations led me more and more towards a holistic, vegetarian lifestyle. Through perseverance, trial and error, I learned over the course of many years which foods, diets, remedies, healing techniques, therapies, and modalities would be good for me and which ones I should avoid. This, in the late seventies, was a lonely, uphill struggle, one that was not yet fashionable in mainstream society. I became informed and educated about Alternative Health Care. Since I eat at least three meals a day and didn't have an in-house health professional to advise me daily, I started on a course of self-healing with the basics - learning what and what not to eat for my particular condition. I also had to become informed and discriminating about which healing (and self-healing) modalities would be consistent with and permissible to my Torah values.

Am I cured? I do not believe that there is a permanent cure for anything as long as we live. Life is perpetual motion and ever-changing, and therefore always a stressful condition. But our bio-computers have the built-in software that automatically strives for homeostasis (balance) every second of our lives. The main thing is that we do not disrupt the flow of the God-given energy, which is our life force, through an unhealthy lifestyle and a negative mind-set, resulting in a lack of emotional poise.

To remain reasonably healthy is a life-long commitment that requires our full participation in our health maintenance on a daily basis. It is not necessarily the easiest road to take, as it requires making informed, educated, and intelligent choices from day to day, and sometimes from hour to hour. But if we make the effort, the innate wisdom of our bodies will guide us on the road to self-healing, where body, mind, and spirit become one whole, balanced, and integrated unit. And only then can we truly serve God with the particular uniqueness that He bestowed on each of us.

MY ELEVEN-DAY WATER FAST

OR

THE STUFF MY DREAMS WERE MADE OF

Many years ago, I underwent an eleven-day water-fast at a small Fasting Institute near Cleveland, Ohio, in order to de-toxify and thereby rid myself of a 25-year bout with chronic arthritis. On the first day, as I was lying in my small room, I found myself having to make an important decision. My alarm clock, ticking away relentlessly and cockily on the tiny night table, was a constant reminder of the real world outside and of my voluntary exile, in stark contrast to the quiet and subdued atmosphere hovering in my room. Once the clock was silenced and out of sight in a bottom drawer, I could turn to the business at hand, which was doing nothing with my time. This proved at first very difficult and stressful to a sociable, go-go person like me. But apparently my unconscious mind knew exactly where it wanted to go, and I found myself doing the next best thing to eating, which was hallucinating about it.

I remember the first day dreaming about hot mushroom crêpes drenched in a rich, smooth mushroom sauce, the way they were always served by the caterer in our *Shul*, (synagogue). I could see them, smell and taste them. The following day, which was a Friday, I fantasized all day about chicken soup with *knaidlach* (dumplings). As the aroma of the yellow-golden broth wafted up to my nostrils, I could even visualize a few rings of fat bumping into each other on the surface of the soup. I could feel the *knaidlach* dissolving on my tongue, soft as a summer cloud. Some kindred spirit had also sprinkled fresh, chopped parsley and dill over the soup, adding immeasurably to my aesthetic and gastronomic pleasure.

But that kind of culinary ecstasy lasted only two days. Everyday, as I continued my solitary water fast, my mind became clearer and I was able to devour one health book after another and listen to countless audiotapes on the subject of dietary and lifestyle changes, healing and self-healing - and I became hooked.

On the twelfth day, when my fast was broken, I was given a four-ounce glass of freshly squeezed orange juice for breakfast. The effect was electrifying. As I sipped the heavenly-tasting elixir, I felt a surge of energy flowing through my whole body all the way to my fingertips and toes. Unfortunately, it didn't last long, and for the next 2 1/2 hours I had to contend myself with dreaming about the four ounces of carrot juice that would be my lunch.

The rest is (my) history, as I walked out of there, weighing much less than when I signed in. But what I lost in weight I gained in so many other ways. I had acquired born-again taste buds. This would allow me to embark on a more natural and wholesome diet without the damaging excess of animal protein and conventionally processed food. It would eventually also help me to forego allopathic medicine in favour of alternative and complementary medicine. Thus, I started on the long and arduous road towards healing and, ultimately with the ever-present and moment-to-moment help of the Almighty, acquired the knowledge for self-healing and, in some small measure, for helping others who are suffering.

HEALTH WARNING:
No one should do a water or juice fast for more than one day without the advice and supervision of a competent Health Professional.

A Trip to the Supermarket

OR

The Seductive Evils of Processed Food

OR

Why Bad Food Tastes so Good

Do you ever wonder why supermarket buggies are so big? I can hardly maneuver mine around, as I seem to have a knack for picking one that always wants to go in the opposite direction of where I want to go. When standing in line at the check-out counter, what is there to do but to peep into other people's buggies, and what I find there is that the fuller the buggy the less healthful is the food in there. My buggy has mostly paper goods, white vinegar with which to wash my vegetables, sugar cubes to add to my fresh flowers, and organic fruits and vegetables. While we are in the supermarket, let me tell you that I am not ever charmed by the miles and miles of meticulously-organized, spanking-clean, attractively-presented, consumer-friendly, splendiferous display of food stuff, with its eye-catching, glossy, shimmering gold and silver and multi-coloured wrappers, boxes and packages. I actually have a conspiracy theory about the relationship between the food industry and the general public but, sorry, I'm getting ahead of myself. With degenerative and terminal diseases and obesity in North America on the rampage and the healthcare system badly in need of healing, it behooves us to examine the evils of processed food from a little closer up.

In general, North Americans are over-fed and undernourished on the SAD (Standard American Diet). This is a heavily processed diet where most of the essential nutrients have been removed by the manufacturers and substituted with chemical additives in order to make their products look more attractive, have a longer shelf life and be financially more lucrative. This process continuously adds inorganic matter to those who eat this diet, for which their bodies were not programmed. Not being live, whole or natural food, it is neither health nor life-supporting. **Because of our natural programming by the original Master Programmer, any of the nutrients that the manufacturers remove from their products have to be made up by our bodies every time we eat and, thus, are constantly being leached from our bones and organs.** Since inorganic matter cannot be converted by our bodies into nutrients, it sooner or later becomes toxic overload, leading to ill health or worse. Besides the host of chemicals, processed food is loaded with salt, sugar, hydrogenated fats and refined oils.

I once tried to acquaint myself with some of the thousands of food additives currently in style. This was no easy task since having chosen English Literature in my undergraduate studies, I missed out on "Chemistry 101". I gave up after I counted about seventy-five additives. Here is my short list and, I promise you, I didn't make it up: Propylene glycol alginate, polysorbate 60, monocalcium phosphate, thiamine mononitrate, acetylated tartaric acid, chloropentafluoroethane, carboxymethilcellulose, silicon dioxide, monosodium glutamate, disodium ethylene diaminetetraacetate, disodium guanylate, calcium chloride, sodium benzoate, calcium silicate, monocalcium phosphate, sodium tripolyphosphate, acetate, zinc sulphate, calcium pantothenate, pyridoxine hydrochloride, benzoyl peroxide, ammonia alginate, disodium phosphate, Frankly, I wouldn't want my kitchen floor washed with any of that stuff. You could just as well melt down your old nylon blouse or use some anti-freeze from your car and add it to your soups.

Here is some more food for thought. When we support the cult of consumerism we make the food industry richer and ourselves poorer in terms of our health. The food industry uses the most sophisticated methods in order for the consumer to be unable to stop eating their respective products. If you carefully read the labels on processed foods, you will often read: "**Artificial flavour enhancers added**". What the uninformed and unsuspecting consumer doesn't know is that these flavour enhancers are **chemical appetite stimulants**. They serve only to create a continuous biochemical dependence on each product. Do you know anyone who can eat just one salted, roasted peanut or just one barbequed potato chip?????????? (Even my keyboard is binging). No one needs to feel guilty about not having enough self-control when munching through a bag of chips or cookies in one go; they have merely been chemically wired for it by the manufacturers. A healthy habit to start while moseying around your supermarket would be to start reading the fine print on all products so that you won't be fooled by the **bold** print. If you are over forty, get glasses instead of *Botox*! Here's another bit of unsolicited advice. If you want more whole health from your packaged food try to buy only products that have no more than five items listed on their ingredient list!! Whenever you feed yourself or your family processed food, you, your children and your children's children will be munching on oodles of chemicals in one product. The food industry lives and thrives on the ignorance or indifference of the general public, which is not able to curb its consuming passion and break the spell of the seductive evils of processed food.

The story goes that scientists did an experiment one time. They gave a control group of laboratory mice the contents of a processed food package to eat, and a second group of mice they gave only the box to eat, which had been pulverized without the actual food in it. Guess which mice lived longer?

Going back to the supermarket, I dare someone to get up on a soapbox near the entrance or the exit, and proclaim the following announcement to those coming and going:

"North Americans live in a salt-infested, sugar-coated, chemically-flavour-enhanced, trans-fatty-greased, barbequed, microwaved, ketchup-splattered, styrofoamed, medically over-pre-scribed, obesity or anorexic oriented society, drowning in Coke and diet drinks; and for dessert they have antacid tablets, and their children have *Ritalin*."

THE FOOD SPECTRUM

FOOD SPECTRUM
⟷

ALKALINE		ACID
EXPANSIVE		**CONTRACTIVE**

ALKALINE
EXPANSIVE

DRUGS
LIQUOR
BEER
WINE
COFFEE
TEA
COCOA
CHOCOLATE
SUGARS
SYRUPS
FRUIT JUICES

PLANT DERIVATIVE

WHOLE
NATURAL
CENTERED
PLANT FOOD

ANIMAL DERIVATIVE

ACID
CONTRACTIVE

MEAT
FOWL
FISH
EGGS
CHEESE
BUTTER
MILK
(SALT)

FRUITS
LEGUMES
VEGETABLES
MOTHER'S MILK
NUTS & SEEDS
GRAINS

THE NUTRILICIOUS PANTRY

Favourite Brands That I Absolutely Prefer In My Culinary Adventures

There are a few brand name products that I use exclusively in all the recipes where they are required. I have chosen these particular items, after carefully trying, testing and tasting many other similar ones; none of which have come up to the standard of my healthy taste buds and quality control. As far as I'm concerned, these products are top quality, consistently fresh, flavourful and health-promoting, and have stood the test of time each and every time.

1 **Bragg™**, liquid soy, is an all purpose seasoning, which can be used interchangeably with any other organic soy sauce. Lately, I have been using mostly the same amount of Bragg instead of any other organic soy sauce. I find that it has a lighter substance and therefore leaves a less salty-lingering flavour on my tongue. (www.bragg.com)

2 **Herbamare® Original**, produced by A. Vogel, Bioforce, can be used interchangeably with sea salt. Its subtle flavour comes from additional organic herbs and vegetables used in its manufacture. Herbamare should be used after cooking. (www.bioforce.com) Even though Herbamare does not have kosher certification marked on its packaging, it is under the kosher supervision of *B'datz Basil*.

3 **Nasoya® All Natural Nayonaise®** Soya-based Sandwich Spread, by Vitasoy USA, Inc. For my fabulous All Purpose 30-second Dressing **Nayomaise**, see page 119. (www.vitasoy-usa.com)

4 **Rice Dream® non-dairy frozen dessert** is manufactured for distribution by Imagine Foods, a division of The Hain-Celestial Group, Inc. RICE DREAM ® comes in many flavours; my favourite is "Cocoa Marble Fudge." (www.imaginefoods.com)

Rice Dream® non-dairy beverage is a rice milk that comes in various flavours.

Living in a metropolitan city, I am fortunate to have all-natural products readily available with kosher certification. However, those living in smaller areas can avail themselves of these products through their company websites or reputable health food stores. You may also find some of these items in regular supermarkets, in kosher groceries and in kosher bakeries.

BAKING
Aluminum-free baking powder
Baking soda
Oat bran
Organic cocoa powder
Pure vanilla extract
Whole spelt flour (unbleached, not sifted)
White spelt flour (unbleached and sifted)
Whole wheat flour

BEVERAGES
Coffee substitutes (Plant-based)
Herbal teas
Rice Dream® non-dairy beverage
Water (bottled or filtered)

"DAIRY MILK IS THE PERFECT FOOD - FOR COWS!"

HELPFUL HINT:
To keep flours fresh, store them in airtight containers in the fridge or freezer.

CANNED GOODS (ORGANIC)
Baked beans
Chickpeas/Garbanzos
Lima beans
Sardines (best quality)
Tomato paste
Tomato sauce
Tomatoes (whole)

HEALTHFUL HINT:
I keep canned beans only for those frantic, frenetic and frazzled days when I need short-cuts to supper meals. You may stock any other canned beans of your choice.

CONDIMENTS
Gomasio (see page 182)
Miso paste (needs always to be refrigerated)
Organic soy sauce (low sodium)
Dill pickles (in brine)
NASOYA® All Natural Nayonaise
Stone ground mustard

DRIED FRUITS (ORGANIC UNSULPHURED)
Apricots
Cranberries
Dates
Golden raisins
Prunes
Thompson raisins

FROZEN FOOD (Organic)
Corn kernels
Basil cubes, frozen
Garlic cubes, frozen
Ginger cubes, frozen
Green peas
Raspberries, organic, unsweetened
Strawberries, organic, unsweetened
Rice Dream® non-dairy frozen dessert

HELPFUL HINT:
The frozen basil, ginger, and garlic cubes come in 4" x 5" packaged red trays, and are stored in the frozen food section of some supermarkets.

GRAINS
Barley (pot and pearl)
Brown rice (long grain, short grain, basmati, wild)
Cracked wheat/bulghur
Millet
Oats (flakes, groats, steel cut)
Quinoa
Rye kernels
Wheat berries

HERBS (DRIED)
Basil
Bay leaves
Dill
Marjoram
Parsley

LEGUMES
Adzuki beans
Chickpeas
Kidney beans
Lentils (brown, red and French)
Lima beans
Navy beans
Pinto beans
Split peas (green & yellow)

MISCELLANEOUS
Apple butter (organic and unsweetened)
Arrowroot Powder
Corn Meal (coarse or fine)
Dried Shiitake Mushrooms (packaged)
Fresh Ginger Root
Jams (sweetened with pure fruit juices)
Organic Tofu
Tahini (sesame paste)

NUTS & SEEDS (RAW AND ORGANIC)
Almonds
Cashews
Hazelnuts/Filberts
Pecans
Walnuts
Flax seeds
Sesame seeds (unhulled)
Sunflower seeds (hulled)

HELPFUL HINT:
Please be sure to always keep your nuts and seeds in the refrigerator or freezer; they tend to go rancid very quickly, which would make them a toxic food.

OILS (Unrefined and/or Organic)
Canola/Rapeseed oil
Corn oil
Grapeseed oil
Extra-virgin olive oil
Flaxseed oil
Safflower oil

HEALTHFUL HINT:
These oils need to be refrigerated once they are opened, except the extra-virgin olive oil; as they do not contain any chemical additives to prevent them from going rancid.

PASTAS
Brown rice pasta
Couscous (whole wheat)
Durum semolina pasta
Spelt pasta
Whole wheat pasta

SEASONINGS
Bragg™ liquid soy
Herbamare® Original
Organic Soy Sauce

HEALTHFUL HINT:
Iodized table salt is a no-no. If you respect your kidneys, try using sea salt or Herbamare instead!

SEA VEGETABLES (DRIED)
Kombu
Wakame

HELPFUL HINT:
Kombu and wakame can be bought, packaged, in a health food store.

SPICES
Allspice
Black pepper
Cinnamon (ground and sticks)
Cloves (ground and whole)
Coriander
Cumin
Curry powder
Garlic powder
Ginger (ground)
Nutmeg
Onion powder
Paprika
Sea salt
Tumeric

SWEETENERS
Brown rice syrup
Pure maple syrup
Stevia (powder or liquid)
Whole cane sugar (granulated, unrefined and unbleached)

HELPFUL HINT:
There are various brands of whole, natural sweeteners to be found at health food stores; have a sweet time exploring them!

VINEGARS
Apple cider vinegar
Brown rice vinegar
Umeboshi vinegar

Please check the expiration date on all packages!

VEGETABLES
&
SALADS

VEGETABLE AND SALAD RECIPES

VEGETABLES

THE BEST LIFE INSURANCE WE CAN BUY

(Memoirs of a Vegeholic)

Vegetables and fruit are nutritional powerhouses like no other food. While fruits supply us with invaluable and health-promoting vitamins, which act as healing antioxidants and are cleansing, vegetables are our builder-uppers. They have no cholesterol and will never put plaque on our veins. Plaque is the stuff that can lead to atherosclerosis, strokes and heart attacks, which are the number one killers in North America. Vegetarians, according to statistics, have lower incidences of cancer, high blood pressure, diabetes, strokes, osteoporosis, food poisoning, kidney stones, gallstones and obesity. One of the reasons for this is the fact that plant-based diets tend to be low in fat and high in fibre.

Vegetables offer a huge array of antioxidants, vitamins and minerals, as well as high-quality carbo-hydrates and good, clean protein. Antioxidants inhibit the growth of cancer cells by stopping free radicals from binding to DNA in our bodies. Thus, they support the body's own ability to repair itself on a continuous basis. What many people may not realize is that minerals and vitamins work synergistically in vegetables and are dependent on each other for keeping organs functioning properly. This natural phenomenon makes vitamins useless to our bodies without minerals. Vegetables also contain a variety of phytochemicals, which are substances found only in plants. Scientific studies have also concluded that antioxidants in supplement form do not measure up to the benefits of eating the whole vegetables from which they are derived.

For your sake and for the sake of your 'e-steamed' vegetables, I have a number of healthful and helpful hints so you can get the most nutritional benefits in the shortest time possible. Vegetables can be prepared in many different ways: par-boiled (blanched), steamed, sautéed, stir-fried, baked, roasted, broiled and stewed. They can be made into soups, casseroles, kugels, quiches and patties. Last but not the least, vegetables can be made into delicious, colourful and health-promoting salads.

CLEANING VEGETABLES TO MAKE THEM KASHRUS ACCEPTABLE

For cleaning vegetables to make them **kashrus-acceptable**, please refer to the rabbinic literature of your choice. (I follow the *Halachic Guide To The Inspection Of Fruits And Vegetables For Insects*, by Rabbi Pesach Eliyohu Falk of Gateshead, England, and *The Orthodox Union Guide To Preparing Fruits and Vegetables*, New York.)

METHODS OF PREPARING VEGETABLES

Steaming is the quickest and easiest way to cook most vegetables for 21st century short-order cooks. My stainless steamer is always standing on one of my back burners, and is only put away *L'Koved Shabbos* (for the honour of the Sabbath). I use neither a collapsible nor a bamboo steamer because I think they are not practical for daily use. It is too easy to burn your hands using one of those, and for speed there is nothing like a good stainless steamer with only one long handle. If you can find one in a store, grab it, even if you have to break your piggy bank.

Other fat-free methods of cooking vegetables are: water-sautéing and par-boiling. Many vegetables can also be baked, roasted or broiled. Onions, potatoes, yams, carrots, beets, squashes, peppers, turnips, and kohlrabi can all be brushed with a little oil, seasoned and oven-cooked.

ORGANICALLY GROWN PRODUCE

Whenever possible, it is preferable to buy organic food. "Organic" food is grown in harmony with nature, without pesticides, herbicides, insecticides, fungicides, artificial fertilizers, or other sundry chemical preservatives. Another benefit of organically grown produce is that it is not genetically modified.

FROZEN VEGETABLES

I am aware that many people use frozen vegetables in place of fresh ones, and I well understand their reasons. However, since food is a conductor of energy, it is much more health-promoting to eat vegetables fresh whenever possible. Why not be your own judge and compare the look and taste of frozen compared to freshly prepared vegetables?

PEELING VEGETABLES

Peel skins of all vegetables that are not organically grown.

SOAKING VEGETABLES

Do not soak vegetables for any length of time, as many vitamins are water-soluble and will leach into the water!

OVERCOOKING VEGETABLES

Do not overcook vegetables, as heat over 112°F destroys a lot of their valuable enzymes and vitamins!

VARIETY

Variety is the key to health on any diet. Just because someone in your family loves broccoli, doesn't mean it should be the sole vegetable served all the time. We need to avail ourselves of the many diverse nutrients which are abundant in a large variety of vegetables. It is not enough to eat only a bowl of green salad every day to maintain sound health into old age. I will share with you below some of the methods of preparation that have worked best for me and my vegetables, and I sincerely hope that my enthusiasm about the rainbow range of veggies will also colour your world in the future.

Green, Leafy Vegetables: Spinach, collards, mustard greens, beet greens, chard, and bok choy are the richest sources of minerals and vitamins in our diet. They are abundant in beta-carotene, iron, zinc, selenium, iodine and calcium. Besides their incredible and wondrous health benefits, they need a minimum of steaming and add colour, flavour and flair to many dishes.

Cruciferous Vegetables: These include: kale, cabbage, broccoli, Brussels sprouts and cauliflower. They are high in cancer-fighting endoles, containing antioxidants, carotene, vitamins C and E and calcium. For example, one serving of broccoli (1 cup, chopped) furnishes about 90% of our daily vitamin A requirements, 200% vitamin C, 6% niacin, 10% calcium, 10% thiamin, 10% phosphorus, and 8% iron. Talking about nutrient-dense food - you get all this for only 45 calories! Broccoli is also rich in potassium, provides about 25% of our daily fibre needs and contains 5 grams of protein. Many people seem to be unaware of the fact that vegetables contain protein. I am forever asked: "From where do you get your protein?" For your information, spinach has 49% of its calories from protein (no wonder Popeye's muscles were bulging); broccoli has 45% and Brussels sprouts have 44%.

Carrots: Carrots are in a class by themselves. Their colour energy vibrates with our own for a feeling of warmth and vitality, and their beta-carotene content stimulates our immune system. One large carrot contains 11,000 units of vitamin A. Carrots are versatile, and dependable, sweet and colourful, and good for all reasons and all seasons. They can be prepared in many different ways: boiled, par-boiled, steamed, baked, stewed, sautéed, puréed, or eaten raw. They can be added to salads, soups, mashed potatoes and stews, kugels and quiches, and used in cakes. I use carrots every day in some form or other.

Root Vegetables: Beets, carrots, turnips, rutabagas, parsley root, parsnips, celeriac and radishes, share their earthy strength and medicinal properties with us, especially during the rugged winter months. Daikon, also a radish, when grated raw and added to a meal, will neutralize any animal fat present, making digestion easier. Baking or roasting the rooties caramelizes them and thus brings out their succulent flavours, yielding a natural, sweet taste.

Other Mild-Mannered Greens: There are other delicious vegetables that can be eaten raw or cooked, and used very interestingly in salads. Frozen green peas thrown into a winter soup add a touch of spring. The ever-upright and slender asparagus add elegance to any meal. Green beans are an old stand-by. Celery can be used raw or cooked in many dishes. (I often add 2 - inch pieces of steamed celery to our dinner plates.) Leeks, the cousins of onions, are delicious in soups and sauces.

Orange Vegetables: To continue our tour of the veggie rainbow, there are the sweet and mild tasting squashes, pumpkins, sweet potatoes and yams. They contain high amounts of beta-carotene and other valuable minerals. I add yams to a number of my soups, as they impart wonderful flavour, texture and nutrition.

Nightshade Vegetables: Potatoes, tomatoes, peppers and eggplant are all part of the 'nightshade' family. Arthritics and those who suffer from osteoporosis, atherosclerosis, kidney stones and such, are advised to refrain from eating these vegetables until their symptoms have disappeared. However, those who can enjoy the nightshades can derive many healthful benefits. Tomatoes and bell peppers are full of vitamin C and other sorely needed antioxidants. And who doesn't love potatoes in one form or another? (What would we do without baked potatoes when there's no time to cook?)

Mushrooms: Mushrooms are not really a vegetable, but edible fungi. Some of them have the potential to treat a host of modern diseases. Studies have verified for a long time, and new research has constantly spot-lighted, their ability to boost the immune system, inhibit tumor growth, fight cancer, liver disease and high cholesterol, and protect the heart. They also have a calming effect on the nervous system. Mushrooms come in various and exotic shapes and sizes. It is however, shiitakes, reishis, and maitakes, that have the most medicinal properties. These can also be purchased in their dried state and rehydrated as needed. However, the popular white button mushrooms, the brown crimini, and the sometimes humongous portobellos do not have much nutritional value, containing mostly water.

Garlic and onions: The lowly smelling roses from the lily family have so many medicinal properties that the list is almost endless. They contain over 200 vitamins, amino acids, enzymes and minerals. Garlic and onions are packed with the germ-fighting chemical allicin and the anti-cancer agent selenium. They are nature's best antibiotic, with their anti-fungal, anti-bacterial, anti-viral, anti-inflammatory and anti-nausea properties. They are healing for stomach, lung and liver cancer, high blood pressure, heart disease, strokes and hardening of the arteries. They fight harmful cholesterol and can also lower blood sugar. Onions and garlic are most effective for the above conditions in their raw state; however, they supposedly retain much of their benefits when cooked. (Store onions in a cool, dry place away from potatoes, as the onions cause potatoes to sprout and go bad!)

I beg forgiveness from any vegetables that I may have forgotten to mention.

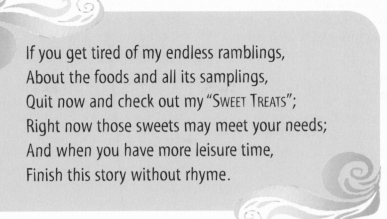

If you get tired of my endless ramblings,
About the foods and all its samplings,
Quit now and check out my "SWEET TREATS";
Right now those sweets may meet your needs;
And when you have more leisure time,
Finish this story without rhyme.

HERBS

While I don't use a large variety of fresh herbs on a daily basis, I am partial to fresh parsley, fresh dill and fresh basil, or, when not on hand, I will substitute with the dried ones. I also like marjoram, but use it mostly dried.

Parsley: Parsley is full of nourishing and medicinal properties. It contains vitamin A and D and is rich in calcium, potassium and magnesium. This makes it a blood purifier and good for the kidneys and brain. There are two kinds of parsley; one is flat-leafed, also called Italian parsley, and the other is curly parsley. I use flat-leaf parsley mostly in food preparations, and curly parsley for decorating. Parsley should not be cooked and should always be added at the end of food preparation. I will add parsley to just about anything that is vaguely related to the vegetable kingdom, as I am hooked on the stuff. I always have a large bouquet of fresh parsley in my refrigerator, arranged in a jar with water. That way, every time I open my fridge I take delight in its ever-green magic, and I can almost feel its curative energy spreading throughout. I also use the stems of parsley, finely chopped, in salads and soups, as I love their almost sweet crunchiness. Surely, they contain as many nutrients as their leaves, or more.

Washing & Storing Parsley: To wash parsley, fill a large white plastic bowl with warm water and thoroughly swish the parsley around in it. Rinse a few times with fresh water and, finally, fill the bowl with water, to which two tablespoons plain vinegar have been added. Let the parsley soak in this for about three to five minutes. Now rinse again until the water is totally clear of even the tiniest speck. Place parsley between two towels, gently roll up and squeeze lightly, and let sit on the counter for a while. Store in a jar with water in your refrigerator.

Dill: Fresh dill lends a most aromatic garden flavour to soups, stews and salads, etc. As a decoration for my little 'food paintings' it's ever-so picturesque; a few fronds of dill atop a cold appetizer adds a wisp of delicate elegance. I also use the stems of dill, finely chopped, in salads and soups; the same way I use those from parsley.

SEA VEGETABLES - *Mining Precious Trace Minerals*

Since our vegetables at this point in time are depleted of most trace minerals and may be two weeks old or more before we can buy them, cooking with sea vegetables is more important than ever. They are the richest source of essential and micro-nutrients that are available to us. They have more fibre, vitamins, minerals, enzymes, amino acids, protein and trace minerals than any other food group. Sea vegetables are also the richest source of iodine and are therefore, especially recommended for salt-free

A NOTE OF CAUTION: Since more is not necessarily better, it is advisable to use moderation when eating sea vegetables, because of their highly concentrated mineral sources. A one - inch piece of dried kombu or wakame a day is all that is needed to receive their nutritional and medicinal benefits on a regular basis.

diets. Because of their vitamin B12 content, sea vegetables are essential for vegetarians and vegans, who may become deficient in this vitamin..

Another powerful asset of sea vegetables is their antioxidant quality, which boosts the immune system, and can help fight cancer and other autoimmune diseases. Sea vegetables protect the heart by reducing the fat cells in blood, and can help regulate blood pressure. They are also anti-inflammatory, anti-viral, anti-fungal and anti-bacterial. Their detoxifying properties can remove heavy metals and radioactive elements from the body, making it invaluable in recovery from chemotherapy and radiation treatment. Thus, a small amount of sea vegetables can give nutritional balance to all diets, and particularly to commercially processed ones..

I use only kombu and wakame in my cooking, and leave nori and such to the yuppy-trendy-sushi-eaters when they congregate for their power lunches. Kombu lends a special depth of flavour and mellowness to soups and stock because of its glutamic acid, which is a natural flavour enhancer. This is much healthier than eating soups from packaged mixes and restaurant soups, as both of these are usually loaded with monosodium glutamate, salt and other flavour enhancers, known to be contributing factors in promoting cancer cells. I use kombu in my stocks and in all legume dishes, as it tenderizes the legumes and aids in digestion, eliminating their gas-forming properties. Wakame, when soaked, has greenish-black ruffled fronds, and I use it mainly in soups or stews.

To prepare sea vegetables for cooking: Break the pieces into the desired measurements, place into a small bowl, cover with warm water, and let it soak for about 8 minutes. (Kombu will expand to 8 times its original size). Remove from the bowl, cut into 1/4 - 1/2 inch pieces, and add to the particular dishes at the beginning of cooking..

JUICING VEGETABLES - *Instant Raw Energy!*

In every generation there have been doctors and healers who promulgated the incredible and unsurpassed benefits of raw food. Juicing raw vegetables is a great nutritional booster, particularly for those on a conventional SAD (Standard American Diet). Vegetables, when juiced, give our bodies the nutrients that promote healing and protect us from disease. Whenever we consume live foods, we bathe trillions of God-given cells in our bodies with plant-derived nutrients. Since the fresh enzymes in juices are already pre-digested, and enter the bloodstream almost instantly, they give us a quick energy boost.

Juicing, however, is not meant to be a substitute for eating fresh fruits and vegetables. It does not replace a proper vegetable or salad meal, which gives us the necessary fiber for healthy digestion. Fiber needs our chewing; remember we don't have teeth in our stomachs!!

In order to juice vegetables, a good, solid vegetable juicer is needed. They can be pricey, but are a definite asset to our survival kit. Drink vegetable juices as soon as possible after they have been juiced, so as to preserve their potent vitamin and mineral contents!

The following vegetables can be juiced in various combinations: carrots, celery, beets, cabbage, parsley,

A NOTE OF CAUTION: Many people think that more is better, but that is definitely not the case when dealing with nutrition, where less can often be more. For anyone not familiar with or used to drinking fresh juices, it is best to go slow at the beginning. Drink only a total of 4 - 6 ounces of juice a day at first, and see where that will take you. Beet juice, pure or in combination, should not be used more than three times a week, as the beet is a very powerful rootie. Juices should always be consumed before solid food.

It is advisable for anyone changing their diet to consult a competent Health Professional, preferably one who understands the connection between nutrition and health (a Holistic Practitioner or one who practices complementary medicine).

romaine, spinach, cucumbers, apples, and more. For samples of a few detoxifying, energizing and rejuvenating cocktails, see the following recipes; each one makes one serving.

BETA BUNNY-HOPPING COCKTAIL

2 medium carrots
2 stalks celery
1/2 small apple

BEETNIK COCKTAIL - 'CAN'T BE BEET'

2 medium carrots
1/2 medium beet
1/2 small apple

TOP O' THE MORN' COCKTAIL - 'RISE 'N' SHINE!'

1 small orange, peeled
4 - inch piece English cucumber
1 large stalk celery
3 - 4 dark romaine lettuce leaves

HIGH OCTANE PUNCH - RAW GREEN POWER

1 large carrot
1/2 small apple
A small handful of parsley with the stems, rolled up in a romaine lettuce leaf

— ✿ —

VARIATIONS:

Join our C.N.N. Club - become Creative, Natural and Nourishing (no connection to Atlanta's CNN). Mix and match different vegetables that will suit your personal tastes and needs.

"If God wanted us to drink packaged fruit juices, he would have grown orange juice groves, tomato juice bushes, bottled apple juice orchards and canned pineapple juice trees."

A COUNTER REVOLUTION IN JERUSALEM

I did not realize that the vegetable juicer in my kitchen was slightly damaged. When one fine morning I made myself a glass of carrot and celery juice, some of it spilled onto the counter under the machine, unnoticed by me. I drank my juice and fortified with live enzymes I went about my business, which happened to be that morning dusting the ultra-fine Mediterranean sand from the whole house.

When I returned to the kitchen some time later, a demonstration seemed to be in full swing. Thousands of tiny ants had assembled on my *Schajish* (Jerusalem marble counter top). As I watched in horror, a steady flow of reinforcements came on the scene, quietly taking over my kitchen. The first question that came to mind was how I was going to take control of this mob. I knew I had to find the leader of this operation in order to bring a halt to this low-keyed but massive border incursion.

As I watched from close-up, my initial horror gave way to quiet amazement. Swimming in blissful euphoria, everyone was frolicking in what seemed a ritual bath. A sense of order and shared joy pervaded the whole spectacle. A few renegades did the back stroke, a few individualists strayed away holding hands, and still a few others climbed the walls of my juicer, evidently overcome by the pure vitamin "A" stimulants. The most welcome fact was that no one was throwing stones; they were not even carrying nasty-slogan signs.

Contemplating strategy, I realized that there was no leader or, if there was one, he was indistinguishable from the rest of the crowd. In order to negotiate a peaceful withdrawal, I was willing to offer them every morning in the garden my carrot/celery cocktail, but I had no one to talk to.

I marveled at their "corps d'esprit". This had always been my private fantasy. To belong to a group or an organization where everyone was playful and happy, content and joyful, cooperative and responsible, peaceful and loving; where everyone knew whether they were coming or going and precisely what they were doing.

Be that as it may, all good things must come to an end (I often wonder why?). Since I found co-existence to be an impossible solution, I had to take action. As my knees started to buckle, I closed my eyes and slammed a cold, wet dishtowel over the entire assembly.

The next morning there was a new generation of ants frolicking on my kitchen counter, without the lure of carrot juice or even one whole wheat crumb. They were a much tougher breed, and my guilt at having committed "anticide" the day before vanished instantly. What were my options now to deal with this "counter-revolutionary" crisis ? I was told by well-meaning but discouraging friends: "*You'll never get rid of them*". I did not fancy a house call from an exterminator because he stays one minute and leaves a 24-hour stink. I am all for peaceful coexistence, but sometimes the line must be drawn somewhere, and "they" had crossed that line already in droves. Since the survival-of-the-fittest theory is not part of my religious belief system, I was neither going to try and battle with them directly, nor was I going to wait until a weak-strained generation would produce strong degenerates (a fat chance in such a happy, loving and cooperative society).

Under these circumstances, I had nothing to lose by convincing the intruders that we go together to the U.N. (United Nincompoops) to settle my grievances (they had none, they loved my place). After a few stormy sessions, each side agreed to abide by the following resolutions:

RESOLUTION 110: The "Antians" would recognize and respect my right to the entire kitchen as the legitimate boundaries of my territory, and they would stop their rebels from any further intrusionary forays, friendly or otherwise.

RESOLUTION 111: A strict food embargo would be imposed immediately by me.

RESOLUTION 112: I would have my vegetable juicer repaired.

RESOLUTION 113: I would ignore the presence of a few rebels and infidels and refrain from any retaliatory or aggressive action.

Three years have passed and I have not had the visit of even one ant and, in my kitchen, all is quiet on the Eastern front.

STEAMED ASPARAGUS AS AN APPETIZER

These slender, elegant and upright stalks are the aristocrats of the vegetable kingdom. They even have the distinction of being the only vegetable Miss Manners allows one to eat with the hands. The green tips of asparagus are high in vitamin A, making them a good blood builder. Asparagus can be steamed, parboiled, or stir-fried and eaten hot, at room temperature, or cold. One of the ways I like to serve asparagus is, as in this recipe, steamed whole as a light appetizer. I often serve it to our guests on Friday evenings. It's simple, elegant, and whets the appetite, but is not too filling.

Serves 4

16 asparagus spears

4 medium lettuce leaves

1/2 sweet red pepper, sliced and steamed (1 1/2-inch strips)

4 tbsp **Nayomaise** (see page 119)

8 tomato wedges

2 sour dill pickles, sliced (1/8-inch slices)

Curly parsley for garnish

1   Wash asparagus and remove the tough bottom parts by breaking them off with your fingers.

2   Steam asparagus whole for 4 minutes and immediately rinse under cold running water to stop the cooking process.

3   On each individual plate, place a lettuce leaf and arrange 4 asparagus spears on top.

4   Drape a few slices of pepper crosswise over the asparagus, and drizzle Nayomaise over the top.

5   Decorate each portion with 2 tomato wedges and pickle disks, and garnish with parsley.

HELPFUL HINTS:
1. When purchasing asparagus, make sure the tips are firm.
2. To store asparagus, stand stalks in a jar of water in the refrigerator, or wrap in a damp towel for up to 4 days.

FOR PESACH:
Pesach mayonnaise and Pesach pickles may be substituted for the ones above.

Matzo-Veggie Kugel

This is a great main course or side dish for Pesach or any other *Yomtov* (holiday). Leftovers taste delicious when broiled until sizzling.

Serves 8-10

4 whole wheat matzos

1/2 cup chopped onions

2 tbsp extra-virgin olive oil

1 cup sliced mushrooms

1 cup packed chopped spinach

3/4 tsp sea salt or Herbamare

1/4 tsp black pepper

1/2 tsp ground paprika

1/4 tsp ground nutmeg

1-2 tsp finely chopped ginger or 1/2 tsp ground

3/4 tsp garlic powder

1 medium carrot steamed whole, and cut into small cubes

3 medium potatoes, boiled mashed and cooled

3 organic eggs, beaten

1. Preheat oven to 350° F.

2. Break up the matzos into 2-inch pieces, soak for 10 minutes in a large bowl filled with warm water, drain, squeeze out all the water and reserve.

3. Grease either a 13 x 9 x 2 - inch baking pan, or a 10 - inch pie plate, and reserve.

4. In a large skillet, sauté the onions in oil until translucent.

5. Add the mushrooms and sauté for 3 minutes, stirring a few times.

6. Add the spinach, sauté 3 minutes, stirring a few times.

7. Add salt, pepper, paprika, nutmeg, ginger and garlic powder, and mix well.

8. Transfer the veggie mixture to a large bowl, add the matzos, carrots, mashed potatoes and eggs, mix thoroughly (best done with your hands) and adjust seasoning.

9. Transfer the contents of the large bowl to the prepared baking dish or pie plate, and bake for 45 - 50 minutes.

HELPFUL HINT:

If this kugel needs to stay in a warming oven for any length of time, it should be covered with parchment paper and then with foil.

FOR PESACH:

Omit the nutmeg, and the oil should be substituted with Pesach oil.

Can't-be-Beet Roasted Beets

These vitamin-and-mineral-packed beets (so good for the liver and gall bladder) delight us with their gorgeous royal colour, their crunchy texture, and their distinctive succulent flavour, when combined with caramelized onions.

Serves 4

6 small beets, peeled and quartered

1 medium onion, cut into 8 wedges

2 tsp garlic powder

1 - 2 tsp umeboshi vinegar

1 Preheat oven to 400° F.

2 In a medium bowl, place the beets and onions, add garlic powder, oil, water and vinegar, and toss well until all pieces are coated.

3 Place in an ovenproof dish, and bake uncovered for 30 - 40 minutes, turning the beets over once.

HELPFUL HINT:

Leftovers can be served the next day at room temperature, or diced into a green salad.

"Choose your veggies the same way teenagers choose their polos at the mall; go for all the colours of the rainbow!"

Colour-Me-Purple Stew

This is the perfect recipe for practicing **Planning Ahead** and **Cooking in Stages** (see page 242), in this age of frenetic multi-tasking, or doing food with only one foot in the kitchen. Don't be put-off by the title; this is not a slow-cooking stew at all (I just don't know what else to call it). Once the preliminary preparations have been made, it is a cinch to put together. It is full of health-promoting ingredients, melding the various flavours into a succulent dish.

Serves 3-4

1/2 cup chopped onions

2 tbsp extra-virgin olive oil

2 medium potatoes, peeled, steamed and sliced (1/4 - inch pieces)

2 medium beets, steamed, peeled and sliced (1/4 - inch pieces)

1 medium yam, steamed, peeled and sliced (1 - inch pieces)

1/2 tsp garlic powder

2 pinches black pepper

1 tbsp umeboshi vinegar

3 cups chopped greens, steamed (1 - inch pieces)

1/2 cup cubed firm tofu (1/2 - inch pieces)

1   In a large skillet, sauté the onions in the oil for about 3 minutes, or until translucent.

2   Add the potatoes, beets and yams, toss together, cover and simmer for 6 - 8 minutes.

3   Add the garlic powder, pepper and vinegar, and stir gently until all is mixed.

4   Add the greens and the tofu, gently toss (with 2 utensils) and cover.

5   Simmer until heated through and serve immediately.

VARIATIONS:

1. 1/4 cup chopped flat-leaf parsley can be substituted for the greens, if necessary.

2. A pinch or 2 of cumin can be substituted for the black pepper.

BROCCOLI

THE GREATEST GREEN THING SINCE THE GARDEN OF EDEN

Why not join the lean 'n green revolution, mobilizing your broccoli brigade
to declare war on the SAD (Standard American Diet)!!!

I use fresh, organic broccoli almost daily, added to some part of my menu, because I'm hung up on its tremendous nutritional healing properties. One cup of fresh broccoli provides about 90 percent of our daily requirement for Vitamin A, 200 percent of Vitamin C, and a wealth of other vitamins and minerals. One serving also provides about 25 percent of our daily fibre needs.

HELPFULL & HEALTHFUL HINTS:

1. To clean broccoli to make it *kashrus*-acceptable, please refer to the rabbinic literature of your choice.

2. To cook broccoli, steam florets for 5 minutes and serve immediately.

3. If you want to reserve the broccoli to add to other dishes for later use, rinse immediately after cooking under cold, running water to stop the cooking process.

4. For a quick stir-fry, after cooking, rinse the broccoli under cold running water, to stop the cooking process, add a little oil to a skillet, garlic powder and soy sauce to taste, and stir-fry 2 - 3 minutes and serve.

5. Steam extra broccoli, to be used in other dishes such as pastas and grain dishes. I sometimes sneak florets into my green salads and, camouflaged, no one suspects they are eating healthy. This is my contribution to off-set the fast-food-convenience food-microwaved-food trend; so please don't let the cat out of the bag!!

6. Peel the stems, slice into thin rounds and steam along with the florets. I always slice them into our salads raw, because that way they are delicious, sweet-tasting and tender.

*"The road of the western diet is paved with fast food,
junk food and antacid tablets."*

Sweet 'n' Sour Red Cabbage

This is a delicious and succulent side dish that goes well with mashed potatoes or any grain dish that is fairly bland, like millet, quinoa, or whole wheat couscous.

Serves 4-5

1/3 cup chopped onions

1 tbsp extra-virgin olive oil

2 cups peeled and chopped apple (1/2 - inch pieces)

4 cups chopped red cabbage (1/2 - inch pieces)

1 large bay leaf

1 1/2 cups water

Sea salt or Herbamare to taste

Black pepper to taste

1 - 2 tsp umeboshi vinegar

1 1/2 tbsp brown rice vinegar

2 tsp pure maple syrup

1 tbsp arrowroot powder

1 tbsp water

1   In a medium saucepan, sauté the onions in oil for 3 minutes.

2   Add the apples and continue sautéing for 3 - 4 minutes.

3   Add the cabbage, bay leaf and water, stir well, cover and cook on low heat for 15 - 20 minutes. (The cabbage should still be crisp.)

4   Add the salt, pepper, vinegars and maple syrup, and bring to a boil.

5   Make a paste with the arrowroot powder and one tablespoon water, add to the cabbage and stir continuously until thickened.

6   Remove bay leaf, adjust seasoning and serve.

HELPFUL HINT:
Serve leftovers at room temperature. Do not reheat!

OVEN-BAKED BUTTERNUT CHIPS

A yummy and nutritious substitute for french fries; not French but trés élégant.

Serves 4

1 large or 2 medium butternut squash
1/2 tsp onion powder
1/2 tsp garlic powder
Black pepper to taste
1 1/2 tbsp organic soy sauce
1 1/2 tbsp extra-virgin olive oil

1 Preheat oven to 450° F.

2 Cover a large baking pan with parchment paper, and reserve.

3 Peel the squash, remove the seeds, cut into quarters, then into eighths, and finally into french-fry style pieces.

4 In a large bowl, place the squash pieces and add onion powder, garlic powder, soy sauce and oil, and toss thoroughly to make sure all the pieces are well coated.

5 Spread the squash pieces onto the baking sheet, making sure the pieces do not overlap, and bake for 15 minutes.

6 Serve immediately, or turn off the oven and leave the chips in the oven until they are as crisp as you like them.

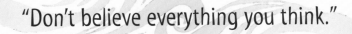

"Don't believe everything you think."

FRIED CAULIFLOWER

Mark Twain allegedly said: *"A cauliflower is nothing but a cabbage with a college education."* Here's a sophisticated way to serve up the graduates. This recipe is very suitable for a *Yomtov* (holiday) meal, as it can be prepared in advance.

Yields 25-30 pieces

1 medium cauliflower, cut into 1 - inch florets

1/2 cup white spelt flour for dredging

2 organic eggs, beaten

2 tbsp extra-virgin olive oil

Breading Mixture:

2 cups matzo meal (preferably whole wheat)

Sea salt or Herbamare to taste

1/2 tsp onion powder

1/2 tsp garlic powder

1   Steam the florets for 4 minutes (not a second longer), and immediately rinse under cold running water to stop the cooking process, and reserve.

2   Have ready: a small bowl with the dredging flour, another small bowl with the eggs, and a medium bowl with the breading mixture.

3   Dredge the florets in the first bowl and reserve on a large plate.

4   Dip each floret into the egg mixture, shake off excess egg, and coat thoroughly in the breading mixture.

5   Fry the florets in oil on both sides until golden brown, and drain on paper towels.

6   Serve immediately, or place uncovered in a warming oven until needed.

HELPFUL HINT:

This recipe can be prepared in advance up to and including step 5. To reheat, place uncovered in a 250° F oven for about 15 minutes.

FOR PESACH:

Substitute potato starch or Pesach flour for the flour in this recipe, and use Pesach oil.

CAULIQUETTES

These patties make a delicious side dish to any menu, or a healthful and tasty snack any time; they also freeze well.

Yields about 1 dozen patties

1 large head cauliflower
1 tbsp extra-virgin olive oil
1 cup finely diced onions
1/2 cup finely diced celery
1/2 cup finely diced carrots
2 tbsp organic soy sauce
1/4 tsp sea salt or Herbamare
1/4 tsp garlic powder
Ground nutmeg to taste
Black pepper to taste
2 tbsp finely chopped flat-leaf parsley
1/4 cup oat bran
1/8 cup white spelt or whole wheat flour or whole wheat matzo meal
1/4 cup tahini
Unhulled sesame seeds for garnish

1   Preheat oven to 350°F.

2   Cut the cauliflower into bite-size florets, wash and steam for 10 minutes.

3   Cover a large baking pan with parchment paper, and set aside.

4   While still warm, mash the cauliflower with a potato masher and reserve.

5   In a skillet, sauté onions for 3 - 4 minutes, add the celery and carrots and sauté for 5 minutes.

6   Add the soy sauce, salt, garlic powder, nutmeg, and pepper and mix.

7   In a large bowl, place the cauliflower, the sautéed vegetables, parsley, oat bran, flour, and mix thoroughly.

8   Mix in the tahini, adjust seasoning and mix well once more.

9   Form 2 - inch diameter patties and arrange on the baking sheet.

10 Sprinkle patties with unhulled sesame seeds, and bake for about 15 minutes; turn over and bake 10 minutes more.

Mystery Latkes

These incredibly delicious latkes are a practical standby for any *Yomtov* (holiday) meal or party fare. I call them mystery latkes; because no one has ever guessed what they're made of!

Yields about 12 latkes

2 medium celeriac (celery root) peeled and sliced (1/4 - inch slices)

1/2 cup white spelt flour for dredging

2 organic eggs, beaten

2 tbsp extra-virgin olive oil

Breading Mixture:

1/2 cup matzo meal, preferably whole wheat

Sea salt or Herbamare to taste

1/2 tsp onion powder

1/4 tsp ground paprika

1/2 tsp garlic powder

1/4 tsp ground ginger

1 Steam the celeriac for 3 - 4 minutes, or until barely soft.

2 With a spatula, lift the celeriac slices from the steamer and place on a large plate to cool.

3 Have ready: a small bowl with white spelt flour for dredging, another small bowl with the beaten eggs and a medium bowl with well-combined breading mixture ingredients.

4 Dredge the slices of celeriac, and reserve on a large plate.

5 Dip each slice into the egg mixture, shake off excess egg, and coat thoroughly in the breading mixture.

6 Fry the latkes in oil on both sides until golden brown, and drain on paper towels.

7 Serve immediately or place uncovered in a warming oven until needed.

HELPFUL HINT:

This recipe can be prepared in advance up to and including step 5.

FOR PESACH:

Substitute Pesach cake meal for the whole spelt flour for dredging, and use Pesach oil of your choice.

STEAMED CELERY

Celery may be underrated in terms of its various health benefits. It is low in calories, high in fibre, an excellent blood purifier, and beneficial to the brain and nervous system. It is also a very useful vegetable to have on hand, as it stores well, and can be used in countless ways in cooking, or as finger food with dips and pâtés. For the juicing crowd, there is nothing like an energizing vitality cocktail of freshly made celery-carrot-apple juice to 'rise 'n' shine' in the morning!

For our weekday suppers, I often serve steamed celery as a side dish. You will need about 1/2 cup sliced celery for each serving.

1   Wash the celery ribs, break all the large ribs into halves and then into quarters which makes it easy to pull off the veins.

2   Cut each rib into 1/2 - inch pieces on the diagonal.

3   Steam for 7-8 minutes for crunch or 10 - 12 minutes for a softer texture.

"If we eat wrongly, no doctor can cure us,
if we eat rightly no doctor is needed"

-Victor G. Rocine

STEAMED AND GLAZED GREENS

It is a nightly ritual for me to steam 'n' glaze my veggies. There are many greens to choose from: Broccoli, Brussels sprouts, Swiss chard, kale, collards, spinach and baby spinach, bok choy and baby bok choy, beet tops, etc. You can mix and match or use each one separately. (Please read, **Vegetables - *The Best Life Insurance we can Buy***, page 20). For each serving, use one cup packed raw greens.

Serves 4

1 tsp arrowroot powder

1/4 cup **Kombu-Shiitake Stock** (see page 105) or **Vegetable Stock** (see page 104) or water

4 cups chopped raw greens

1 tsp extra-virgin olive oil

1/2 tsp garlic powder

2 dashes organic soy sauce, or to taste

Sea salt or Herbamare to taste (optional)

1   Combine the arrowroot with the stock or water, stir to make a paste, and reserve.

2   Steam the greens until they are almost tender, and remove from steamer.

3   In a skillet, on medium heat, add the greens and sauté for about 3 minutes in the oil.

4   Add the garlic powder, soy sauce and salt, if used, and sauté until heated through.

5   On high heat, add the arrowroot mixture to the skillet, and keep stirring continuously until the contents have thickened.

6   Adjust seasoning and serve immediately.

HEALTHFUL HINT:

I often mix left-over greens into rice or other grain dishes, pasta or soups (when re-heating them). Or, there is always my salad bowl, which will welcome these lovely greens.

KALE – LEAN 'N' GREEN HAUTE CUISINE

Kale is a very sturdy and hardy vegetable. In its raw state, it keeps fresh in the refrigerator for up to a week, and cooked it keeps three to four days. This curative nutrition booster is nature's high-powered antioxidant, packed with vitamin A, vitamin C, B and iron, and, last but not least, high amounts of calcium. Kale is actually a much better and purer source of calcium than milk, as the calcium content of milk is not well assimilated by the human body and, thus, causes a host of health problems. There seems to be udder confusion about milk; yes, it is a perfect food - for cows!

Kale comes in three varieties. Besides the curly one, there is one that has long, deeply furrowed leaves, called *lacinato* or *dinosaur kale*. Kale also comes in purple. You may have seen it used as a table decoration by not-so-trendy caterers at receptions. Come to think of it, the caterers would actually serve their clients' health better if they would serve them for their dinner the purple kale and use their main dinner course as table decorations at the reception. I could envision a lovely boarder of overlapping, rare roast beef slices arranged along the sides of the tables, resting on snow white linen and accented by dabs of mustard, forming a pattern running towards the floor.

I use kale almost daily. Some of it will invariably end up, cooked, in salads, grain dishes and pastas. I often add kale, shredded and cooked, to soups when re-heating them. When used in combination with other foods, kale has no real flavour, and fussy eaters (and which family doesn't have at least one of those) will never suspect they are eating something healthy.

HELPFUL AND HEALTHFUL HINTS:

1. To clean kale, take apart each leaf and remove the hard stems. Cut all the leaves across into 1 - inch pieces, check each piece and discard any bad parts.

2. Place the kale into a large white plastic bowl filled with warm water, and let soak for 5 minutes. Lift the kale out of the bowl into a colander, change the water, add 3 tablespoons vinegar, and let soak for another 5 minutes. Lift the kale out of the water again, place into the colander, and inspect the water. Keep rinsing the kale until the water is sparkling clean.

3. Dry in a salad spinner, or roll between two towels until dry. Store in a plastic bag (Ziploc bags are best for this purpose) in the refrigerator.

4. Compared to other greens, kale needs more cooking to bring out its flavour. It can be boiled, steamed, or water sautéed.

5. Keep cooked kale on hand and add to other cooked dishes such as: stir- fries, soups, grains, pasta, salads and sauces.

6. When reserving the kale to add to other dishes, rinse immediately after cooking under cold, running water to stop the cooking process. However, when storing cooked kale, it needs to be thoroughly dried, which can be done either between 2 towels or layers of paper towels.

7. Reserve the mineral-rich cooking water for stock!

8. Sprinkling unhulled sesame seeds or **Gomasio** (see page 182) over the kale, when serving same, will add crunch, flavour and protein.

Boiled Kale

Serves 2

1 cup chopped kale, packed (1/4 - inch pieces)

2 - 2 1/2 cups water

1 In a medium pot, bring water to a boil, add the kale and cook for about 8 minutes.

2 Lift out kale with a slotted spoon and serve immediately, or reserve as per instructions above.

Steamed Kale

Serves 2

1 cup chopped kale, packed (1/4 - inch pieces)

1 Steam kale for about 8 minutes and serve immediately, or reserve as per above instructions.

Water-Sautéed Kale

Serves 3

1 cup water

3 cups chopped kale (1/4 - inch pieces)

Sea salt or Herbamare or organic soy sauce, to taste

1 tbsp arrowroot powder

Unhulled sesame seeds or Gomasio (see page…), for garnish (optional)

1 In a medium saucepan, bring water to a boil, add the kale, cover, lower heat, and simmer for about 8 minutes.

2 Turn up the heat, sprinkle arrowroot powder over the kale, and stir continuously until thick.

3 Adjust seasoning and serve immediately.

KALE AT ITS SAUCY BEST

Served in this basic béchamel sauce, the hardy kale is transformed into a smooth, scrumptious side dish, or, it can be poured as a sauce over grains, mashed potatoes, pasta, etc. This is healthful eating at its best!

Serves 2
as a side dish

2 tbsp white spelt flour

3/4 cup liquid (cooking water, stock, or water)

2 cups sliced steamed kale (1/4 - inch strips)

Organic soy sauce or sea salt or Herbamare to taste

1/2 tsp garlic powder

1   In a small bowl, place the flour and add only enough from the liquid to make a paste.

2   In a medium saucepan, bring the remaining liquid to a boil.

3   Add the flour paste, and keep stirring continuously until the sauce has thickened.

4   Add the kale, soy sauce or sea salt or Herbamare and garlic powder, stir, and simmer the sauce until heated through.

5   Adjust seasoning and serve.

HELPFUL HINT:

This recipe can also be found under **Sauces** (see page 114).

"It's not only the food in our life that counts but the life in our food."

WATER-SAUTÉED LEEKS

Leek is often called *"the poor man's asparagus"*. Closely related to onions and garlic, it nevertheless has a much milder flavour, without the pungent smell of its cousins. Leek is a good blood purifier, good for the liver and the respiratory system, and takes very little time to prepare. It is a great side dish, and can also be used sauced over grains, pasta and mashed potatoes, etc.

Yields 2 cups, serves 4 as a side dish

1 1/2 cups sliced leeks (light and darker parts mixed), cut into 1/2 - inch pieces

1 1/2 cups water

1/2 tsp garlic powder

2 tbsp organic soy sauce

2 tbsp arrowroot powder dissolved in 2 1/2 tbsp cold water

1   In a large skillet, place the leeks, water, garlic powder and soy sauce, and cook, covered, on low-medium heat for 8-10 minutes.

2   Turn heat to high, add the arrowroot mixture, and stir continuously until sauce has thickened and is smooth.

HELPFUL HINT:

White spelt or whole wheat flour can be substituted for the arrowroot powder (the ratio will remain about the same).

QUICKIE VARIATION:

If you don't have time to be saucy, do what I do sometimes; slice leeks into 1 - inch chunks, steam and serve.

"Humour is to health what water is to a steamer."

MUSHROOM PÂTÉ

All types of mushrooms beckon us today at the stores, from simple white button mushrooms to more exotic and strange-looking creatures. Their distinctive, strong flavours enhance many a dish.

This pâté makes a delectable appetizer, using 1/4 - 1/3 cup pâté for each portion, served on a lettuce leaf and colourfully decorated, or as a tasty snack on crackers, rice cakes or bread.

Yields about 2 cups; serves 6-8 as an appetizer

2 tbsp extra-virgin olive oil

2 cups coarsely chopped onions

1 lb coarsely sliced mushrooms

2/3 cup raw organic walnuts

1 tsp sea salt or Herbamare

Black pepper to taste

1   In a large skillet, heat oil and sauté the onions and mushrooms until onions become translucent (about 8 minutes).

2   In a food processor, chop the walnuts, add the mushrooms and onions, salt and pepper, and process until well blended.

3   Transfer to a bowl, adjust seasoning, and serve chilled or at room temperature.

HEALTHFUL HINT:

For the weight watchers, the yo-yo dieters and the health-conscious, place a dollop of this mouth-watering pâté on a medium, firm lettuce leaf, roll up and snack to your heart's content.

FOR PESACH:

Substitute Pesach oil for the extra-virgin olive oil.

CREAMED MUSHROOMS WITHOUT THE CREAM

Mushrooms hold a special place in my bio-food file. This goes back to my childhood when I was taken to weddings of family or my parents' friends, and the invariable first course was mushrooms in a smooth sauce served in patty shells, which were called *Pasteten*. This recipe can be served as a side dish.

Serves 4-5 as a side dish

1 tbsp white spelt flour

Enough water to make a smooth paste

1 tbsp extra-virgin olive oil

3/4 cup chopped onions

2 cloves garlic, minced

4 cups diced button mushrooms (1/4 - inch pieces)

1 cup water

1 tbsp organic soy sauce

1/4 tsp sea salt or Herbamare

1/8 tsp black pepper

1/4 cup chopped flat-leaf parsley

1 In a small dish, mix the flour with the water to make a paste and reserve.

2 In a large skillet, sauté the onions in oil on medium heat for about 5 minutes.

3 Add the garlic and sauté 2 minutes more.

4 Add the mushrooms and sauté for 3 minutes.

5 Add the water, soy sauce, salt and pepper, cover, and bring to a boil.

6 Lower heat and simmer for 5 minutes.

7 Bring sauce back to boil, add the flour paste and stir continuously until sauce has thickened and is smooth.

8 Adjust seasoning, mix in the parsley and serve.

HELPFUL HINTS:

1. For a more intense flavour, substitute the white mushrooms with Portobello mushrooms, or go rich and nutritious with fresh shiitake mushrooms.

2. Add leftovers to soups, or use as a sauce over grains, pasta, etc. This recipe can also be found in the section for Sauces.

3. Always store fresh mushrooms, unwashed, in a paper bag in the refrigerator.

APPETIZER:

Serve hot, poured over individual slices of challah or light toast, or fill into warm patty shells. (Half a cup serves one person as an appetizer).

FOR PESACH: Substitute 2-3 teaspoons potato starch for the flour, 1/2 teaspoon salt for the soy sauce, and use Pesach oil.

SAVOURY BAKED PEPPERS 'N' ONIONS

This easy-to-prepare dish will add geschmack to your food arsenal. Serve over grains, mashed potatoes, add to a green salad, or just heap on toasted bread. It also makes a good appetizer (see below).

When it comes to peeling peppers, I have always been a klutz. My peppers, no matter what I tried, never wanted to give up their skins willingly, even after I broiled them and forced them into a brown paper bag to cool down. Since I don't have as much time as they seem to have, I now use them unpeeled, which seems to be o.k. with them.

*Yields 1 1/4-
1 1/2 cups*

1 cup seeded and chopped sweet red pepper (2 - inch x 1/4 - inch pieces)

1 cup chopped onions (2 - inch x 1/4 - inch pieces)

1 - 2 tsp extra-virgin olive oil

1 - 2 tbsp organic soy sauce

1 clove garlic, minced

1 tsp umeboshi vinegar

2 pinches black pepper

1 Preheat oven to 350°F.

2 Cover a medium baking pan with parchment paper, and reserve.

3 In a small bowl, place the peppers and onions, add the oil, soy sauce, garlic, vinegar and pepper, and toss well until all is coated.

4 Transfer to the baking pan and bake for 30 - 35 minutes.

5 Remove the peppers and onions from the oven and cool before storing; keeps well in the refrigerator for one week.

— —

APPETIZER:

Toast, or warm in the oven, small slices of bread or challah, top with a generous portion of the peppers and onions, add some freshly chopped parsley and voila! You have savoury crostini.

BAKED 'N' BROILED POTATOES

This is a no-pots-no-pans recipe for busy people on the go, and can be a side dish, or a health-promoting snack (much better than a pizza or a bag of potato chips).

1 large potato per person

1 large potato

Extra-virgin olive oil

Sea salt or Herbamare to taste

Ground paprika to taste

Onion powder to taste

Garlic powder to taste

Dried parsley or dill (optional)

1   Bake 1 large potato per person.

2   Cool the potatoes slightly, cut in half, make a slash in the middle of each piece, and brush with oil.

3   Sprinkle sea salt or Herbamare, paprika, onion powder, garlic powder and parsley or dill, if used, over the top of the potatoes and broil until golden brown.

4   Serve immediately

HELPFUL HINT:
The potatoes may be baked a day in advance and prepared when needed (as in step 2).

———— 🎔🎔 ————

DECADENT VARIATION:
Substitute butter for the oil, if you dare!

"Your body doesn't lie - listen to it!"

POTATO KNISHES WITH A DIFFERENCE

This recipe was handed *up* to me by my charming granddaughter, Devorah, who happens to be an outstanding cook.

Yields 10-12 knishes

4 large potatoes

3/4 cups chopped onions

1 tbsp extra-virgin olive oil

1/4 cup whole spelt or whole wheat flour

1 organic egg

3/4 tsp sea salt or Herbamare

2 pinches black pepper

2 pinches ground nutmeg

1/4 cup chopped flat-leaf parsley

1 organic egg yolk for glazing the top

Unhulled sesame seeds for garnish (optional)

1   Preheat oven to 350°F.

2   Cover a large baking pan with parchment paper and reserve.

3   Peel potatoes, cut in 1 1/2 - inch chunks and boil until done.

4   Drain the potatoes and mash (save the cooking water for stock).

5   Sauté onions in oil until translucent (about 8 minutes), and cool slightly.

6   In a large bowl, place the mashed potatoes, sautéed onions and flour and mix well.

7   In a small bowl, beat the egg, add salt, pepper, nutmeg and parsley and stir well.

8   Add the egg mixture to the mashed potato mixture, mix well and adjust seasoning.

9   Using a tablespoon, scoop out and place potato mounds on the baking pan.

10 Brush each scoop completely with egg yolk and sprinkle sesame seeds on top, if used. Bake for about 30 minutes.

11 Serve immediately, or keep in a warming oven until needed.

HERB ROASTED POTATOES

Herbs, which have been around since the Garden of Eden, are apparently the latest discovery of trendy caterers and the new breed of food stylists. They are being used with utter abandon in just about everything that's edible. (Imagine vanilla - rosemary ice cream!) Here is a recipe using my favourites; you may substitute any other herbs of your choice.

Serves 2-3

1 1/2 tbsp extra-virgin olive oil

1 1/2 tbsp organic soy sauce

2 tbsp water

1/2 tsp garlic powder

1/2 tsp onion powder

2 tsp stone-ground mustard

1 tbsp chopped basil or 1 tsp dried

1 tbsp chopped oregano or 1/2 tsp dried

4 medium red-skinned potatoes, unpeeled, scrubbed, and sliced into 1 - inch cubes

1 Preheat oven to 450° F.

2 Cover a large baking pan with parchment paper, and reserve.

3 In a small bowl, place oil, soy sauce, water, garlic powder, onion powder, mustard, basil and oregano, and mix well.

4 In a large bowl, place the potatoes, add the herb mixture and toss until all pieces are well coated.

5 Transfer the potatoes to the baking pan, preferably arranging them in a single layer, and bake for 20 minutes.

6 Turn off the oven, turn over the potatoes, and leave them in the oven until they are as crisp and golden as you like them (they love to lazy around in hot weather).

BAKED GREEN POTATO LATKES

When my freezer went on the blink recently, I found (among other things) a bag of spinach, totally defrosted, staring up at me and wondering what I would do with it. Having been brought up on the dictum, "Waste not, want not" - which incidentally is so in again - I tried to do damage control, and that's how the greening of my latkes came about!

Yields 15 latkes

4 medium potatoes, peeled and sliced (1 - inch pieces)

1/4 cup whole wheat couscous

1/2 cup water

1/2 cup chopped onions

1 tbsp extra-virgin olive oil

1 1/4 cups steamed, squeezed dry, finely chopped packed spinach

Sea salt or Herbamare to taste

1/4 tsp garlic powder

Pinch ground nutmeg

1 tbsp organic soy sauce

1/4 cup oat bran

1 - 2 tbsp whole spelt or whole wheat flour

Unhulled sesame seeds for dredging

1 Preheat the oven to 350° F.

2 Cover a medium baking pan with parchment paper, and reserve.

3 Cook the potatoes, mash, and reserve.

4 Place the couscous in a small saucepan, add water, bring to a boil, cover, turn off the heat, and let stand for 15 - 20 minutes.

5 Sauté the onions in oil until translucent.

6 In a large bowl, place the potatoes, couscous, sautéed onions, spinach, salt, garlic powder, nutmeg, soy sauce, oat bran and flour, and mix well.

7 Form medium-sized patties, dredge in sesame seeds, place on the baking sheet, and bake for 20 minutes.

8 Turn the patties over, bake for another 15 minutes, and serve hot or at room temperature.

MASHED POTATOES WITH A DIFFERENCE

This velvety-smooth dish is as good for your immune system as it is delicious, and is a perfect way to sneak in some vitamin A.

Serves 6

3 medium potatoes, peeled and cubed (1 - inch cubes)

2 medium carrots, sliced (1/4 - inch rounds)

1/3 cup chopped onions

Water to barely cover the vegetables

Sea salt or Herbamare to taste

Garlic powder to taste

2 tbsp finely chopped flat-leaf parsley

1   In a medium pot, place the potatoes, carrots, onions and water and boil on low heat for 20 minutes.

2   Drain the vegetables and reserve the cooking water.

3   Mash the vegetables and add from the cooking liquid until the desired consistency is reached.

4   Add salt, garlic powder and parsley, adjust seasoning and serve piping hot.

─────── ❧ ───────

YUMMY VARIATIONS:

1. Substitute one large yam for the carrots.

2. Make extra mashed potatoes and reheat under the broiler until golden brown.

3. Leftovers make great patties. Just add any one of the following until they hold together: oat flour, oat bran, or white spelt flour. Add a pinch of nutmeg, adjust seasoning, form patties, and bake on a baking pan at 350° F for 30 minutes.

"The greatest threat to our health is ignorance and processed food."

ROOTIE ROAST

In winter we need rooties,
They warm like babies' booties,
And lift blue seasonal moodies.

Neither snowstorms nor wind chill factors can dampen our spirits when we go back to our roots. Root vegetables may not look as glamorous as the elegant asparagus, the snow-white cauliflower, the voluptuous broccoli, or the frizzy kale, but they infuse us with their earthy and steadfast strength when we most need it. Roasting them concentrates their natural sugars and yields a sweet, caramelized taste and meaty texture.

Serves 4

6 cups any combination of the following vegetables: carrots, potatoes, yams, shallots or onions, beets, turnips, parsnips, and rutabaga (use at least three different vegetables for a tasty dish).

Dressing:

4 tbsp organic soy sauce

2 tbsp extra-virgin olive oil

2 tbsp water

1 tsp garlic powder

1 tbsp chopped basil or flat-leaf parsley, or 1 tsp dried

1   Preheat oven to 450° F.

2   Cover your largest baking pan with parchment paper, and reserve.

3   Peel the vegetables, cut into 1 1/2 - inch cubes, and place in a large mixing bowl.

4   In a small bowl, whisk the dressing ingredients.

5   Pour the dressing over the vegetables, and toss well until all the pieces are thoroughly coated.

6   Arrange the vegetables on the baking pan in a single layer, bake for about 30 minutes, and serve immediately.

HELPFUL HINT:
When I'm in a hurry, I sometimes roast only a combination of any two of the vegetables together.

PIQUANT SPINACH PÂTÉ

Spinach brings back childhood memories for me. As "good children" we were expected to finish whatever was put on our plates. The humongous portions of spinach turned quickly to cold mush. My brothers, being less good and less intimidated than us girls, used to solve their spinach problem by putting a portion of their spinach on the empty seat where our unsuspecting nanny would eventually sit, thereby providing us with our weekly entertainment.

This low-cal, mineral-packed pâté has incredibly piquant flavours and is ever so versatile. My guests don't necessarily know exactly what's in it, and maybe we can all keep my little secret. It can be served as a side dish, or spread thickly on bread, crackers or rice cakes; it also makes a very succulent appetizer (see below).

Yields about 2 cups

10 oz. bag regular or baby spinach (about 4 cups tightly packed)

1/4 cup finely chopped onions

1/8 tsp garlic powder

1 tsp umeboshi vinegar

1/2 tsp stone-ground mustard (optional)

1 tbsp **Nayomaise** (see page 119)

Sea salt or Herbamare to taste

2 organic hard-cooked eggs, chopped

1 Steam the spinach for about 30 seconds (this may have to be done in batches), cool and squeeze out the liquid.

2 Finely chop the spinach, place in a bowl, add the onions, garlic powder, umeboshi vinegar, mustard (if used), nayomaise, salt and eggs, and mix thoroughly.

3 Adjust seasoning and serve at room temperature.

APPETIZERS:

1. Peel a cucumber, slice into long diagonal pieces (1/4 - inch thick), pile the pâté on top and decorate. Wow! Is that ever succulent and refreshing.

2. Spread the pâté thickly on small slices of *challah*, (plain or lightly toasted), whole grain bread or rice cakes, and garnish.

HEALTHFUL HINTS:

1. Spinach is a rich source of iron, sodium, potassium, calcium and magnesium. But spinach also contains oxalic acid, which when eating it, has the tendency to inhibit the body's absorption of the other minerals in it. It is therefore advisable, when eating spinach, to combine it with a protein food, as in this recipe. Supposedly, the above problem does not hold true when eating spinach in its raw state.

2. 1/3 cup cubed medium tofu may be substituted as an added protein for those who do not eat eggs.

MINIATURE YAM PUFFS

These delectable and nutrilicious immune-boosting morsels go with any kind of menu.
They also make delicious party fare and after-school snacks, and they freeze well.

Yields about 30 2-inch puffs

2 tbsp tahini

3 tbsp organic soy sauce

1/4 cup finely chopped onions

1/4 cup finely chopped celery

1/4 cup finely chopped sweet red pepper

1 1/2 tbsp extra-virgin olive oil

1/4 tsp sea salt or Herbamare

3/4 tsp garlic powder

1/4 - 1/2 tsp ginger powder

4 medium yams, peeled, boiled or steamed, and mashed

1/2 cup cooked millet

1/3 - 1/2 cup oat bran

Unhulled sesame seeds for garnish

1 Preheat oven to 350° F.

2 Cover a large baking pan with parchment paper, and reserve.

3 In a small bowl, whisk the tahini with the soy sauce.

4 In a large skillet, heat oil and sauté the onions, celery and peppers for 7-8 minutes.

5 Add salt, garlic powder and ginger and mix well.

6 In a large bowl, place the yams, millet and oat bran, add the sautéed vegetables and tahini-soy sauce mixture, mix well, and adjust seasoning.

7 With a tablespoon, drop the yam mixture onto the baking pan to form puffs; do not flatten the puffs!

8 Sprinkle with sesame seeds and bake for 30 minutes.

9 For extra crispness, broil the puffs for a few minutes.

10 Serve immediately, or let sit and serve at room temperature.

PIQUANT YAM STEW

This is a flavourful dish that goes well with just about anything else on your supper menu - it's particularly good with rice and steamed greens. Don't let the word 'stew' fool you; it's a quickie to prepare!

Serves 4-6

4 large yams, steamed with the peel and cooled

1 tbsp extra-virgin olive oil

1/4 cup chopped onions (1/2 - inch pieces)

1/4 cup diced sweet red peppers (1/2 - inch pieces)

2 tbsp organic soy sauce

1/4 tsp garlic powder

1/4 tsp ginger powder

1 Peel the yams, slice into 1 - inch pieces and reserve.

2 In a large skillet, sauté the onions and peppers in the oil for 5 minutes, or until the onions are translucent.

3 Add the soy sauce, garlic powder and ginger powder.

4 Add the yams, toss gently, cover, and simmer for 6 - 8 minutes, stirring once.

5 Serve immediately, or transfer to an oven-proof dish, cover and keep warm in a 225°F oven.

HELPFUL HINTS:
1. The yams can be steamed a day ahead, or the whole dish can be prepared in advance, and reheated as needed.
2. This stew is an excellent choice for a Friday evening menu, because it will not dry out in the oven or on a *blech* (stove top).

BROILED YAM BOATS

These boats add a sweet touch and nutrition to any meal. Remember: orange-coloured food is "*in*"! Yams contain high amounts of antioxidants that forever take up the fight against free radicals in our bodies (which develop as a result of unhealthy lifestyles). Use one large yam per person.

Serves 4-5

4 large yams, baked, peeled, and cut in half lengthwise

Extra-virgin olive oil

Sea salt or Herbamare to taste

Onion powder to taste

Garlic powder to taste

Dried herb of your choice (optional)

1 Preheat broiler.

2 Brush each half yam lightly with oil and sprinkle with salt, onion powder, garlic powder and herbs, if used.

3 Broil until heated through and serve immediately.

HEALTHFUL HINT:

Serve these boats with brown rice or another grain, steamed greens, and a big interesting salad!

FOR PESACH:

Substitute Pesach oil and use dried herbs, if used, with a Pesach hechscher (kosher certification).

YAM-PRUNE CASSEROLE

This is a favourite with our Friday night guests. The delicate flavours come from the combination of the sweet yams and the succulent prunes. Besides tasting yummy, this casserole has great nutritional benefits, as the yams and prunes add the antioxidants we need to stay well and to age gracefully with most of our equipment intact (with the gracious help of God) .

Serves 8

5 medium yams

20 - 25 pitted sun-dried prunes

1 tbsp orange zest

1/2 tsp sea salt or Herbamare

1 Preheat oven to 325° F.

2 Steam or boil the yams until soft, peel and reserve.

3 In a small saucepan, place the prunes, cover with water, bring to a boil and simmer on medium heat for 8 - 10 minutes.

4 Drain the prunes and reserve the liquid for another use.

5 Place yams into a food processor, add orange zest and salt and process until smooth.

6 Place the yam ingredients into an oven-to-table casserole dish and decorate with the prunes.

7 Bake covered for 20 minutes.

> **HELPFUL HINT:**
>
> This casserole can be made up to, and including, step 6, and frozen. When needed, bake covered for about 45 minutes without first defrosting it.

TO DECORATE WITH THE PRUNES:

Form a border of prunes all around, placing one next to the other on top of the yam mixture inside the rim, and arrange a few prunes in the middle. Press each prune gently into the yam mixture.

YUMMY BAKED YAM CUBES

These succulent morsels are quick 'n' easy to prepare, and enhance any kind of meal. Kids love them; what a great immune-boosting after-school snack!

Serves 4-5

1 tsp sea salt or Herbamare

1 tsp garlic powder

1 tsp onion powder

1 tsp ground ginger

Black pepper to taste

2 tbsp organic soy sauce

4 tbsp water

2 tbsp extra-virgin olive oil

3 large or 6 medium yams, peeled and cubed (1 - inch cubes)

1 Preheat oven to 425° F.

2 Cover a large baking pan with parchment paper and reserve.

3 In a small bowl, blend salt, garlic powder, onion powder, ginger, pepper, soy sauce, water and oil.

4 In a large bowl, place the yams, pour the sauce on top, and toss gently until all the pieces are well coated.

5 Arrange the yam cubes on the baking pan, trying not to overlap them, and bake for 20 minutes.

6 With a spatula, turn the yams over and bake for another 10 - 15 minutes.

7 Turn off the oven and serve, or leave the yummies in the oven for a while. Don't worry about over-exposure; the yams love to socialize in hot weather!

FOR PESACH:

Substitute Pesach oil for the extra-virgin olive oil and skip the soy sauce, adding perhaps more of the other seasonings.

YAM-CRAN CASSEROLE

This is an easy-to-prepare casserole that complements any festive meal. Our Friday evening guests often take second helpings.

Serves 8

5 medium yams

1 package cranberries (10 ounces)

1/3 cup pure maple syrup

1/4 cup water

1/2 tsp sea salt or Herbamare

1 tbsp arrowroot powder

1 tbsp cold water

1 Preheat oven to 325° F.

2 Steam or boil the yams in their skins, until soft, cool, peel and reserve.

3 In a small saucepan, combine the cranberries, maple syrup and water, bring to a boil, and simmer for 5 minutes. Remove from heat and reserve.

4 Dissolve the arrowroot powder in 1 tablespoon cold water to form a paste.

5 Place yams in a food processor, add salt, and process until very smooth.

6 Place the yam mixture in a 9 - inch, round, oven-to-table casserole dish and cover with the cranberry sauce.

7 Bake uncovered for 20 minutes, and serve.

HELPFUL HINTS:

1. The rim of my particular casserole dish measures 3 inches in height.

2. This casserole can be prepared up to and including step 7, and frozen. When needed, bake covered for about 45 minutes without first defrosting it..

YAM LATKES

Everyone loves these immune-friendly latkes: the young, the old, the sandwich generation, and even the *"DINKS"* (Double-Income-No-Kids). They're perfect for any *Yomtov* (holiday) meal, as they can be made in advance and complement any menu. When finished, hide them until serving time or they'll never make it to the table.

Serves 8-10

8 medium-large yams

1 1/2 - 2 cups cornmeal or matzo meal for dredging

Sea salt or Herbamare to taste

2 tsp onion powder

2 tsp garlic powder

2 tsp ginger powder

Extra-virgin olive oil

1   Wash the yams and steam or boil until 'barely' soft.

2   Cool yams and peel, and refrigerate until cold.

3   Slice carefully into 1/4 - inch rounds and place on a large tray or platter.

4   In a suitable bowl, mix the cornmeal or matzo meal with the salt, onion powder, garlic powder and ginger powder, and dredge all the yam slices on both sides.

5   Pan-fry the latkes in a minimum amount of oil on medium heat on both sides until they are brown, and drain on paper towels.

HELPFUL HINTS:

1. These latkes can be prepared ahead of time, frozen and reheated in a 250° F oven as needed. When reheating, keep the latkes uncovered so they remain crisp.

2. You can make your own matzo meal by processing whole wheat matzos in a food processor or blender.

FOR PESACH:

Substitute Pesach oil for the extra-virgin olive oil, and use matzo meal for dredging.

MINI ZUCCHINI PATTIES

These crunchy cocktail patties are loved by everybody. When you are done pan-frying them, hide them until mealtime or they'll never make it to the table! They are also mouth-watering as appetizers.

Yields about 28 patties, 2-inch diameter

2 medium zucchini, coarsely grated and squeezed dry

1 small onion, finely grated

1/4 cup whole spelt or whole wheat flour

2 pinches nutmeg

1/4 cup bread crumbs

1 organic egg

1/4 - 1/2 tsp sea salt or Herbamare

Black pepper to taste

Extra-virgin olive oil for pan-frying

1 In a large bowl, combine the zucchini, onion, flour, nutmeg, bread crumbs, egg, salt and pepper, and mix well (best done with your hands).

2 In a large skillet, pan-fry the patties in oil by dropping them from a tablespoon, 4 - 5 minutes on each side, or until golden brown.

3 Drain well on paper towels and serve immediately.

FOR PESACH:
Substitute matzo meal for the flour and the bread crumbs, and Pesach oil for the extra-virgin olive oil.

"Fry now - pay later."

ZUCCHINI-TOMATO SAUCE

Zucchini is a bland-tasting vegetable, but here it is jazzed up as a succulent, ultra-versatile chunky sauce, served either as a side dish or sauced over grains, mashed or baked potatoes and pasta. It also can be an elegant appetizer (see below). Left-overs make great winter lunches, poured hot over toasted bread.

Serves 6-7 as a side dish or appetizer

1/2 cup chopped onions

1 1/2 tbsp extra-virgin olive oil

2 cloves garlic, minced or 1/2 tsp garlic powder

4 cups unpeeled chopped zucchini (1/4 - inch chunks)

1 1/4 cups water, divided

2 large bay leaves

3 tbsp white spelt flour

1/3 cup tomato paste

2 - 3 tbsp organic soy sauce

2 tbsp umeboshi vinegar

Black pepper to taste

2 tbsp chopped dill or 2 tsp dried

1 In a large saucepan, sauté the onions in oil until translucent, about 5 minutes.

2 Add the garlic and sauté another 2 minutes.

3 Add the zucchini, 1 cup water and the bay leaves. Cover and simmer for 5 minutes, or until the zucchini is almost done, stirring once.

4 In a separate bowl, combine the flour with the remaining 1/4 cup water, add the tomato paste, soy sauce, vinegar and pepper and mix.

5 Turn up the heat under the saucepan, add the flour mixture and stir constantly until the sauce has thickened.

6 Remove bay leaves, adjust seasoning and add the dill.

HELPFUL HINTS:
1. This sauce will keep in the refrigerator 4 - 5 days; can also be frozen.
2. Always taste zucchini raw before using it. If it is not fresh and firm, it may taste bitter and should be discarded. Sometimes only the peel is bitter; in that case it can be used peeled.
3. This recipe can double as a scrumptious sauce (see page 113).

— 🍃 —

APPETIZER:

Serve on individual plates. Pour the hot sauce generously on small slices of toasted bread or plain challah, or spoon into and over oven-warmed patty shells and serve immediately. DEELICIOUS!

BROILED ZUCCHINI BOATS

Simplicity is the key to most vegetable cooking. This recipe is quick and easy to prepare and delectable in a savoury kind of way, as long as you spice up this otherwise "*blah*" vegetable.

Serves 8-10 slices

1 medium unpeeled zucchini

Extra-virgin olive oil for coating

Sea salt or Herbamare to taste

Onion powder to taste

Garlic powder to taste

Black pepper to taste

1 Preheat broiler.

2 Scrub the zucchini, slice on the diagonal into 1/4 - inch x 2 - inch slices, and lay on a large broiling pan in single file.

3 With a pastry brush, lightly brush the top of each slice with oil, and sprinkle some sea salt or Herbamare, onion powder, garlic powder and black pepper on each slice.

4 Broil for 5 - 6 minutes or until golden on top. Do not stray from your kitchen, as these boats can easily burn.

HELPFUL HINTS:
If you have smaller zucchini, they can be cut in half lengthwise, and prepared the same way as above, but may need more time under the broiler.

FOR PESACH:
Substitute Pesach oil for the extra-virgin olive oil.

Zucchini-Tomato Pizzetta

This is a quick, flavourful and succulent snack with real pizzazz for lunch or anytime, provided you have the sauce stocked in the refrigerator, or defrosted. It is a health-promoting, lean-cuisine alternative to the common pizza with its low-grade ingredients, and my absolute favourite lunch.

Serves 1

2 slices whole spelt, whole rye, or whole wheat bread
1 cup **Zucchini-Tomato Sauce** (see page 113)
1/2 tsp dried basil (optional)

1 Preheat broiler.

2 On a broiling pan, place the bread, pour the sauce over it, and sprinkle with basil, if using.

3 Broil for about 5 minutes (Keep a close watch over it; the bread will burn quickly!).

"Human beings are the only critters in the world that overeat. There are no diet workshops or M.D.'s in the jungle. When animals get sick, they stop eating and rest until they are well again."

BASIC STIR-FRY

This basic stir-fry can be enhanced by adding other veggies, to increase the healing factor in our food.

Serves 2-3

1/2 cup **Kombu-Shiitake Stock** (see page 105) or **Vegetable Stock** (see page 104) or water

2 tsp arrowroot powder or white spelt flour

2 tbsp organic soy sauce

1/8 tsp sea salt or Herbamare

1/8 tsp black pepper

2 tsp extra-virgin olive oil

1/2 cup chopped onions

1 clove garlic, minced

1/4 cup sliced carrot (1/8 - inch rounds)

1/3 cup chopped celery (1/4 - inch pieces)

1/4 cup sliced sweet red pepper (1/8 - inch strips)

1 In a small bowl, combine stock or water with the arrowroot powder or flour, soy sauce, salt and pepper, and reserve.

2 In a large skillet, on medium heat, sauté the onions in oil for 2 - 3 minutes.

3 Add garlic and sauté another minute.

4 Add carrots, celery and peppers, and sauté 5 - 7 minutes.

5 Turn up heat, pour the liquid mixture over the vegetables, and stir continuously until the sauce thickens.

6 Adjust seasoning and serve immediately.

HELPFUL HINT:
Leftovers can be used in soups, grains, stews, pasta, patties, etc.

— ✎ —

VARIATION:

For a more substantial stir-fry, you may add any other vegetables that are hangin' out in your fridge; e.g. zucchini, mushrooms, broccoli, kale, spinach, bok choy, green onions, etc... (This will increase the volume of your stir-fry accordingly).

VEGETABLE CASSEROLE

This succulent, layered, main-course dish is one of my favourite comfort foods, but don't do it with one foot in the kitchen.

Serves 4-5

3 tbsp arrowroot powder or white spelt flour

3 3/4 cups **Kombu-Shiitake Stock** (see page 105) or **Vegetable Stock** (see page 104) or water

2/3 cup tomato paste

1-2 tbsp organic soy sauce

Sea salt or Herbamare to taste

Black pepper to taste

1 tsp garlic powder

1 tsp dried marjoram

4 medium potatoes, peeled and chopped (1/2 - inch chunks)

2 medium yams, peeled and chopped (1/2 - inch chunks)

1 1/2 cups chopped onions

2 cups sliced carrots (1/4 - inch rounds)

2 cups sliced celery (1/4 - inch pieces)

1 1/2 cups sliced leeks (1/2 - inch pieces)

2 medium zucchini, sliced (1/4 - inch rounds)

3 large bay leaves

1 Preheat oven to 350° F.

2 In a small dish, mix the arrowroot powder or flour with a bit of cold water to make a paste.

3 In another bowl, combine the stock or water, tomato paste, soy sauce, salt and pepper, garlic powder and marjoram with the arrowroot paste.

4 In a large, lightly-oiled oven casserole, layer the vegetables as they are listed and tuck the bay leaves in between.

5 Pour the liquid mixture over the casserole.

6 Bake, covered, for 55 - 60 minutes.

7 Remove bay leaves before serving.

HELPFUL HINTS:
1. To speed up preparation, use a food processor to chop and slice some of the vegetables (celery needs to be cut by hand).
2. You may add or substitute other veggies and herbs at your discretion, e.g. cauliflower, broccoli, etc…

BASIC WINTER VEGGIE STEW

This stew is especially good during the winter months when we need more warming foods. Once the veggies are all cut up, it takes only minutes to cook. My favourite winter lunch consists of pouring this hot, saucy stew over a few slices of steamed bread with a sprinkle of toasted sesame seeds. For best results, you will need at least 5 different vegetables to make this a tasty stew.

Serves 4-6

1/2 cup thinly sliced celery

1/2 cup shredded cabbage

1/2 cup sliced carrots (1/4 - inch pieces)

1/2 cup sliced leek (1 - inch pieces)

1/2 cup sliced zucchini (1/4 - inch pieces)

1/2 cup diced turnips (1 - inch cubes)

1/2 cup small cauliflower florets

1 1/4 cups water

2-3 tbsp organic soy sauce

1 tbsp umeboshi vinegar

1/2 tsp onion powder

3/4 tsp garlic powder

1/4 tsp dried marjoram

2 tbsp arrowroot powder

1 - 2 tbsp cold water

1   In a large bowl, place all the vegetables and toss well.

2   In a large skillet, bring water, soy sauce, vinegar, onion powder, garlic powder and marjoram to a boil.

3   Add the vegetables to the skillet, toss until all the vegetables are immersed in the boiling liquid.

4   Cover, turn off heat, and let stand on the element for 4 - 5 minutes, stirring once.

5   In a small bowl, mix the arrowroot powder with the cold water.

6   Bring the stew back to boil, add the arrowroot paste, and stir continuously until the sauce bubbles.

7   When the sauce has thickened, remove the skillet from the heat, put the cover back on, and let it stand for 8 - 10 minutes before serving.

HELPFUL HINTS:

1. You may substitute other veggies of your choice.

2. When reheating the finished stew, do not bring back to boil.

3. Leftovers can be added to soups, grains, pasta dishes and salads.

No-Fuss Potato Bake

There are no particular health benefits from eating potatoes (they are a nightshade vegetable and arthritics should avoid them) but most of us love them in all shapes, flavours and manner of cooking. Here's an easy way to prepare them and, eaten as soon as they are ready, they are a yummy comfort food

Serves 2-4

4 medium potatoes, unpeeled and scrubbed

2 tbsp extra-virgin olive oil

2 tbsp **Kombu-Shiitake stock** (see page 105) or **Vegetable stock** (see page 104) or water

1 tsp garlic powder

1 tsp paprika

1/2 cup chopped onions (1/4 - inch pieces)

1 tbsp dried parsley

Sea salt or Herbamare or organic soy sauce, to taste

1 Preheat oven to 450° F.

2 Cut potatoes into 3/4 - inch cubes and place in a mixing bowl.

3 Add the oil, stock or water, garlic powder, paprika, onions, parsley and salt or soy sauce, and mix well.

4 Transfer potatoes to an ovenproof baking dish, cover, and bake for 15 minutes.

5 Turn off the oven, leaving potatoes inside for about 3/4 of an hour.

6 Gently stir potatoes once, about halfway through.

7 Serve immediately.

HELPFUL HINT:
These potatoes do not like to hang around in the oven for more than one hour.

THE ABC OF CULINARIA - MY COOKING BIBLE & WORK ETHIC
(one hundred seventy ways to cook)

Add, adjust, arrange, assemble, bake, baste, blanche, blend, boil, braise, broil, brush, burn the food, chill, chop, coat, coddle, combine, cook, cool, cover, crimp, crumble, crush, curdle, cut, decorate, defrost, dice, dip, discard, dissolve, divide, drain, dredge, dress, dribble, drop, dry, dump in the garbage, dust, emulsify, fill, flip over, flute, fold, form, freak out, freeze, frost, fry, fuss, fuss, fuss, garnish, glaze, grate, grease, grill, grind, halve, heat, hull, hurry, ice, juice, julienne, layer, line, marinate, mash , measure, meld, melt, mince, mix, moisten, oil, omit, over-cook, pan fry, parboil, pat dry, peel, pick over, pile, pinch, place, plan, plan, plan, plunge, poach, pound, pour, press, proteinize, pulverize, puree, put-aside, quarter, reduce, reheat, remove, reserve, rinse, roast, roll, sauté, scoop, scrape, sear, season, seed, serve, set aside, shake, shallow-fry, shave, shred, sift, simmer, skim, slice, slide, soak, soften, sort, splash, spoon over, spread, sprinkle, spritz, sprout, squeeze, steam, stir, stir-fry, stock, stuff, substitute, swirl, take out the garbage, taste, tear, test, throw out, tilt, toast, top off, toss, transfer, trim, turn over, undo, vex, warm, wash, water-sauté, weigh, whip, whisk, wilt, worry, worry, worry, x-tract, yield, zest.

Dear Reader: Please ignore this list entirely. I guess this is just my way of displaying my passion to play with words. I have done most of these chores over and over again by trials, tribulation and trepidation in order for you to be able to sail with ease and the least amount of time through most of my recipes. If you enjoy this book, that will be my ample reward.

THE RAW DEAL ON SPROUTING
LIFE INSURANCE FOR PENNIES

Sprouts are a SUPERFOOD. A sprouting seed is the most alive and nourishing food known to humankind and therefore one of the most perfect foods. No amount of chewing grains and seeds can fully unlock their complete nutritional potential; only soaking and sprouting will do that. Sprouts contain from 50 - 1350% more of certain vitamins (A, B, C and E), minerals (calcium, potassium, magnesium, iron, selenium, and zinc), trace minerals, enzymes, cell salts, antioxidants, fibre, essential amino acids and protein than do the same seeds in their dry state. They increase our energy, add alkalinity to our system, cleanse our blood and cells and rid the colon of toxins. They enter the blood stream almost immediately after eating, since their high level of simple sugars requires little digestion. Sprouts are low in calories and contain no fat or cholesterol, and are the only food that can be organically grown anywhere, even in the tiniest kitchen. However, buying them ready - grown from a vegetable or supermarket may at times carry certain health hazards which do not apply in a private kitchen with clean water facilities. Here are my two favourite, easy-to-do sprout recipes.

ALFALFA SPROUTS

Yields 2 cups

You will need:
1 tbsp alfalfa seeds
1 wide-mouth jar
1 elastic band
1 piece of cheesecloth or old nylon hose
1 warm, dark space in your kitchen

1 Place the seeds in the wide mouth jar and fill with distilled or filtered water.

2 Cover the jar with the cheesecloth and affix the elastic band.

3 Let soak overnight in a dark corner or on your counter.

4 In the morning, drain off the water but do not remove the cheesecloth.

5 Rinse the seeds several times by filling the jar with fresh water, swishing it around gently and pouring off the liquid.

6 Fill the jar again with water, return it to its place, leaving the jar face down at a 45° angle, so it can drain.

7 Repeat steps 5 and 6 in the morning and evening until the seeds begin to sprout.

8 The alfalfa sprouts are ready to eat in 5 - 6 days, at which time they need to be thoroughly drained and stored in an airtight container in the fridge.

LENTIL SPROUTS

*Yields 1 1/2 -
2 cups*

You will need:

1/4 cup green lentils

1 wide- mouth jar

1 elastic band

1 piece of cheesecloth

1. Please follow steps 1 - 7 of the Alfalfa Sprouts recipe. The lentil sprouts are ready to eat in 2 days and should be stored in an airtight container in the fridge.

HELPFUL HINTS:

1. At the first stage of soaking, it is always necessary to use distilled or filtered water, as otherwise the seeds may not germinate well. Tap water for rinsing is fine.

2. When finished, throw the sprouts into your soup just before serving; sprinkle them into or onto your salads and or sandwiches. They will add protein and crunch and a distinctly earthy flavour to your dishes.

"Stop being brainwashed by the false notion that only animal food contains adequate protein."

- Dr. Joel Fuhrman MD

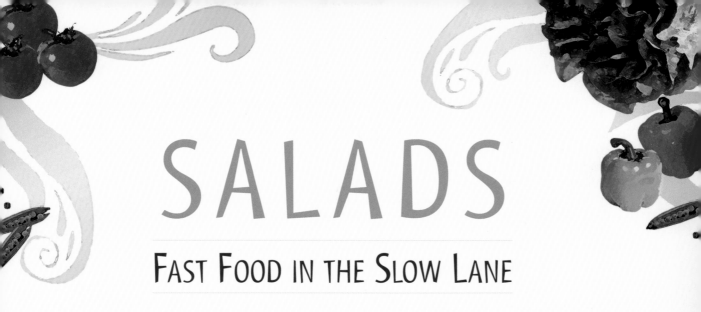

SALADS

FAST FOOD IN THE SLOW LANE

When I meet people socially, we invariably begin or end up talking 'food' or 'diet'. It is quite apparent that I somehow acquired a reputation, over many years, as some kind of a 'health nut', who deprives her husband of the culinary pleasures of eating anything that has been remotely in the vicinity of a butcher shop, or any other store than a health food store. Usually my friends and acquaintances want to know either what we eat and how we survive, or they want to give me their opinions as to why a vegetarian diet wouldn't work for them. If and when we do get to talk about actual food and cooking, I am usually told: "Oh, we have a large salad every night." But life in the slow lane is not quite so simplistic. A big salad every day is great, but it is not enough to keep us, in the polluted-frenetic-21st-century-time-zone, healthy and ageing gracefully. We need a large variety of vegetables on a regular basis. Many vegetables can actually be incorporated into one big salad. These combinations look gorgeous, taste scrumptious, are nutritious and great time-savers, provided you can get your kitchen act together (No, of course I don't mean YOU!) (see **How to Cook in Stages & Other Timeless Timesavers**, page 242).

It's 'cool' nowadays for the diet-conscious or yo-yo-dieting woman of the 21st Century to order a fresh salad without dressing over a schmoozie lunch with a bunch of like-minded females. (Of course, we don't want to know what she packs in from the back of the fridge when she gets home).

> Become Your Own C.E.O
> C - Creative and Consistent
> E - Experimental and Efficient
> O - Original and Orderly

If your imagination and/or your organizational skills in the kitchen are lacking, or you are tired or frazzled, having all your energies tied up either in a career (trying to shatter the 'glass ceiling' perhaps), or in any other boring or fascinating job away from home, or volunteering, or if it seems like you are carpooling all day, or if your kids are climbing the walls, or crayoning on your dining room silk-brocade-baroque-style wallpaper, or swinging from the chandelier while nanny is polishing her toe nails - and if you are still with me - I will be glad to offer you my phantasmagoric veggie-combo-salad ideas.

In order to make a good salad, I like to begin with a large bowl; and it should be twice as big as your quantity of salad. This makes it possible to mix your salads well with your dressings. I always start with romaine as the basic ingredient. In comparison, romaine lettuce has twice the potassium and folic acid, six times the vitamin C and eight times the beta-carotene that iceberg lettuce has, even if it does come washed, chopped and rusty-around-the-edges in a plastic bag, with a kosher seal. Since romaine has such sturdy leaves, I often shred it by hand into my salads (1/4 - inch pieces). The varieties of salads that can be prepared are virtually endless. Most vegetables turn up sooner or later, raw or steamed, in my salads along with other sundry edibles. For instance, the young 'n' pale yellow - green leaves from celery stalks add a delicate, understated hint of celery taste. This is where the Edith Principle comes in: "Whatever is not nailed down in my kitchen or hanging from the ceiling is power for the cause".

There are a variety of salad greens that in small quantities can enhance a basic salad and are equally as nutritious - some even more so! These are: dandelion; arugala (rocket), which has a peppery bite and is rich in both calcium and beta-carotene; radicchio, which adds a lovely red colour, crunch and a slightly bitter taste; frizzy lettuce; watercress, which supposedly has more iron than spinach; sorrel and Belgian endive, which has a mild taste and has as much potassium as bananas. A salad tastes best when its lettuce leaves are dry. I don't necessarily use a salad spinner, but will wrap the salad leaves between two towels after they have been washed, lightly roll them up for awhile, and then store the leaves in a plastic container. Who has not heard of Tupperware, which was perhaps one of the greatest kitchen ideas for the 20st Century housewife-cook?

A basic salad will often have tomatoes, cucumbers and red bell peppers in it. I often add raw or lightly steamed grated carrots to my salads. There are few limitations when adding vegetables to a green salad. Any freshly cooked or left over vegetables add nutritional and special interest value to a salad.

For proteinizing and simplifying my meals, I often throw cooked adzuki beans or chickpeas into my salad. Sunflower seeds add a special crunch and flavour, and walnuts give a Waldorf twist.

One of my favourite ways to eat a green salad is a lettuce and fruit combination. For a cooling midsummer luncheon, or for that matter all year 'round, I will mix any of the following sliced fruits into a green salad: orange, tangerine, grapefruit, mango, pear, strawberries, cranberries and raisins. (See **Summer Salad Supreme** page.78)

Fresh parsley, fresh dill, or dried marjoram, always adds an extra bit of herbal sophistication to any salad.Taste wise, fresh herbs are always better than dried ones. I also routinely add finely chopped purple (red) onions, as they lend a special and savory bite to salads.

There are literally endless variations to mixing and matching your own in-house salads (even if you don't have a salad chef). Being a confirmed 'vegeholic', I create new rainbow combinations everyday - just can't help it.

ABOUT DRESSINGS

In spite of the current 'foodies' trend to fancy up our salads with aromatic oils and exotic vinegars, housed in artistically-shaped bottles, giving the illusion of sun-drenching on a mediterranean sea-side patio, or better still being on a cruise, I do not buy into the illusion. I am a firm believer in simplifying my life and building health on the home front. Therefore, I stick more or less to the same ingredients for most of my dressings.These are: one or more of the following vinegars: umeboshi vinegar, apple cider vinegar or brown rice vinegar, flaxseed oil, sea salt or Herbamare, fresh parsley, fresh or dried dill, or dried marjoram. **Nayomaise** (see page 119), is added where and when suitable.

Speaking of dressings, this really happened in England between a woman and her au-pair girl, in the kitchen. The au- pair was repeatedly asked to dress the chicken, until she finally took the courage to say, practically in tears; "But, madame, I don't know where her clothes are."

BEYOND THE RAINBOW SALAD

No veggies, raw or cooked, are safe from my passion for this vita-packed, mix 'n match salad. It is especially good for those poor souls who don't like vegetables but need their immune-building properties.

Serves 5-6

4 cups shredded packed romaine lettuce

1/4 cup shredded packed radicchio

1/4 cup shredded packed Belgian endive

1/3 cup finely sliced purple onion

2 - inch piece English cucumber, shaved with a vegetable peeler

1 small carrot, shaved with a vegetable peeler

1 celery stalk, shaved with a vegetable peeler

1/8 cup finely chopped dill

2-3 tbsp flaxseed oil

3 tbsp brown rice vinegar or 1 - 2 tbsp apple cider vinegar

2 tbsp umeboshi vinegar

1 tbsp dried marjoram

1 In a large bowl, place all the vegetables and dill and toss well.

2 Pour the oil and vinegars and marjoram over the salad, toss well, adjust seasoning and serve immediately.

———————— ❧ ————————

BEYOND THE RAINBOW VARIATIONS:

More colour in your salad means more energy for you, and adds to your daily vitamin and mineral account. Add to this salad any of the following according to your taste: finely sliced raw mushrooms, finely grated raw or cooked beets, yellow or red sweet peppers, cut into fine strips. You can also sneak in some steamed kale or broccoli. Served with some kind of grains, pasta or wholesome bread, this salad can become a main course.

A SPECIAL OCCASION SALAD

I often serve this fruity salad at our Friday evening meals by itself after the soup and before the main course, when we have guests.

Serves 4-6

4 cups shredded packed romaine lettuce (iceberg is a nutritional no-no!)

1/4 cup shredded packed Belgian endive

1/4 cup shredded packed radicchio

1/3 cup shredded packed arugula

1/3 cup finely sliced purple onions

1 medium or 2 small oranges, peeled and chopped (1/2 - inch pieces)

1/4 cup dried organic cranberries

2 - 3 tbsp brown rice vinegar

1/2 tbsp umeboshi vinegar

2 - 3 tbsp flaxseed oil

1/8 cup finely chopped flat-leaf parsley or dill

1   In a large bowl, combine the lettuce, endive, radicchio, arugula, onions, orange pieces and cranberries.

2   Add the vinegars, oil and parsley or dill, and toss well.

3   Serve immediately.

VARIATIONS:

1. Substitute 1/2 cup diced tangerine slices, sweet ripe pear or mango for the oranges.

2. Substitute organic Thompson raisins for the cranberries.

3. The lettuce may be torn by hand rather than shredded in all salads; in fact, the lettuce may prefer it for being much gentler on their system.

"Attractive, colourful and health-promoting food is to my stomach
what music is to my ears, what flowers are to my eyes,
what kindness is to my heart and what love is to my spirit."

CLEOPATRA SALAD

This is a heart-smart salad, the perfect antidote to the ever-popular restaurant stand-by, the Caesar salad. Its only drawback is that you have to get into your kitchen and actually prepare it yourself, notwithstanding the likelihood that Cleopatra had more than one salad chef. The grated Parmesan cheese of the Caesar salad is replaced here by hard-boiled eggs, and the anchovies, which are too salty and oily for my taste, are replaced by a zesty dressing.

Serves 2-3

1 1/2 cups shredded packed romaine lettuce

1 medium tomato, cut into thin wedges

1/4 cup finely slivered purple onions

1/4 cup chopped green onions (1/4 - inch pieces)

1/4 cup thinly sliced or finely shaved cucumber

1 tbsp umeboshi vinegar

2 tbsp brown rice vinegar

1 1/2 tbsp flaxseed oil

1/4 cup finely chopped flat-leaf parsley or dill

1 - 2 organic hard-cooked eggs, coarsely chopped

1   Place all the vegetables in a large bowl.

2   Add the vinegars, oil, and parsley or dill, and toss well.

3   Sprinkle the egg over the salad and toss gently again.

4   Serve at room temperature.

HELPFUL HINT:

For best results, the greens in this salad should be fresh, crisp, and completely dry.

SUMMER SALAD SUPREME

What is supreme about this salad? It's as refreshing as a cool breeze on a hot summer day. I eat it all year 'round, whenever I need a light lunch and some vitamin C. Whenever we combine fruit with salad greens, we slow down the absorption of sugars from the fruit into our bodies. This enables us to keep our energy level up longer and prevents us from getting hungry again too soon.

Serves 2

2 cups shredded packed romaine lettuce (iceberg is a nutritional no-no!)

1 large orange or 2 tangerines, peeled and chopped (1/2 - inch pieces)

1 small grapefruit, peeled and chopped (1/2 - inch pieces)

1 tbsp freshly squeezed lemon juice

2 tbsp **Nutty-Edith Crunch** (see page 181)

1 - 2 tsp flaxseed oil

A small handful organic golden raisins or dried organic cranberries

1 In a medium bowl, combine all the ingredients, toss well and serve.

HEALTHFUL HINT:
In addition to the numerous health benefits of all grapefruit, pink grapefruit has 40% more beta carotene than white grapefruit.

VARIATIONS:

1. Substitute ripe pear or mango pieces for the orange or tangerine.
2. Substitute sunflower seeds for the Nutty-Edith Crunch.

"If life hands you a lemon, squeeze it into your salads."

DILLICIOUS CARROT SALAD

This slightly sweet 'n sour salad is a healthy complement to any menu, with its life-supporting antioxidants, and is especially good with steamed rice or mashed potatoes.

Serves 2-3

2 medium carrots, steamed whole and cooled

2 tsp umeboshi vinegar

1 tsp flaxseed oil

1 tsp water

1 1/2 tsp pure maple syrup

1 tsp stone-ground mustard

1/2 tsp grated ginger or 1/4 tsp ground ginger

1 tbsp finely chopped dill

1 Coarsely grate the carrots and place in a medium bowl.

2 Whisk together the vinegar, oil, water, maple syrup, mustard, ginger and dill, and pour over the carrots; toss well, and serve at room temperature.

⎯⎯ 🍃 ⎯⎯

SUNNY VARIATION:

Add 1 tablespoon sunflower seeds to this salad.

KALE 'N' CARROT SALAD

This sturdy, easy-to-make salad keeps well in the refrigerator for a few days, so you can double the recipe and serve several times. It goes well as a side dish with any type of carbohydrate main course.

Serves 4

2 cups shredded packed kale, steamed

4 small carrots, steamed and sliced (1/4 - inch slices)

1/3 cup cooked chickpeas

2 tbsp chopped onions

2 tsp sunflower seeds

1/4 tsp stone-ground mustard

2 tsp umeboshi vinegar

1 tbsp apple cider vinegar

Sea salt or Herbamare to taste

Black pepper to taste

1 tsp **Nayomaise** (see page 119)

2 tsp flaxseed oil

1 In a medium bowl, place the kale, carrots, chickpeas, onions and sunflower seeds and toss.

2 Whisk together mustard, vinegars, salt, pepper, Nayomaise and oil until well blended, add to the bowl, mix well, and serve at room temperature.

"There is absolutely no nutrient, no protein, no vitamin, no mineral that can't be obtained from plant-based foods."

– Michael Klaper, MD

CELERY-CELERIAC SALAD

Even though celeriac (celery root) and celery grow up together, each has its own distinct taste and texture, which gives this salad its interesting flavour.

Serves 4-6

1 medium celeriac, peeled

2 large celery ribs, sliced (1/4 - inch pieces)

1/2 cup finely chopped purple onions

1/4 cup finely chopped flat-leaf parsley

2 tbsp brown rice vinegar

1 tbsp umeboshi vinegar

1 tbsp flaxseed oil

Black pepper to taste

1 Cut the celeriac into quarters and slice each wedge thinly into 1/4 - inch pieces.

2 Steam celeriac for 5 minutes, and cool.

3 Steam celery for 8 - 10 minutes, and cool.

4 In a bowl, toss the steamed vegetables with the onions, parsley, vinegars, oil and pepper, mix well, adjust seasoning and serve at room temperature.

BEETIFUL SALAD

This mineral-rich and health-promoting salad 'beets' to a different drummer.

Serves 3-4

2 medium beets, peeled and steamed or boiled,

1/8 cup diced purple onions

2 tsp apple cider vinegar or brown rice vinegar

2 tsp umeboshi vinegar

Sea salt or Herbamare to taste

Black pepper to taste

2 tsp **Nayomaise** (see page 119)

1 tbsp finely chopped flat-leaf parsley

1 Into a medium bowl, coarsely shred the beets and add the onions, vinegars, salt, pepper, Nayomaise and parsley, and toss well.

2 Adjust seasoning and serve at room temperature.

HELPFUL HINT:

Cook extra beets and grate or finely dice into green salads, adding colour, texture, flavour and nutrition.

HEALTHFUL HINT:

Please do not discard the full-of-nutrition stems! I chop them into 1/4 - inch pieces, steam them for about 8-10 minutes, and add them to green salads.

COLOUR-ME-PURPLE SALAD

If you are not a vegan, you may have had a peek into my fish department and noticed the recipe for Herring salad. This succulent salad is a take-off from that one minus the herring, but tastes very similar. It makes great party fare at a buffet, and is an excellent choice as an appetizer (see below).

Serves 6-7

1/2 cup peeled steamed or cooked beets (1/4 - inch cubes)

1/2 cup steamed sliced carrots (1/4 - inch cubes)

1/2 cup steamed sliced celery (1/4 - inch cubes)

1/2 cup peeled steamed or cooked potatoes (1/4 - inch cubes)

1/2 cup sliced apple (1/4 - inch cubes)

1/4 cup finely chopped purple onions

1/4 cup finely chopped sour pickle

1/4 cup finely chopped flat-leaf parsley

Dressing:

2 tsp umeboshi vinegar, or to taste

2 tsp apple cider vinegar, or to taste

1 tbsp flaxseed oil

1   Make the dressing.

2   Place all the other ingredients in a large bowl, and mix thoroughly.

3   Pour the dressing over the ingredients in the bowl, toss everything together and adjust seasoning.

4   Serve at room temperature.

─────── 🍃 ───────

HELPFUL HINT:
Keeps well refrigerated about three days.

SCHMALTZY VARIATION:

If you are a herring lover, check the recipe for **Herring Salad** (see page 192) for a similar culinary experience, however it'll be fishy.

APPETIZER:

Serve 1/3 - 1/2 cup individually on a large lettuce leaf!

Fresh 'n' Frooty Spinach Salad

This elegant, luscious salad is a real quickie to prepare, and makes a mouth-watering, enticing side dish or appetizer. Popeye would have loved it.

Serves 4 as a side dish, or 6 as an appetizer

4 cups packed baby spinach

1/2 cup finely chopped purple onions

1/2 orange or 1/2 mango, peeled and chopped (1/2 - inch pieces)

1/4 cup organic golden raisins or dried organic cranberries

1 1/2 tbsp flax seed oil

2 tsp umeboshi vinegar

2 tsp apple cider vinegar

2 pinches black pepper

1 In a large bowl, combine the spinach, onion, orange or mango and raisins or cranberries.

2 In a small bowl, whisk together the oil, vinegars and pepper.

3 Pour dressing over the spinach mixture and toss well, adjust seasoning and serve at room temperature.

VARIATIONS:

1. The orange or mango can be substituted with chopped soft anjou pear or with fresh, sliced strawberries.

2. To proteinize this gorgeous salad, add a small handful of sunflower seeds or a few chopped walnuts.

"The quality of food we eat is a major contributor to the quality of our life."

TASTES FROM A MAGNIFICENT HERB GARDEN

Herbs have tremendous healing powers besides their inimitable flavours. The use of fresh herbs seems to be the stuff that nowadays defines a good cook. There is a tendency afoot for chefs, gourmet cooks and self-styled foodies to use herbs in utter profusion and with total abandon. Their dictum seems to be "more is better", but I follow the dictum "less is more" when it comes to flavouring food. Herbs should enhance and not overpower a dish.

My own experience with fresh herbs came many years ago when my husband and I spent ten days at a Health Clinic in Switzerland. Raw, whole, organic fruits and vegetables, picked hourly fresh from the gardens, was the order of the day. Don't get the wrong idea, you steady spa clients! This was a far cry from a North American or European fancy-schmancy spa. The most pampering we got was thermos bottles in our room each evening with our own personalized and tailored-to-our-health, ghastly-tasting, herbal teas.

You would not dare to talk in the dining room while eating as you were supposed to chew each morsel of food fifty times before swallowing. The portions were extremely moderate, certainly not in line with the price of the place. At lunch time, with Swiss punctuality at exactly twelve noon and not a second later, each person was served their own elegantly-arranged all-raw salads in an attractive bowl. The herbs that went into these unforgettable salads were picked fresh from the magnificent gardens literally minutes before being served. And the taste of these exquisite, sensational salads will probably remain forever in the food files of the clients' bio-computers.

SOUPS
&
SAUCES

SOUP AND SAUCE RECIPES

SOUPS

THE COMFORT FOOD FOR ALL OCCASIONS

Satisfying, Original, Utilitarian, Pleasurable, Savoury

Most people love soup, especially in winter to start a meal. We, of the daily-soup-eating club, however, enjoy soups all year 'round. Hot weather does not deter us; we simply eat some of our soups cold or, to put it more elegantly, "chilled."

First and foremost, soup is a comfort food for body and soul. It warms us in the winter and cools us in the summer. It quickly satisfies our appetite and cravings and it's usually easy to digest. But I suspect soup's appeal may also have something to do with nostalgic feelings originating in childhood, when the lucky ones were nurtured on more than just a physical level. When I was choosing the topic for my Masters thesis in Adlerian psychology, had I known then what I know today, I would not have agonized for a whole year psychoanalyzing the tragic figure of Willie Loman in Arthur Miller's "*Death of a Salesman*." Instead, I would have written about the comforting and psychological effects of eating a good homemade soup cooked by a loved one.

Preparing a soup is always a great opportunity for me to use up leftovers, making it a practical, economical, creative and delicious way to implement my No-Waste-Food-Policy. Anything that is not nailed down in my kitchen may end up in my soups. When frequently asked by our guests "*What's in this soup?*" I always reply quite honestly: "*I don't remember.*"

One of the many healthy benefits of making vegetarian, home-cooked soups is the fact that most people are willing to eat ingredients in soup that they might otherwise not so readily eat if served on a dinner plate. And if you can keep it a secret, they don't necessarily need to know that there may be kale or yams in their soup to support a healthy immune system.

If you are pressured for time, a hearty soup can be the centre of your meal. Soups freeze well, but they should never be brought back to a boil when being reheated, because heat over 112 degrees destroys their valuable vitamins and enzymes. I freeze my soups in glass jars, but they can easily be frozen in Ziploc bags. To defrost my soups, I take off the cover and place them in a warming oven for an hour or more. If you have the time, cook soups for the freezer, especially in winter, or make doubles and freeze. Defrosted soups will come in handy for those frantic, fretful, frazzled, frenetic and frenzied days. (If you don't have any of those, please tell us your secret!)

My soups are all made without fat or oil. If you prefer to sauté some of the ingredients first, you may do so and then continue with my recipes.

I use the sea vegetable, wakame, in many of my soups, as it is the richest source of essential and micro-nutrients available to us in our diet (see **Sea Vegetables**, page 27).

There are endless variations to cooking vegetarian soups, the only limitations being your imagination and the size of your pot. Most vegetables get along fine together in one vegetable soup. Adding any of the grains to your soups will make them more filling and more nutritious. Fast cooking grains, such as oats, quinoa, millet, bulgur, and couscous, can be added at the beginning of cooking soup. Longer-cooking grains, such as barley, rice, wheat berries, rye kernels and kamut kernels, are best cooked separately and when finished added to a basic vegetable soup.

Adding legumes to your grain soups will constitute a complete protein dish, which can be your main course, and needs no other protein for that meal. Lentils can be added at the beginning of cooking, while slower-cooking legumes, such as dried peas, chickpeas, adzuki beans and all other beans, are better cooked separately and added at the end. What a delicious, practical, and health-promoting way to get your protein without the negative side effects of eating animal protein in today's over-chemicalized world. If you don't particularly care for legumes in your soups, you can always make a bean salad and serve it with your grain meals in order to get the complete nutritional benefit. Or, simply enhance your green salads by adding some cooked beans.

When cooking fresh vegetable soups, there are a few tricks that will enhance their flavour and appearance:

- Always use celery leaves along with their stalks.

- Use the stems of all vegetables, chopped into small pieces.

- Throw in some fresh-frozen peas to add an aura of summer.

- Adding yam pieces will give your soups a delicately sweet flavour and a golden, smooth texture when processed.

- Tomato paste will add extra flavour and colour to certain soups.

- Dried, soaked and chopped shiitake mushrooms add an earthy and meaty flavour to soups; they also have a calming effect on nerves.

- Adding tiny tofu cubes to a cooked soup supplies easily-digestible protein.

Whenever you can, garnish your soups with herbaceous greens, such as fresh parsley or dill. Parsley is full of calcium and other blood-building components, and dill always adds a delicate culinary and aesthetic pleasure. Lately, I have started chopping up the stems of fresh parsley, and sprinkling them on soups and salads when serving, adding a touch of earthy crunch and aromatic flavour. I avoid garnishes such as pine nuts, as they are often rancid and can spoil the flavour of the whole soup. I love croutons in certain soups, but they are usually too greasy for my conscience.

Any soup can be blended or processed to be served to a baby or to a 100-year-old person. It can also be a booster to patients who have digestive problems or difficulty in swallowing. To serve puréed soups cold in summer is a delightful and refreshing treat. I have, this summer, puréed a bean soup and served it cold, which proved a filling and delicious dish. For an elegant appetizer, serve your 'chilled' soups in attractive china bowls or cups. Of course, one has the choice to always use plastic or throw-away bowls and clutter up the universe.

So what are you waiting for? Get in your kitchen, put on your apron - if you are old-fashioned like me - take out your biggest pot, count how many big mouths you have to feed and start cooking soups!

HERBED SOUP CAROTENE

The acidity of the tomatoes and the sweetness of the carrots make for a most flavourful combination in this soup. Served chilled at the start of a summer meal, it is positively elegant.

Serves 4

4 medium carrots, peeled and halved crosswise

4 medium, ripe tomatoes

3 cups water

2 cloves garlic, minced

2 tbsp organic soy sauce

2 tbsp umeboshi vinegar

1 tsp chopped basil or 1/4 tsp dried

Chopped dill for garnish

1 Steam the carrots for 8 minutes and reserve.

2 Plunge the tomatoes into boiling water for 30 seconds, remove the peel, and chop coarsely.

3 Place the tomatoes in a saucepan with 3 cups water and garlic, cover, and bring to a boil.

4 Turn heat to low and simmer for 10 minutes.

5 Strain the soup and reserve the liquid.

6 Purée the tomatoes and carrots with a hand-held electric mixer, or in a blender or food processor, and add from the reserved liquid until the desired consistency is reached. (Keep unused liquid for stock.)

7 Pour the soup back into the saucepan, add the soy sauce, vinegar, and basil, adjust the seasoning, and simmer five minutes more.

8 Garnish with dill, and serve hot or chilled, depending on the season.

TEN-KARAT SOUP

This semi-precious, velvety soup is loaded with vitamin A, which has the function to feed the good soldiers in our bodies that are fighting for a healthy immune system against the "free radicals", created by a diet of processed and junk food.

Serves 8-9

10 medium carrots, sliced (1/4 - inch rounds)

1 medium white potato, cubed (1 - inch cubes)

1 medium onion, diced

3 cloves garlic, minced

1 1/4 - inch piece ginger, grated

6 cups water

3 tbsp organic soy sauce

2 tbsp umeboshi vinegar

Black pepper to taste

Chopped curly parsley or dill for garnish

1. In a large pot, add the carrots, potato, onion, garlic, ginger and water, cover, and bring to a boil.

2. Reduce heat to low and cook for about 30 minutes.

3. Cool slightly and purée with a hand-held electric mixer, or in a blender or food processor.

4. Return the soup to the pot, add the soy sauce, vinegar, and pepper and simmer for another 8 minutes.

5. Garnish liberally with parsley or dill before serving.

———— 🍀 ————

PRECIOUS VARIATION:

If you insist on a 14 - karat soup, increase the quantity of carrots and the other ingredients in the recipe accordingly.

SIMPLY YAM SOUP

This is the smooth, creamy soup our lovely daughter-in-law, Esther, serves us when we come for *Shabbos* (Sabbath). Being the mother of all mothers, she also allows her father-in-law to have a side dish of chicken soup with a few fluffy *kneidels* (dumplings), which he cannot get at home because we do not have a *fleischike* (meat) kitchen.

Serves 7-8

6 cups water

4 medium yams, chopped (1 - inch chunks)

1 cup chopped onions

1/2 cup oatmeal (not the quick-cooking kind please!)

2 cloves garlic, minced

2 large bay leaves

1/2 tsp grated ginger

2 - inch piece wakame

1 - 2 tbsp organic soy sauce

2 tbsp umeboshi vinegar

3/4 tsp ground cumin

Chopped curly parsley or chopped dill for garnish

1   In a large saucepan, add the water, yams, onions, oatmeal, garlic, bay leaves, ginger, wakame, soy sauce, vinegar and cumin, and simmer for 25 - 30 minutes.

2   Remove the bay leaves, and purée with a hand-held electric mixer, or in a blender or food processor.

3   Adjust seasoning, garnish with parsley or dill and serve.

———————— ✤ ————————

CALCI-YUMMY VARIATION:

Add one cup finely shredded kale at step 1.

VIVALDI SOUP

This heart-friendly and comforting Four-Seasons soup provides you with lo-cal, no-fat plant protein, and is a mouth-watering meal starter, served hot or cold.

Serves 8

4 - inch piece wakame

1 cup yellow split peas, soaked overnight in 3 cups water

8 cups water

2 medium yams, peeled and sliced (1 - inch pieces)

1 cup coarsely chopped onions

3 cloves garlic, minced

3 bay leaves

3/4 cup sliced celery (1/2 - inch pieces)

1 tsp grated ginger

5 tbsp organic soy sauce

3 tbsp umeboshi vinegar

1/2 tsp ground cumin

Black pepper to taste

Chopped curly parsley for garnish

1   Soak the wakame in a bit of warm water for 8 minutes, cut into small pieces, and reserve.

2   Strain the peas and discard the soak water.

3   In a large pot, place the peas, wakame, water, yams, onions, garlic, bay leaves, celery and ginger, cover and bring to a boil.

4   Cook on medium-low heat for 30 minutes.

5   Cool slightly and purée with a hand-held electric mixer, or in a blender or food processor.

6   Put the soup back in the pot, add the soy sauce, vinegar, cumin, and pepper; adjust seasoning and simmer for another 8 minutes.

7   Remove the bay leaves, garnish with parsley, and serve.

CREAMED CAULIFLOWER SOUP

This is a velvety-smooth, low calorie soup, with its own simple and delicate flavour. Served hot or cold, it is a perfect meal-starter, and is an elegant addition to a buffet.

Serves 7-8

5 cups small cauliflower florets (1 small cauliflower)
6 cups water
1 cup coarsely chopped onions
1/2 cup oat flakes
1 medium potato, cut into chunks
1 tsp sea salt or Herbamare
2 - inch piece ginger with peel
1/2 tsp ground nutmeg
1 1/2 tsp umeboshi vinegar
1/4 tsp ground turmeric
1 tbsp organic soy sauce
2 tbsp chopped dill for garnish

1 In a large pot, place the cauliflower, water, onions, oat flakes, potato, salt, and ginger, cover and bring to a boil.

2 Cook on medium - low heat for 20 - 25 minutes.

3 Remove the ginger.

4 Cool slightly and purée with a hand-held electric mixer, or in a blender or food processor.

5 Pour the soup back into the pot, and add the nutmeg, umeboshi, turmeric and soy sauce, adjust the seasoning and simmer for another 8 minutes.

6 Garnish with the dill and serve.

———— 🍂 ————

CALCI-YUMMY VARIATION:
Add 1 cup finely shredded kale at step 1.

Velvety Zucchini Soup

This mellow soup with its emerald hue is one of my favourites. Its low - keyed flavour masks a simple elegance. If you like creamy soups, marry off your vegetables with oatmeal. It will give you a smooth and velvety soup each time, and is much healthier without the dairy cream. In her very generous and loving way, our daughter-in-law, Chani, makes bucketsful every time we come to visit in Monsey.

Serves 6-8

2 large zucchini, chopped (1/2 - inch chunks)

1 large or 2 medium potatoes, peeled and sliced (1/4 - inch rounds)

1 cup chopped onions

2 cloves garlic, chopped

2 bay leaves

6 cups water

1/2 cup oat flakes

1 - 2 tbsp organic soy sauce

Sea salt or Herbamare to taste

Black pepper to taste

2 pinches ground nutmeg

2 tbsp finely chopped dill or 1 tsp dried, for garnish

1   To a medium or large pot, add the zucchini, potatoes, onions, garlic, bay leaves, water and oat flakes, cover and bring to a boil.

2   Lower the heat to medium-low and cook for 30 minutes.

3   Cool slightly, remove the bay leaves and purée with a hand-held electric mixer, or in a blender or food processor.

4   Return the soup to the pot, add soy sauce, salt, pepper and nutmeg, adjust seasoning and simmer for another 6 - 8 minutes.

5   When serving, garnish with dill.

"When we sit down to a meal, we should eat with our eyes, digest with our mouths, be calm with our minds and be grateful with our hearts."

SIMPLY PEA SOUP

This is an easy recipe, especially for a beginner who wants to dabble in legumes, get away from flesh foods, and get into 'comfort food'. Eaten with a grain dish, it is a delicious way to get your proteins.

Serves 8-9

1 1/2 cup green or yellow split peas, soaked overnight

8 cups water

1 1/2 cup coarsely chopped onions

3 cloves garlic, minced or 3/4 tsp garlic powder

3 bay leaves

3 medium carrots, cut into quarters, crosswise

1 tsp sea salt or Herbamare

1/2 tsp ground cumin

1 - 2 tbsp organic soy sauce

2 tbsp chopped flat-leaf parsley

1 Drain the peas.

2 To a large pot, add the water, peas, onions, garlic, bay leaves and carrots, cover and cook for 30 minutes.

3 Add salt and cook for another 25 - 30 minutes or until the peas are soft.

4 Cool slightly, remove the carrots and reserve; remove the bay leaves and discard.

5 Purée the soup with a hand-held electric mixer, or in a blender or food processor.

6 Put the soup back into the pot, add the cumin and soy sauce, adjust seasoning and simmer for another 8 minutes.

7 When serving, garnish with 1 or 2 pieces of the carrots and the parsley.

POTATO-LEEK SOUP

This simple soup is filling and heart-friendly; truly *nouvelle cuisine*, as its flavour does not depend on *beurre blanc* or *crème fraiche*. Served cold, it becomes *vichyssoise*, which is a signature dish for students at the exclusive *Cordon Bleu* cooking school in Paris.

Serves 6
- 4 - inch piece wakame
- 6 cups water
- 3 cups peeled and cubed potatoes
- 3 cups sliced leeks (1 - inch pieces)
- 2 cloves garlic, minced
- 1/2 tsp dried marjoram (optional)
- Pinch ground nutmeg
- Sea salt or Herbamare to taste
- Black pepper to taste
- 2 tbsp organic soy sauce
- 2 tbsp chopped dill or 2 tsp dried

1. Soak the wakame in a bit of warm water for 8 minutes, and cut into small pieces.

2. In a medium pot, place the water, potatoes, leeks, garlic, and soaked wakame, cover, and bring to a boil. Simmer for about 25 minutes.

3. Purée the soup with a hand-held electric mixer, or in a blender or food processor.

4. Pour the soup back into the pot, add marjoram (if used), nutmeg, salt, pepper, soy sauce, and dill; adjust the seasoning and simmer for another 8 minutes.

5. Serve hot or chilled, depending on the season.

BARLEY-BEAN SOUP

This is one of those classic, no-fuss grain/legume combos, where no other protein is needed. Served with a big salad, it can be a one - pot meal.

Serves 6-7

1/3 cup baby lima beans
4 dried shiitake mushrooms
2 - inch piece wakame
5 cups water
1/2 cup barley
1 small yam, peeled and cubed (1/2 - inch cubes)
1/2 cup chopped onions
2 cloves garlic, minced
1/2 cup sliced carrots (1/4 - inch rounds)
1/2 cup sliced celery (1/2 - inch pieces) (also the leaves if available)
2 large bay leaves
2 tbsp organic soy sauce
1/8 tsp ground cumin
1 tsp dried marjoram
Black pepper to taste
1/4 tsp sea salt or Herbamare
Finely chopped flat-parsley, for garnish

1 Soak the lima beans overnight, drain, and reserve.

2 Soak shiitake mushrooms in warm water for 15 minutes; chop small, discarding only the hard ends.

3 Soak wakame in warm water for 8 minutes, and slice into 1/4 - inch pieces.

4 In a medium pot, place the lima beans, shiitake, wakame, water, barley, yam, onions, garlic, carrots, celery, bay leaves, and cover.

5 Bring to a boil, and cook on medium-low heat for 50 minutes, or until beans are soft.

6 Add soy sauce, cumin, marjoram, pepper and salt, adjust seasoning and simmer another 8 minutes.

———————— 🍀 ————————

NUTRILICIOUS VARIATIONS:

1. Substitute adzuki beans for the limas.

2. Substitute 3/4 cup fresh, sliced, white or brown button mushrooms for the dried shiitake.

3. Add 1/4 - 1/2 cup tomato paste to the soup near the end of cooking, to add a stronger flavour.

BARLEY-LENTIL SOUP

With its grain-legume combination, no other protein is needed when this soup is on the menu. It can also be placed into a crock-pot, and served as a vegetarian cholent on *Shabbos* (Sabbath) for lunch, which is a heart-smart delight to body and soul.

I just read in the newspaper that Crock Pots are 'in' again. That's how I found out that, apparently, they were 'out' for about thirty years. I've used the same slow cooker for my weekly cholent soup for more years than I care to tell you. Usually, I seem about twenty-five years behind certain trends but, ironically, as trends do resurface in a cyclical manner, sometimes I find myself ahead of my time, even though I'm so 20th Century.

Serves 7-8

4 dried shiitake mushrooms
3 - inch piece of wakame
1/2 cup lentils
1/2 cup barley
1 cup chopped onions
1 cup sliced carrots (1/4 - inch rounds)
6 - 7 cups water
2 cloves garlic, minced
2 bay leaves
Black pepper to taste
1/8 tsp ground cumin (optional)
2 tsp sea salt
4 tbsp organic soy sauce
1/3 cup tomato paste

1 Soak shiitakes in warm water for 15 minutes, and chop into small pieces, discarding only the hard ends.

2 Soak wakame in a bit of warm water for eight minutes, and slice into 1/4 - inch pieces.

3 To a large pot, add the shiitake, wakame, lentils, barley, onions, carrots, water, garlic, bay leaves, pepper, and cumin.

4 Cook on low-medium heat for 30 minutes.

5 Add salt, soy sauce and tomato paste and cook another 20 - 25 minutes.

6 Remove bay leaves, adjust seasoning and serve.

— 🌿 —

VARIATION:

For a week-day Barley-Lentil Casserole: When almost done, transfer the soup into a casserole dish and bake, uncovered in a 350°F oven, for about 25 minutes.

LENTIL-QUINOA SOUP

The protein-rich quinoa, which is an especially high-quality grain, adds extra nutrition to this hearty legume soup.

Serves 8-10

4 - inch piece wakame

1 cup green lentils

1/2 cup quinoa, thoroughly rinsed through a fine sieve

10 cups water

3 cloves garlic, minced

1 cup chopped onions

3 bay leaves

1 cup sliced carrots (1/4 - inch rounds)

1 cup sliced celery (1/4 - inch pieces - also the leaves, if available)

1/2 cup sliced leek (1/4 - inch pieces)

1 large tomato, chopped or 1/2 cup tomato paste

1/8 tsp ground cumin

3 tbsp organic soy sauce

Sea salt or Herbamare to taste

Black pepper to taste

1/3 cup finely chopped parsley, flat-leaf or curly

1   Soak wakame in a bit of warm water for 8 minutes, and slice into small pieces.

2   In a large pot, place the lentils, quinoa, water, garlic, onions, bay leaves, carrots, celery, leek, and tomato (if used); cover and bring to a boil.

3   Add the wakame; turn heat to medium-low, and cook for about 40 minutes.

4   Add the cumin, soy sauce, and tomato paste (if used); add salt and pepper, and simmer for another 8 minutes.

5   Remove the bay leaves and stir in the parsley.

—— 🐝 ——

VARIATION:

Millet, oats, or couscous can be substituted for the quinoa.

Spicy Red Lentil-Yam Soup

This light soup, with its gorgeous golden colour, is a nutri-yummy meal-starter any time of the year. It is also a most pleasant way to add to your (and your family's) vitamin A and protein account.

Serves 6-7

3 - inch piece wakame

8 cups water

2 medium yams, peeled and cut into 1 - inch cubes

1 cup red lentils

1 cup coarsely chopped onions

2 cloves garlic, coarsely chopped

2 large bay leaves

2 tsp grated ginger

1/2 tsp ground cumin or to taste

1 tsp ground coriander or to taste

3 tbsp organic soy sauce

1 - 2 tbsp umeboshi vinegar

Finely chopped dill or curly parsley, for garnish

1 Soak the wakame in a bit of warm water for 8 minutes, and cut into 1/4 - inch pieces.

2 In a large pot, place the 8 cups water, yams, lentils, onions, garlic, bay leaves, ginger, and wakame; cover, bring to a boil, and cook on medium heat for 40 - 50 minutes.

3 Cool slightly, remove the bay leaves, and purée with a hand-held electric mixer, or in a blender or food processor.

4 Pour the soup back into the pot, add the cumin, coriander, soy sauce and vinegar, adjust seasoning, and simmer for another 8 minutes.

5 Garnish with dill or parsley and serve.

HELPFUL HINTS:

1. For party-time or special occasions, serve hot in mugs or in elegant china cups.

2. In summer serve chilled.

Naomi's Hodge-Podge Barley & Whatever-Else Is-Around Soup

This is invariably the soup which our daughter Naomi prepares for us lovingly whenever we arrive in Israel. We are by far not the only recipients of her gourmet goodies, but that's for another book. Also, her daughter, our granddaughter, Shuli, prepares yummy vegan dishes for our Yom Tov (holiday) delight.

When I asked Naomi for the precise recipe, she couldn't really oblige, and could only tell me that she puts into this soup "whatever is around" at the time.

Since at this time I have a deadline to meet with my publisher, I will tell you the ingredients and ask you to make up your own recipe this one time, if you so desire.

Barley, Carrots, Potatoes, Onions, Garlic, Yams,
Pumpkin or Squash, Mushrooms, lots of fresh dill, etc.

"God gives us homework and the assignment is different for everyone, but He neither writes it on the blackboard nor posts it on the internet."

WHOLE VEGETABLE SOUP

This is a versatile, multi-purpose soup to have on hand. I make large quantities a̶ freeze it. Any combination or all of the veggies listed below can be used; the mo̶ merrier, as they all seem to get along well with each other. Quantities depend on large your soup pot is and how many big mouths you have to feed.

4 - inch piece of wakame

10 cups water, or water to cover the veggies plus 3 - inches more

5 cups of your choice of the following vegetables: Cabbage, carrots, cauliflower, celeriac, celery (with the leaves), daikon, kale, leeks, mushrooms, onions, parsley root, rutabaga, tomatoes, turnips, yams, zucchini, etc.

2 - 3 cloves garlic, finely minced

2 - 3 bay leaves

1/3 - 1/2 cup tomato paste

Organic soy sauce or sea salt or Herbamare to taste

1/4 cup finely chopped parsley or dill

1 Soak wakame in a bit of water for 8 minutes, and slice into small pieces.

2 In a large pot, bring the water to a boil.

3 Decide which veggies you are going to use. (You will need at least 6 different ones to give this soup a good flavour).

4 Cut the vegetables into as equal-sized pieces as possible and add to the pot.

5 Add the garlic, bay leaves and the wakame, cover the pot and bring back to a boil.

6 Lower the heat and cook gently for 30 - 35 minutes.

7 Remove the bay leaves, add the tomato paste, soy sauce or salt, tomato paste and parsley or dill, and adjust seasoning.

8 Cool the soup and store in the refrigerator (will keep 3 - 5 days), or freeze in usable portions.

—————— 🐝 ——————

CREAMED SOUP VARIATION:

This soup can be pureed in a blender or processor to serve to a convalescent person, or to any fuss-pots who don't like pieces in their soup.

HELPFUL & HEALTHFUL HINTS:

1. When reheating this soup, do not bring back to boil.

2. For a more filling soup, add rolled oats or couscous and simmer 6 - 8 minutes, or add any cooked grains or tiny-sized pasta.

3. For extra protein, add cubed tofu or cooked beans.

4. For a touch of summer, add some frozen or fresh garden peas.

LOW-CAL 'N' LEAN VARIATION:

For the weight watchers and the yo-yo dieters, or for the woman who desperately needs to get back into her machateineste (mother-in-law) gown for the next simcha (occasion), simply omit the carrots and yams and ess, ess, ess! (eat, eat, eat!)!

FOR PESACH: Omit the chometz vegetables.

BARBARA'S VEGETABLE STOCK

This recipe was given to me by the wonderful chief cook and bottle-washer at 'True North Health Education Center', in California.

Veganistas and vegeholics can use this broth the same way conventional cooks use chicken stock. It serves as a base for - or an addition to - many dishes, including quickie soups, risotto, sauces, etc.

Yields 12-14 cups

1 piece wakame (8 - inches)

20 cups water

2 cups unpeeled quartered onions

3 cups sliced carrots (1/4 - inch rounds)

2 cups sliced celery, with leaves (1/2 - inch pieces)

1 cup sliced leeks, both white and darker green parts (1- inch pieces)

3 cups shredded packed Swiss chard (also the stems)

4 cloves garlic, crushed

1 Soak the wakame in a bit of water for 8 minutes, and cut into 1/4 - inch pieces.

2 In the largest pot you own, place the wakame, water, onions, carrots, celery, leeks, chard and garlic, cover, bring to a boil, and cook on medium-low heat for 1 1/2 - 2 hours.

3 Cool and strain the stock, discarding the vegetables.

4 Store stock in the refrigerator, where it will keep 3 - 5 days, or freeze in usable portions.

—— 🌱 ——

FOR PESACH:

Omit the wakame.

KOMBU-SHIITAKE STOCK

This is my chicken soup, but without the steroids and antibiotics the poor chickens are fed. When eating chicken soup, we cannot avoid ingesting these drugs into our systems, which may make us immune to antibiotics when we, God forbid, need them for a real emergency. I use this recipe whenever stock is called for, as it is simpler and faster to make than vegetable stock. Kombu, being a sea vegetable, supplies us with much-needed trace minerals and an abundance of other invaluable nutritional ingredients. (see **The Benefits of Sea Vegetables**, page 25).

Yields about 8 cups

10 cups water

4 dried shiitake mushrooms

5 - inch piece of kombu

1 cup finely diced onions

2 bay leaves

3 - 4 tbsp organic soy sauce

1 To a large pot, add water, mushrooms and kombu. Cover and bring to a boil.

2 When the water boils, turn off the heat and let stand 15 minutes.

3 Remove kombu and mushrooms with a slotted spoon onto a cutting surface and finely slice (discard only the hard ends of the mushroom stems).

4 Put sliced kombu and mushrooms back into the pot, add onions, bay leaves and soy sauce, and simmer for 30 minutes.

5 Cool stock and store in the refrigerator, where it will keep for 5 days or more, or freeze in usable portions.

"Let thy food be thy medicine, and thy medicine be thy food."

- Hippocrates

MISO SOUP FOR ONE

Miso is an unpasteurized, slow-fermented soya bean paste, which seems to have an amazing amount of health benefits. Some Asian countries consider it a miracle food, and on a macrobiotic healing diet miso soup is eaten daily. It is supposedly one of the most powerful detoxifying foods one can eat. Researchers in Japan have concluded that those who eat miso soup daily are 33% less likely to get cancer than those who never eat it.

Miso provides the enzymes and micro-organisms which aid digestion and restore proper intestinal flora. It can be effective in preventing stomach ulcers, heart and liver disease, and can restore weak kidneys. Miso can also lower cholesterol and can neutralize the effects of environmental pollutants, as well as greatly counteract the effects of chemical poisoning and radiation. Miso can be eaten daily and takes little time to prepare; however, being a salty food, it needs to be used in moderation. Fermented as it is, miso is a gentler source of salt than iodized table salt, and it is not as harsh on the body.

1/2 - inch piece wakame

1/2 - 1 tsp miso

1 - 1 1/4 cup water

4 thinly sliced discs of carrot

1/8 cup finely sliced celery or leek

1/8 cup finely sliced green onions

1 Soak wakame in a bit of warm water for 8 minutes, and dice into 1/4 - inch pieces.

2 Measure the amount of miso used into a small dish and reserve.

3 To a small saucepan, add wakame, water, carrots, celery or leek and onions, and bring to a boil.

4 Lower heat and simmer for 3 - 5 minutes.

5 Add a small amount of the hot liquid to the dish with the miso and stir until the miso is completely dissolved (miso will not dissolve easily in cold liquid).

6 Pour this back into the soup and simmer just below boiling for 1 - 2 minutes. Miso always needs to be simmered for 1 - 2 minutes in order to activate its beneficial enzymes, however, it should never be boiled, which would destroy its enzymes.

HEALTHFUL HINTS:

1. Barley, rice and hatcho misos,which are all dark, can be used daily for miso soup, whereas light-coloured miso is generally used for sauces and spreads.
2. Other food tidbits can be added to your miso soup, such as, left-over tiny tofu squares, a bit of cooked grains, or greens, etc. If I'm in a hurry, I'll just throw in some finely chopped dark-green lettuce leaves, parsely or fresh dill.

7 To serve, pour into a bowl and enjoy.

FLOATING SOUP CLOUDS

This recipe is an upscale change from the traditional *knaidel*, regardless of whether they are floaters or sinkers. You can add these fluffy clouds to any soup, but they are particularly suitable to lighten up a heavy *Yomtov* (holiday) meal.

Serves 6-8

8 cups prepared soup

3 organic eggs, separated

Sea salt or Herbamare to taste

1/4 tsp ground ginger

Pinch of ground nutmeg

2 tbsp finely chopped curly parsley or dill

1 Bring soup to a boil.

2 Beat the egg whites until almost stiff. Add the salt, ginger, and nutmeg, and continue beating until stiff but not dry.

3 Gently fold in the yolks and parsley or dill by hand with a spatula.

4 When the soup has come to a rolling boil, pour the egg mixture over it and spread it out with a spatula to cover the soup like a blanket. Turn heat to low, cover, and simmer for 10 minutes.

5 Turn off heat. With a sharp knife, cut the cloud blanket in half on top of the soup, then in 1/4's, and finally, into bite-size pieces.

HEALTHFUL HINT:
If you are on a low cholesterol diet, you can make this recipe without the yolks. At step 2, use only the whites, and add 1/4 - 1/2 teaspoon turmeric to give it that luscious, golden colour.

FOR PESACH:
The nutmeg may have to be omitted.

Instant-Chicken-Noodle-Style-Soup

Here is a recipe, which may appear rather lengthy to you, but let me put your mind at ease; you do not have to assemble the ingredients. All you have to do is buy a box of this 'marvelous' mixture in your supermarket or grocery store, dump it into a cup of boiling water, wait a few minutes for all the chemicals to get comfortable with each other, and enjoy! I rest my case here.

Enriched wheat flour (thiamine mononitrate, riboflavin, niacin, reduced iron, folic ACD, amylase, benzoyl peroxide, ascorbic acid)

Hydrogenated vegetable oil (canola and/or soy and/or palm)

Potato starch

Modified potato starch

Salt

Dehydrated vegetables (peas, carrot, corn, onion, garlic)

Maltodextrin

Monosodium glutamate

Sugar

Natural flavor (hydrolyzed corn protein, yeast extract, thiamine hydrochloride, partially hydrogenated soybean oil)

Soy sauce powder (soy, salt, wheat)

Turmeric powder

Torula yeast

Canola oil

Silicon dioxide (anticaking agent)

Spices

Guar gum

Potassium carbonate

Sodium carbonate

Sodium tripolyphosphate

Turmeric extractives

Disodium inosinate

Disodium guanylate

BHA & BHT (as antioxidants)

"Tell me what you eat, and I will tell you what you are."

-Jean Anthelme Brillat-Savarin

TO BRING OR NOT TO BRING TECHNOCRACY INTO MY KITCHEN

I'm spending a lot of time in my kitchen lately, not necessarily by choice, but for the sake of my current life's mission; to finish writing a vegetarian cookbook about whole food and whole health. As a result, I'm interested in upgrading my kitchen, technologically speaking. With the now-ancient twentieth century behind us, we can look forward to futuristic gizmos as never before. To me, these present more of a challenge than a convenience since my right-brain seems to be under-developed and my left-brain is definitely working overtime.

The question that pops into my mind is the following: Do I really want a 'smart-alecky' kitchen with a brain? Would I remain in control of my one undisputed domain, given the fact that I am an inherent control freak? Would my rather underdeveloped right brain be able to cope with all that digital stuff? We're talking about a person who has not yet learned how to program her new two-year-old VCR other than to push the "power" and "eject" buttons. Likewise, I have not yet been able to set the clock on the dashboard of my new three-year-old car - it continues to run merrily one hour ahead in complete disregard of the fact that it is no longer Daylight Savings Time. I have therefore decided that when my book is finished, I will work on the Ph.D. I so longed for in my younger days; and it will be a doctorate in "Progressive Harebrained Deficit."

Nevertheless, I am contemplating getting one of those new talking refrigerators. The idea of having a fridge that could talk to me is rather exciting, especially since I spend a lot of time home alone. But the thought that it could also have a computer screen on its door, from which I could access the Internet and send e-mail, is positively daunting. And the prospect of receiving an automatic shopping list that connects to my supermarket without even opening the fridge door is absolutely awesome.

But since I am always concerned about good communication, I wonder how I would interact in a friendly and appropriate manner with my new "frigocrat". What if, for example, he/she/it announces to me that we are running low on baking apples? How do I tell him/her/it that I don't have time this week to bake my apple crisp? Or, when he/she/it reminds me that we are out of zucchini, how do I respond without offending? "Excuse me, Smart One, I'm tired of zucchini; I'm getting into brussels sprouts and fiddleheads."

While we're talking electronic comfort, let me share with you some of my darkest secrets. I do not own a dishwasher, a microwave oven, an electric coffee maker, a toaster oven, an electric frying pan, an electric waffle iron or, for that matter, any of the other new electronic *tschatschkes* that have come on the market since last weekend. Please don't feel sorry for me, though. I am very happy not to surround myself with more electromagnetic waves than are absolutely necessary, since I believe they have a negative effect on our healthy cells, robbing us of our vital energy.

I will probably also forgo the opportunity to purchase a new oven (mine is thirty years old), even though it may be wired with sensors and a voice microchip that announces when my cooking and baking is ready. How do I know that voice will resonate with my own kitchen-counter-culture energy?

But most of all, the futuristic, 'smart' kitchen will lack the atmosphere and nourishing energy of the kitchens of old. It will be stripped of any semblance of warmth, comfort and family togeth-erness. Smelling a lukewarm pizza in a closed take-out carton is not the same as having the sweet aroma of something baking in the oven or something fresh and wholesome simmering on the stove waft around our nostrils. And where better to iron out sticky family issues than late at night at the kitchen table?

No doubt I should hop with both feet into the twenty-first century with all its new-fangled gizmos in order to avoid a millennial inferiority complex. But, unfortunately, I am so "twentieth-century", which is quite natural given the fact that we have spent a great deal of time together. My peculiar habit of using my own brain, my own hands and my own programming are deeply ingrained and probably influenced by the dictum: "If you don't use it, you lose it." So, when all is said and done, I have come to the intelligent conclusion that for me to have a "smart" kitchen would be a stupid idea.

SAUCES

To Make Simple Food Elegant

Sauces are not only an elegant addition to our foods; they are also a practical and flavourful adjunct to a healthful, vegetarian diet. Over the centuries, sauces have been utilized in various ways; either they were served to mask bad food, to make good food taste richer, or to make rich food taste poorer. Since basic vegetarian food is simply prepared, sauces can immeasurably enhance certain foods with extra culinary flavour. Simplicity and only a few ingredients are needed to create good sauces as gourmet standbys. Contrary to the new breed of self-styled, post-modern food aficionados, these sauces are not drenched in tons of butter, oil, wine, cream, cheeses and more cheeses, and other sundry ingredients, or extracted from exotic cans and jars - **and they do not jeopardize anybody's cholesterol**.

BÉCHAMEL SAUCE (WHITE SAUCE)

This is a basic sauce recipe, which can be altered and adapted to enhance any number of simple dishes. Once you've mastered the basic steps, you can practice your skills and, with imagination, creativity and flair, elevate any of your dishes into the sphere of *Gourmania*. This sauce was named after its inventor, Louis XIV's steward Louis de Béchamel.

Yields about 1 cup

Basic Recipe:

2 tbsp white spelt flour

1/4 tsp sea salt or Herbamare, or to taste

1 cup **Kombu-Shiitake Stock** (see page 105) or **Vegetable Stock** (see page 104) or water

1 In a suitable saucepan, mix the flour with a small amount of the liquid, to make a paste.

2 Stir the remaining liquid into the paste until smooth and add salt.

3 Cook sauce over medium heat, stirring continuously until it has thickened.

HELPFUL HINT:

The thickness of the sauce depends on the proportion of flour to liquid. For a thin sauce use 1 tablespoon of flour per 1 cup of liquid. For a medium sauce, use 2 tablespoons of flour per 1 cup of liquid. For a thick sauce, use 3 tablespoons of flour per 1 cup of liquid.

VARIATIONS:

1. Add one or as many as you fancy of the following ingredients: Organic soy sauce, finely chopped herbs (parsley, dill, basil, marjoram, etc.), minced garlic or garlic powder, chopped onions or onion powder, light or dark miso, minced ginger or ginger powder, black pepper, paprika, capers, stone-ground mustard, etc.

2. If making fish, use the cooking liquid to make your sauce.

3. For a luscious Rosé pasta sauce, add some tomato paste or, for the ultimate gourmand experience, add some blanched 'n' peeled, chopped fresh tomatoes.

Luscious Leeky Sauce

Leek is often called "the poor man's asparagus". Closely related to onions and garlic, it nevertheless has a much milder flavour, without the pungent smell of its cousins. Leek is a good blood purifier, good for the liver and the respiratory system, and takes very little time to prepare. This sauce is great over grains, pasta and mashed potatoes, and can also be served as a side dish.

Yields 2 cups

1 1/2 cups sliced leeks (light and darker parts mixed),
cut into 1/2 - inch pieces

1 1/2 cups water

1/2 tsp garlic powder

2 tbsp organic soy sauce

2 tbsp arrowroot powder dissolved in 2 1/2 tbsp cold water

1   In a large skillet, place the leeks, water, garlic powder and soy sauce, and cook, covered, on low-medium heat for 8 - 10 minutes.

2   Turn heat to high, add the arrowroot mixture, and stir continuously until sauce has thickened and is smooth.

HELPFUL HINT:

White spelt or whole wheat flour can be substituted for the arrowroot powder (the ratio will remain about the same).

"Milk is the perfect food - for cows."

Zucchini-Tomato Sauce

Zucchini is a bland-tasting vegetable, but here it is jazzed up as a succulent, ultra-versatile chunky sauce, served either as a side dish or sauced over grains, mashed or baked potatoes and pasta. It also can be an elegant appetizer (see below). Leftovers make great winter lunches, poured hot over toasted bread.

Yields 4-5 cups

1/2 cup chopped onions

1 1/2 tbsp extra-virgin olive oil

2 cloves garlic, minced or 1/2 tsp garlic powder

4 cups unpeeled chopped zucchini (1/4 - inch chunks)

1 1/4 cups water, divided

2 large bay leaves

3 tbsp white spelt flour

1/3 cup tomato paste

2 - 3 tbsp organic soy sauce

2 tbsp umeboshi vinegar

Black pepper to taste

2 tbsp chopped dill or 2 tsp dried

1 In a large saucepan, sauté the onions in oil until translucent, about 5 minutes.

2 Add the garlic and sauté another 2 minutes.

3 Add the zucchini, 1 cup water and the bay leaves. Cover and simmer for 5 minutes, or until the zucchini is almost done, stirring once.

4 In a separate bowl, combine the flour with the remaining 1/4 cup water, add the tomato paste, soy sauce, vinegar and pepper and mix.

5 Turn up the heat under the saucepan, add the flour mixture and stir constantly until the sauce has thickened.

6 Remove bay leaves, adjust seasoning and add the dill.

HELPFUL HINTS:
1. This sauce will keep in the refrigerator 4 - 5 days; can also be frozen.
2. Always taste zucchini raw before using it. If it is not fresh and firm, it may taste bitter and should be discarded. Sometimes only the peel is bitter; in that case it can be used peeled.
3. This recipe can double as a delicious **vegetable side dish** (see page 63).

APPETIZER:

Serve on individual plates. Pour the hot sauce generously on small slices of toasted bread or plain challah, or spoon into and over oven-warmed patty shells and serve immediately. DEELICIOUS!

KALE AT ITS SAUCY BEST

Served in this basic béchamel sauce, the hardy kale is transformed into a smooth, scrumptious side dish, or can be poured as a sauce over grains, mashed potatoes, pasta, etc.

This is healthful eating at its best!

Yields 2 1/2 - 3 cups

2 tbsp white spelt flour

3/4 cup liquid (cooking water, stock, or water)

2 cups sliced steamed kale (1/4 - inch strips)

Organic soy sauce or sea salt or Herbamare to taste

1/2 tsp garlic powder

1   In a small bowl, place the flour and add only enough from the liquid to make a paste.

2   In a medium saucepan, bring the remaining liquid to a boil.

3   Add the flour paste, and keep stirring continuously until the sauce has thickened.

4   Add the kale, soy sauce or sea salt or Herbamare and garlic powder, stir, and simmer the sauce until heated through.

5   Adjust seasoning and serve.

HELPFUL HINT:

This recipe can also be found in the **Vegetable** section as a side dish (see page 43).

CREAMED MUSHROOM SAUCE WITHOUT THE CREAM

Mushrooms hold a special place in my bio-food file. This goes back to my childhood when I was taken to weddings of family or my parents' friends, and the invariable first course was mushrooms in a smooth sauce served in patty shells, which were called *Pasteten*. This recipe can be served as a side dish or used as a sauce, and also makes a yummy appetizer (see below).

Yields 2 cups-
3-4 servings

1 tbsp white spelt flour

Enough water to make a smooth paste

1 tbsp extra-virgin olive oil

3/4 cup chopped onions

2 cloves garlic, minced

4 cups diced button mushrooms (1/4 - inch pieces)

1 cup water

1 tbsp organic soy sauce

1/4 tsp sea salt or Herbamare

1/8 tsp black pepper

1/4 cup chopped flat-leaf parsley

1 In a small dish, mix the flour with the water to make a paste and reserve.

2 In a large skillet, sauté the onions in oil on medium heat for about 5 minutes.

3 Add the garlic and sauté 2 minutes more.

4 Add the mushrooms and sauté for 3 minutes.

5 Add the water, soy sauce, salt and pepper, cover, and bring to a boil.

6 Lower heat and simmer for 5 minutes.

7 Bring sauce back to boil, add the flour paste and stir continuously until sauce has thickened and is smooth.

8 Adjust seasoning, mix in the parsley and serve.

HELPFUL HINTS:

1. For a more intense flavour, substitute the white mushrooms with brown crimini or Portobello mushrooms.

2. If you want more sauce, just add more water and seasoning.

3. Add leftovers to soups, or sauce over grains, pasta, etc., or make extra for that use.

4. Always store fresh mushrooms, unwashed, in a paper bag in the fridge.

5. This recipe can double as a scrumptious side dish to a main course meal. It can also be found in the section for Vegetables.

APPETIZER: On individual plates, spoon the hot sauce over slices of challah or light toast, or fill into warm *vol-au-vents* (patty shells to you!)

FOR PESACH: Substitute 2 - 3 teaspoons potato starch for the flour, 1/4 teaspoon salt for the soy sauce, and use the appropriate oil.

PRIMAVERA TOMATO SAUCE WITH TOFU

This versatile sauce with its Mediterranean flavours is quick and easy to prepare and, when served hot over grains, pasta or mashed potatoes, acquires absolute gourmet status. Also great on bread, crackers or rice cakes which, with a green salad, will make a very comforting winter lunch at home. Or, serve it to your guests, if you are lucky enough to have some of those, as an appetizer (see below). And one final word of advice: If anyone asks you what those little white things in there are, do not tell them its tofu! For all you know they may associate it with Birkenstock sandals or men with ponytails. Just tell them your cooking instructor does not want to you to divulge her ingredients as they are copyrighted.

Yields approximately 1 cup

1 tbsp extra-virgin olive oil

1/4 cup chopped onions

1 clove garlic, minced

1/4 cup finely chopped sweet red pepper

1/2 cup coarsely chopped fresh tomatoes

1/3 cup tomato sauce

1/4 cup cubed firm tofu (1/8-inch cubes)

1 tsp umeboshi vinegar, or to taste

Dash black pepper

Water as needed

A few basil leaves, chopped

1 In a medium skillet, sauté the onions and garlic in oil on medium heat until the onions become translucent.

2 Add the red peppers and tomatoes and sauté 4 - 5 more minutes.

3 Add the tomato sauce, tofu, umeboshi vinegar and pepper, toss well, cover and simmer for 5 minutes.

4 Add just enough water to reach the desired consistency, adjust seasoning and serve.

—— 🦋 ——

APPETIZER:

Serve hot or warm on toast or challah, or fill into warmed patty shells.

Tartar Sauce

Relish this relish. It adds zip and zest to many plain-cooked foods, elevating them to gourmet status. It can be used over fish, patties, any cold cooked vegetables, spread on bread or rice cakes for a quick and savoury snack, or as a dip for raw veggies.

Yields 1 cup

3/4 cup Nasoya Nayonaise

1 tsp finely chopped dill or 1/3 tsp dried

1 tsp finely chopped curly parsley or 1/3 tsp dried

2 tbsp finely diced sour pickle

1 tbsp finely diced green onions

2 tbsp finely diced sweet red pepper

1/2 cup finely diced purple onions or 1/2 tsp onion powder

Sea salt or Herbamare to taste

Black pepper to taste

1 tsp apple cider or umeboshi vinegar

1 In a small bowl, combine all ingredients and mix well.

2 Adjust seasoning and serve.

HELPFUL HINT:
This sauce will keep refrigerated for up to 1 week.

GUACAMOLA EDITA

Avocado is one fatty food that is good for us; as a matter of fact, it is one of our most valuable fats. It can be eaten on a daily basis as a spread on bread or rice cakes, or used as a dip for crudités. It also makes a great appetizer (see below).

Yields 1 - 1 1/4 cup

1 small, ripe avocado

1 tbsp finely chopped onions

1 tbsp finely chopped tomatoes

1 tbsp finely chopped sweet red or orange pepper

2 pinches ground paprika

Garlic powder to taste

2 tsp umeboshi vinegar

2 tbsp chopped flat-leaf parsley

Freshly squeezed lemon juice to taste

1 Remove avocado from the peel, and place into a shallow bowl.

2 Add the onions, tomatoes, peppers, paprika, garlic powder, vinegar and parsley, and mix.

3 Add lemon juice and mash until it is the consistency you like.

APPETIZER:

Place a large lettuce leaf on individual plates, add 1/3 - 1/2 cup guacamole on top, and decorate with tomatoes or red pepper.

HELPFUL HINT:

The avocado is ripe when the flesh will yield to a slight pressure of the fingers. Do not bruise, or you'll end up with a black, arthritic avocado.

30 - SECOND NAYOMAISE

This recipe is the most versatile dressing ever to visit your fridge, taking only 30 seconds to prepare unless you are a turtle. The taste is unique, with a non-rich flavour and texture that is absolutely and irresistibly habit- forming. It can be used on any and all salads, served with fish, dabbed on cold vegetables, to decorate appetizers, or added to upgrade any other cold foods.

Yields 1 cup

3/4 cup Nasoya Nayonaise

2 tsp umeboshi vinegar, or to taste

1 tbsp water

1 tsp dried dill

1 In a small bowl, combine all the ingredients until emulsified.

PIQUANTISSIMO VARIATION:

Substitute apple cider vinegar for the umeboshi vinegar, add Bragg™ to taste and a dried green herb of your choice.

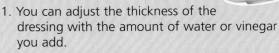

HELPFUL HINTS:
1. You can adjust the thickness of the dressing with the amount of water or vinegar you add.
2. For a stronger flavour you may add a touch of mustard and/or chopped fresh parsley.
3. For "pretty pink" add a touch of beet juice.
4. Will keep refrigerated in an airtight container for weeks.

THE FABLE OF THE TWO FROGS WHO COULDN'T SWIM

Two frogs went gallivanting around the neighborhood and ended up falling into a large pitcher of sweet cream. Neither frog knew how to swim. One frog weakly thrashed about, all the while thinking: "Oh, I don't know how to swim, surely I'm going to drown." And sure enough, according to his self-fulfilling prophecy, he drowned at the bottom of the pitcher. The other frog was a positive creature, and he said to himself: "I must try to survive this ordeal; I will not give up." He thrashed about wildly with all his might and kept going so long until, lo' and behold, he sat atop a mound of butter.

The moral of the story:

Never give up on life, it may eventually turn to butter; but don't let it melt!

GRAINS
&
PASTA

GRAIN AND PASTA RECIPES

WHOLE GRAINS

THE GRAINS OF TRUTH

Grains, high in complex carbohydrates and low in fat, are the ideal food to furnish us with the high-efficiency energy our bodies need to function from day to day. Grains have a low glycemic index and therefore it takes longer before our blood sugar lowers enough to stimulate hunger again. The soluble fibers in grains have proven to be beneficial to certain people with high cholesterol levels.

Many people today engage in "carbohysteria", as they have the mistaken notion that eating grains is fattening and will make them gain weight; especially those enrolled in some popular weight-loss programs. What they do not realize is that it is only processed and highly refined foods that have a high glycemic index, where hunger will be experienced again soon after eating.

BROWN RICE

Brown rice is a good source of many vitamins and minerals, and is packed with protein and fiber. Rice is a good complement to legumes, since both of them lack certain amino acids, when eaten by themselves. When eaten together, they supplement each other, forming a complete protein.

More than 2000 kinds of rice are cultivated throughout the world, but the kind we should never partake of is "white rice". Since the bran and the germ have been removed, there is no nutritional value left. As a matter of fact, all grains should be purchased in their whole and unadulterated form for the reason stated above.

I use mainly long-grain brown or aromatic brown basmati rice (see **Basic Brown Rice**, page 128).

When cooking rice, it's a good idea to make more than needed, as leftovers store well either covered in the fridge for up to a week, or frozen, portioned in individual baggies.

OATS

Oats, with their vast amount of soluble fiber, are truly heart-friendly, as they can help reduce high blood cholesterol levels. They provide substantial levels of the B vitamins thiamin, folic acid, riboflavin and B6, vitamin E, and the minerals calcium, magnesium, iron, potassium and zinc.

Oats come in many forms: whole groats, oat flakes, steel-cut oats and oat flakes ground into flour. While many people think of oats only as breakfast cereal, oats are actually a versatile, wonderful and totally health-promoting grain in all types of dishes.

The following helpful hints will showcase my favorite ways to enjoy oats!

- Cooked oat groats can be substituted for rice in a main course meal. It will have a more hardy and earthy flavour than rice and a more crunchy texture.
- You can grind oats into flour in a blender or processor and use it as a substitute for wheat flour.
- Cooked oat groats can be added to fried rice to give it another culinary dimension (1/3 cup oats to 2/3 cups rice).
- Oats in various forms always create the basis for my **Breakfast Cereals**, (see page 126).

MILLET

Millet is called 'The Queen of Grains'. It is extremely gentle on the digestive system, as it is gluten-free and very alkaline, making it one of the most digestible of grains. Millet is nearly 15% protein, contains high amounts of fiber, B vitamins, and essential amino acids. It is also high in the minerals: iron, magnesium, phosphorous and potassium. Another one of millet's assets, in this cancer-ridden world of ours, is the fact that it contains one of the richest sources of nitrilosides, which are cancer-inhibiting substances. Millet can be used in many ways: as a breakfast cereal, in soups, as a main course in stews, casseroles and patties.

QUINOA

Quinoa is touted as a 'Super-Grain' - a perfect food. As a matter of fact, several studies show that its nutritional composition is the closest of any food to mother's milk. It is the only grain that is a completely balanced protein, with all of its eight essential amino acids in nearly perfect balance. This makes it a complimentary food for legumes, which are low in certain amino acids. Quinoa is gluten-free, easy to digest and can help lower cholesterol levels.

Quinoa is as practical as it is nutritious; it cooks in a mere 12 - 15 minutes. This ancient and versatile grain is great in breakfast cereals, soups, casseroles, patties and salads and, last but not least, can replace brown rice as a main course dish. Always be sure to rinse quinoa thoroughly before cooking to remove its naturally-occurring bitter saponin coating! (For my favorite quinoa recipe, see **Quinoa, Greens and Chickpeas**, page 142)

SPELT AND KAMUT

Spelt and kamut are two ancient cousins to the modern wheat. Nutritionally, kamut and spelt are superior to conventional wheat, containing 25% more protein. They are also high in the B complex vitamins, and are superb sources of fiber. Scrumptious crackers and bread sticks made from spelt or kamut can be bought in kosher bakeries and in some kosher grocery stores as well. A variety of breakfast cereals made from spelt or kamut are also widely available. Their flakes are crunchy and sturdy and hold their shape and backbone in their milk baths, unlike their limpy cousins.

WHOLE-WHEAT COUSCOUS

Made of semolina wheat, couscous is actually a member of the pasta rather than the wholegrain family. It is an extremely convenient food to keep in stock as it can be prepared in minutes, which should be appealing to all 21st century short-order cooks. Couscous can be used on its own, like any other grain, and is great in stir-fries, stews and salads. I also use couscous to thicken a ready-made vegetable soup for instant enjoyment. To prepare couscous, add 1/2 cup dried couscous to 2 cups of boiling water, cover and set aside for 10 minutes. Fluff with a fork. Serves 2 - 3.

Since we share our world with tiny critters, you may want to add 2 bay leaves to each bag or container of grains to keep out unwanted visitors.

To end this grainy saga, here is another way to wrap it all up:

GOING WITH THE GRAINS

Let me introduce you to the family of grains,
So you become familiar with their names.
There's barley, quinoa, kamut, oats 'n rice,
And wheat berries, bulgur and rye kernels are nice;
With spelt, cracked wheat and millet to boot,
You will partake of the most nourishing food.

The grains do happy endorphins emit,
So you'll feel good and emotionally fit;
The first to benefit will be your brains,
And there'll be no fat to stick to your veins.
Grains kick your metabolism into proper drive;
There'll be no need for junk food in your life.

If you decide to eat lots of grains,
Your weight will stay – there'll be no gains;
If lose you must, just eat a grain meal,
And soon you'll see your weight ideal.
There won't be any withdrawal pains,
If you make friends with the family of grains;

The grains are ideal to fuel your muscle;
There'll be no need to always hustle.
Go for the grains that are intact and whole,
Where the bran and the germ play the biggest role.
Stay away from rice that's refined and white!
And you'll know that you are always nutritionally right.

The scientific studies all seem to agree,
Low fat, high fibre, may keep you cancer-free;
If you then add legumes to many of your grains,
You'll have plant protein for nutritional gains.
These complex carbs will de-stress your stress,
So your life won't have to be a mess.

For health and good digestion, here's another clue;
Make sure all your grains, you chew, chew and chew!
Don't take my word for it 'cause it rhymes;
Try it out yourself a couple of times!

THE GRAIN-COOKING CHART

Below is your compass to sail with ease through your grainy journey. Keep in mind that the cooking times are approximate. Please use your discretion to modify the grain-to-water ratio.

Be sure to carefully sort all your grains before washing them and then wash and rinse them thoroughly.

Grains (1 cup dry)	Cups of Water	Cooking Time (minutes)*	Yield in Cups
Barley, pearled	3	50 - 60	3 1/2
Barley, pot	3	75	3 1/2
Barley, flakes	2	30 - 40	2 1/2
Millet	3 1/2	20 - 25	3 1/2
Oat groats	3	30 - 40	3 1/2
Oats, steelcut	4	20	2
Quinoa	2	15 - 20	2 3/4
Rice, brown basmati	2 1/2	35 - 40	3
Rice, brown	2	45 - 55	3
Rice, wild	3	60	4
Rye kernels	3 1/2	60	3
Rye, flakes	2	10 - 15	3
Whole wheat berries	3	120	2 1/2
Whole wheat couscous	1	5	2
Whole wheat, cracked	2	20 - 25	2 1/4
Wheat, bulgur	2	15	2 1/2

Breakfast Cereals

The following recipes are my favourite breakfast foods, as they supply a part of my daily grain requirements in a very pleasant, nourishing way; especially in the winter when snowflakes are tapping at my kitchen window (excuse me for hallucinating - I don't have a kitchen window - but I can dream, can't I?).

Steel-Cut Oats - Quinoa Breakfast

The steel-cut oats remain crunchy and never get mushy like their oatmeal cousins, and the quinoa furnishes a delicious taste and fine-grained texture.

Serves 1-2

2 tbsp steel-cut oats

2 tbsp quinoa

1/2 cup water

1/2 cup Rice Dream® non-dairy beverage

A handful of organic Thompson raisins

2 - 3 pinches ground cinnamon

1 To a medium saucepan, add the above ingredients, bring to a boil, lower heat, cover and cook for 25 - 30 minutes.

2 Stir a few times during cooking to make sure the cereal won't stick.

3 If at this point you are not ready to eat your cereal, place it on a flame deflector to keep it warm. If the cereal has become too thick, you may add more water or Rice Dream® non-dairy beverage.

OAT FLAKES - MILLET BREAKFAST

Serves 1-2

2 tbsp oat flakes

2 tbsp millet

1 1/2 cup water

1/2 cup Rice Dream® non-dairy beverage

1/8 cup organic Thompson raisins

2 - 3 pinches ground cinnamon

2 tbsp **Nutty-Edith Crunch** (see page 181) (optional)

1 To a medium saucepan, add the above ingredients, bring to a boil, lower heat, cover and cook for 25 - 30 minutes.

2 Stir a few times during cooking to make sure the cereal won't stick.

3 If at this point you are not ready to eat your cereal, place it on a flame deflector to keep it warm. If the cereal has become too thick, you may add more Rice Dream® non-dairy beverage or water.

———————— 🎕 ————————

BREAKFAST CEREAL VARIATIONS:

Fruity Variation:
Instead of raisins, you may add chopped dried apricots, prunes, or any other dried fruits, or a raw peeled apple in big chunks, to your breakfast cereal before cooking.

Savory Variation:
Omit the raisins, substitute the Rice Dream® non-dairy beverage with water, and add 1 tablespoon grated carrots, 1 tablespoon chopped green onions, 1 tablespoon finely chopped celery, and 1 tbsp chopped parsley.

Sunny Variation:
Sprinkle with sunflower seeds.

Nutty Variation:
Sprinkle with **Nutty-Edith Crunch** (see page 181)

Omega-3 Variation:
Sprinkle with ground flax seeds.

BASIC BROWN RICE

There are two methods I use to cook brown rice.

Yields 2 cups

Method 1

2 cups water

Pinch sea salt or Herbamare

1 cup brown rice

1 In a medium saucepan, bring water and salt to a boil.

2 Add the rice, bring to a boil again and cover.

3 Reduce heat to low and simmer for 30 minutes, (do not lift the lid and do not stir the rice while it's cooking).

4 Place saucepan on a flame deflector and cook for another 20 minutes.

5 Turn off the heat, fluff gently with a fork, cover again and let sit for another 10 minutes.

Method 2

When I cook more than 1 cup of raw rice, I cook it in the oven, in a covered 3-quart square Corningware casserole dish.

3 3/4 cups water

2 pinches sea salt or Herbamare

2 cups brown rice

1 Preheat oven to 350°F.

2 Place the Corningware dish on the stove, add water and salt, and bring to a boil.

3 Add the rice, cover and transfer to the oven.

4 Bake for 30 minutes, turn oven to 325°F and bake another 25 minutes.

5 Remove the rice from the oven; fluff gently with a fork and let sit, covered, for another 10 minutes.

HELPFUL HINTS:

1. Cooked rice may be stored in a covered container in the refrigerator for up to one week. It can also be packed into meal-sized portions in little baggies and stored in the freezer. (I measure about 3/4 cup of cooked rice per person.)

2. To defrost rice quickly, place into a warming oven for 1/2 - 1 hour, in a covered, ovenproof dish.

3. If you have fussy eaters in your household who claim not to like brown rice without ever having tasted it, make a real good vegetable soup and simply add the cooked rice to the soup. And if you throw in a small portion of cooked beans, you are serving a complete protein meal.

RICE AMANDINE

This is a delectable, aromatic dish for any festive occasion; which for us is usually on Friday evenings. It goes well with just about anything else on your menu.

Serves 4-6

1/2 cup chopped onions (1/4 - inch pieces)

1/8 cup extra-virgin olive oil

1 cup brown basmati rice

2 cups water

1/3 cup coarsely chopped dried organic apricots

1/4 cup organic golden raisins or dried organic cranberries

1/4 tsp sea salt or Herbamare, or to taste

2 pinches black pepper

2 pinches ground cloves

1/2 cup slivered toasted almonds

1/4 cup coarsely chopped flat-leaf parsley

1 In a large saucepan, sauté the onions in the oil 5 - 7 minutes, or until golden.

2 Add the rice and stir for 1 minute.

3 Add water, cover and bring to a boil.

4 Reduce heat to medium, and cook 40 - 50 minutes, or until the rice is soft.

5 Add apricots, raisins or cranberries, salt, pepper and cloves, adjust seasoning, and simmer covered for another 5 minutes.

6 Turn off the heat, stir in the almonds and parsley, and serve immediately. Or, transfer to an oven-proof covered dish, and keep in a warming oven until ready to serve.

"If you want time to be on your side, you have to make time for it; and cooking healthy is no exception."

RISOTTO VERDE AND CHICKPEAS

This is a heart-smart and splendiferous dish that makes a substantial main course. No other protein is needed for this meal; just add an interesting salad. The spinach can be substituted with any other steamed leafy green or chopped vegetables. This dish can be prepared in advance, which makes it very practical to serve on *Yomtov* (holiday).

Serves 6

4 cups cooked brown rice

1 cup cooked chickpeas

3/4 tsp sea salt or Herbamare

1/4 tsp ground cumin

3 tbsp organic soy sauce

3/4 cup chopped onions

2 tbsp extra-virgin olive oil

2 cloves garlic, minced

4 cups coarsely chopped packed spinach leaves

1 cup **Kombu-Shiitake Stock** (see page 105) or **Vegetable Stock** (see page 104) or water

1 Preheat oven to 325°F.

2 In a large bowl, place the rice, chickpeas, salt, cumin and soy sauce, toss together and reserve.

3 In a large skillet, sauté the onions in oil for 4 - 5 minutes.

4 Add the garlic and sauté 2 minutes.

5 Lower the heat, add the spinach, cover and simmer for 1 minute.

6 Add the contents of the sauté pan to the large bowl and toss well.

7 Add stock or water and adjust seasoning.

8 Pour this mixture into a 3 - quart ovenproof casserole dish, cover and bake about 25 minutes, and serve.

> **HELPFUL HINT:**
> If this casserole has to remain in the oven after it is finished for any length of time before being served, make sure that the oven temperature is not above 225°F, and that there is enough moisture in the casserole so that it will not dry out.

―――――― ❧ ――――――

A SALAD-AS-A-MEAL VARIATION:

Make more, or use any leftovers from this dish and turn this recipe into a great salad-as-a-meal, or a buffet party dish!

Add to taste: cooked corn, chopped onions, chopped red pepper, chopped parsley, apple cider vinegar, umeboshi vinegar, Nasoya Nayonaise, sea salt or Herbamare.

RICE-SHIITAKE CASSEROLE WITH GREENS

This easy-to-prepare casserole melds lovely flavours and has real pizzazz. Serve it with **Dahl,** (see page 159) or **Saucy Lentils** (see page 158) to turn it into a splendiferous protein meal.

Serves 8

8 fresh shiitake mushrooms, sliced

1 cup chopped onions

2 tbsp extra-virgin olive oil

2 cups shredded kale, lightly steamed or 2 cups packed baby spinach

4 cups cooked brown rice

2 cups **Kombu-Shiitake Stock** (see page 105) or **Vegetable Stock** (see page 104) or water

1 tbsp umeboshi vinegar, or to taste

1/2 tsp ground curry

1/4 tsp ground cumin

1 Turn oven to 325°F.

2 In a large saucepan, sauté the mushrooms and onions in oil until onions are translucent (4 - 5 minutes).

3 Add the kale or spinach and rice, toss and sauté for 3 minutes.

4 Add the stock, vinegar, curry and cumin, and mix well.

5 Transfer this mixture to a 3-quart oven-to-table casserole dish, cover and bake for 30 minutes.

6 Serve immediately.

HELPFUL HINT:
More stock or water may be needed to keep this casserole moist.

"Rice and veggies don't stick to your arteries."

SHORT-SHRIFT RISOTTO-STYLE RISOTTO

Whenever the word "style" appears behind a food, we know that it's not the real thing. Risotto is the kind of dish that supposedly lends itself to fun-in-the-kitchen-with-your-guests; where they all hang out in your large, state-of-the-art Smart-kitchen. While some of the guests take endless turns adding stock to and stirring the risotto, others prepare the garlic roasted croutons for the salad. The artistic ones among them decide which colour scheme to use for the edible flowers. Well, I have news for you; this is not my idea of fun with my guests. I like my kitchen and I like my guests, but never the twain shall meet. If I don't have time to prepare dinner for them, I don't invite them. Also, my kitchen is rather smallish; you can't even swing a big head of lettuce in it. My short-shrift risotto needs only one short-order cook, and I have developed a basic recipe - good any time - provided you have the required ingredients prepared and on hand (see **Cooking in Stages and Other Timeless Timesavers**, page 242). I call it 'risotto' because I like the name, and I hope the Culinary Police won't come 'round and revoke my license!

Serves 4-5

2 cups **Kombu-Shiitake Stock** (see page 105) or **Vegetable Stock** (see page 104), or water

2 cups cooked brown rice

1/4 tsp sea salt or Herbamare

1/4 tsp onion powder

1/4 tsp dried crushed garlic flakes

A few pinches ground cumin

Organic soy sauce to taste

1 tsp dried parsley or - if you are fresh-obsessed like me - 1 tbsp chopped flat-leaf parsley

1 In a large saucepan, bring the stock to a boil.

2 Add the brown rice, salt, onion powder, garlic flakes, cumin, soy sauce and parsley, stir well, cover and simmer for 5 minutes, or until heated through.

3 Adjust seasoning and serve.

HELPFUL HINT:

If you don't have Kombu-Shiitake Stock or Vegetable Stock on hand, substitute with a mixture of water, soy sauce and seasoning to taste.

— 🌿 —

VARIATIONS:

1. You may add any cooked vegetables (especially green ones) or leftover ones to this basic recipe at step 2.

2. If you add tofu cubes to this dish, or serve it with a bean side salad, you have added to your daily protein account and have earned, perhaps not air miles but, sugar-free brownie points.

Rice 'n' Millet Patties

These substantial patties can be prepared ahead of time and kept in your freezer for those times when the-last-thing-you-want-to-do-is-worry-about-supper. And get someone else to make a large salad for you, if you are that lucky!

Yields 1 dozen patties, 2 1/2 - inch diameter

2 tbsp extra-virgin olive oil

1/2 cup chopped onions

1 clove garlic, minced

1/4 cup finely chopped celery

1/2 cup coarsely grated carrot

1/2 cup diced sweet red pepper

3 tbsp organic soy sauce

1/4 tsp garlic powder

1/4 tsp dried basil

1/4 tsp dried marjoram

1 cup cooked brown rice

1/2 cup cooked millet

1/8 cup tahini

1/4 cup whole spelt or whole wheat flour

1 tbsp finely chopped flat-leaf parsley

1 Preheat oven to 350ºF.

2 Cover a medium baking pan with parchment paper and reserve.

3 In a large skillet, heat oil and sauté onions for about 1 minute, add garlic and sauté for another minute.

4 Add celery and carrot and sauté for 3 - 5 minutes.

5 In a medium bowl, place sautéed vegetables, add the red pepper, soy sauce, garlic powder, basil, marjoram, rice, millet, tahini, flour and parsley, mix well, and adjust seasoning.

6 Divide mixture into 12 equal portions and form patties (for smooth patties, wet hands before flattening each patty).

7 Place patties on the baking pan and bake for 10 - 15 minutes, or until top is lightly browned.

8 Turn each patty over, bake another 10 - 15 minutes, and serve hot, cold or at room temperature.

Rice, Oats 'n' Veggies

This is my favourite way to eat rice. The oat groats add a delicious earthy flavour and chewy crunch to the genteel, soft rice.

Serves 3 as a main dish or 4-5 as a side dish

1/4 cup chopped onions

1 tbsp extra-virgin olive oil

1/8 cup finely grated carrots

1/8 cup finely sliced celery

1/3 cup chopped spinach, steamed for 30 seconds

3/4 cup cooked brown rice

3/4 cup cooked oat groats

1/4 tsp sea salt or Herbamare, or to taste

1/4 tsp garlic powder

1/8 tsp black pepper

1/8 cup chopped flat-leaf parsley

Stock or water as needed

1   In a large skillet, sauté the onions in the oil until translucent.

2   Add the carrots, celery and spinach and sauté for 2 minutes.

3   Add the rice, oats, salt, garlic powder, pepper and parsley, and stir until everything is thoroughly mixed.

4   If the mixture is too dry at this point, add from the cooking liquid of the grains or use stock or water.

5   Cover and simmer until heated through.

6   Adjust seasoning and serve immediately.

—  —

VARIATIONS:

1. You may add or substitute any other greens of your choice.

2. To make this dish into a casserole, prepare up to and including step 3, place the rice-oat mixture into an oven-proof casserole dish, add some stock to keep it moist, cover, and bake at 325° F for 30 minutes.

THE ULTIMATE STIR-FRIED GREEN RICE

This dish will never coat your veins with plaque, and it takes only minutes to prepare, provided you've got your act together (No, of course I don't mean YOU!) and manage to cook in stages. The only other ingredients to make this meal the ultimate health-promoting experience would be: good chewing, a quiet mind and a grateful heart.

Serves 2

1 tbsp extra-virgin olive oil

1/4 cup chopped onions

1/2 cup packed chopped kale, steamed

1 1/2 cups cooked brown rice

2 tsp organic soy sauce

1/4 tsp garlic powder

Sea salt or Herbamare to taste

2 pinches ground cumin

1 In a large skillet, sauté the onions in the oil until translucent.

2 Add the kale and stir 1 - 2 minutes.

3 Add the rice, soy sauce, garlic powder, salt and cumin, toss and cover until heated through.

4 Serve immediately.

VARIATIONS:

1. Baby spinach or any other steamed green vegetable of your choice may be substituted for the kale.
2. To proteinize this dish, add some 1/2-inch cubes of firm tofu at step 3.

> "Investing a few extra minutes of good chewing
> when we eat may add healthful years to our lives;
> try to remember that we have no teeth in our stomachs."

Spiced Quinoa

Serves 2-3 as a main dish or 4-6 as a side dish

1 cup quinoa

1/2 cup chopped onions

2 cloves garlic, minced

1 tbsp plus 1 tsp extra-virgin olive oil

1/2 tsp ground cardamom

1/2 tsp ground coriander

1/4 tsp ground cumin

1 3/4 cup **Kombu-Shiitake Stock** (see page 105) or **Vegetable Stock** (see page 104) or water

1/3 cup chopped dried organic apricots

1/2 tsp sea salt or Herbamare

1/8 tsp black pepper

2 tbsp chopped flat-leaf parsley

1 Rinse quinoa well to remove its bitter saponin coating, and drain.

2 In a large skillet, sauté onions and garlic in oil for 3 - 4 minutes.

3 Add quinoa, cardamom, coriander and cumin, and stir.

4 Add stock or water and apricots, season with salt and pepper and bring to a boil.

5 Reduce heat, cover and cook until all water is absorbed (about 15 minutes).

6 Remove from heat, stir in parsley, and adjust seasoning.

7 Serve immediately, or keep warm in the oven in an oven-proof, covered dish until needed.

"I have no time to be in a hurry!"

QUINOA AND MILLET PILAF

What a delicious way to eat your grains, and what a great *shidduch* (match)! Millet is the queen of grains and quinoa is the grain with the most protein. This pilaf has a light texture and goes well with almost any other food on your menu.

Serves 3 as a main dish or 4-5 as a side dish

1 1/2 tbsp extra-virgin olive oil

1/2 cup chopped onions

1/4 cup finely diced or coarsely grated carrots

1/4 cup diced sweet red pepper

1/4 cup finely chopped celery

2 tbsp dried organic cranberries (optional)

1/4 cup millet

1/4 cup quinoa

1/4 tsp sea salt or Herbamare

Pinch black pepper

2 1/4 cups **Kombu-Shiitake Stock** (see page 105) or **Vegetable Stock** (see page 104) or water

2 tbsp finely chopped flat-leaf parsley

1 In a large saucepan, heat the oil and sauté onions and carrots for 5 - 6 minutes.

2 Add the red pepper, celery and cranberries, if used, and sauté for 5 minutes.

3 Add the millet and sauté for 5 minutes, stirring occasionally.

4 Add the quinoa and sauté for 2 - 3 minutes.

5 Add the stock or water, salt and pepper, cover and bring to a boil.

6 Lower heat and simmer for 20 - 30 minutes.

7 Add parsley, adjust seasoning, fluff with a fork and serve.

"Diets based on deprivation don't work."

EASY MILLET STEW

This is a very alkaline dish, easy on your stomach, on your time and on your budget.

Serves 4-5

3 1/4 cups water
1/2 cup millet
1/2 cup coarsely chopped onions
1/2 cup sliced carrots (1/4 - inch rounds)
1/2 cup sliced celery (1/4 - inch pieces)
1/2 cup cauliflower florets (1/2 - inch pieces)
2 bay leaves
1/2 tsp sea salt
2 tbsp flat-leaf parsley

1 In a medium saucepan or 2 - quart Corningware casserole dish, combine the water, millet, onions, carrots, celery, cauliflower, bay leaves and salt, mix, cover and bring to a boil.

2 Lower the heat to medium-low and cook for 15 minutes.

3 Place a flame deflector under the saucepan or casserole dish, and simmer for 45 minutes. Do not stir the stew while it is cooking!

4 Remove the bay leaves, adjust seasoning, add the parsley and serve.

"People lose their health in search of wealth and spend their wealth in search of health."

Rainbow Couscous

Couscous is not really a grain; it is part of the pasta family. The good thing about couscous is that it hardly needs cooking. This recipe is a very tasty and light dish. Served at room temperature, it makes a nice side dish to a *Shabbos* (Sabbath) lunch. It is also ideal to take along in a container when you have to go somewhere where you prefer your own food, if you have the nerve and the sophistication to do it.

Serves 4

3/4 cups water

1/4 cup finely chopped onions

1/8 cup finely sliced scallions

1/4 cup finely chopped sweet red or yellow pepper

1/4 cup finely diced celery

1/4 cup coarsely grated carrots

2 tsp extra-virgin olive oil

1 tsp organic soy sauce

1/8 tsp black pepper

1/2 tsp sea salt or Herbamare

2 tbsp chopped flat-leaf parsley

1/4 cup whole wheat couscous

1   In a small saucepan, combine the water, onions, scallions, red or yellow pepper, celery, carrots, oil, soy sauce, pepper, salt and parsley, and bring to a boil.

2   Add couscous, stir, cover, lower heat and simmer for 5 minutes, or until all the water has been absorbed.

3   Turn off the heat and let sit for 5 minutes.

4   Adjust seasoning, fluff with a fork and presto! it's ready to eat or go!

FRUITY COUSCOUS SALAD

This is a light and fluffy side dish - a perfect addition to a *Shabbos* (Sabbath) lunch. It can also be taken along on an outing or a picnic, as the ingredients in it would not spoil quickly.

Serves 4-6

1 1/2 cup water

1 cup whole wheat couscous

1/2 cup chopped dried organic apricots

1/4 cup dried organic cranberries

1/8 cup sliced green onions (1/8 - inch pieces)

1/8 cup chopped flat-leaf parsley

Sea salt or Herbamare to taste

Black pepper to taste

1/4 cup coarsely chopped raw organic nuts

1 In a medium saucepan bring water to a boil.

2 Remove from heat, add couscous, stir, cover and let sit for 5 minutes.

3 In a medium bowl, combine the couscous with the apricots, cranberries, onions, parsley, salt, pepper and nuts, and mix well.

4 Adjust seasoning and serve at room temperature.

"Every Torah Jew has an obligation to preserve his or her life and not to jeopardize it with fork and knife, bit by bit and bite by bite."

QUINOA, GREENS AND CHICKPEAS

This combination is quick and easy to assemble, extremely nutritious with its complete protein balance, and is very pleasing to discriminating tastes and uncontaminated palates. It is also a good recipe with which to test your ability to 'cook in stages' (see **Cooking in Stages**, page 242).

Serves 4

1 cup packed spinach

1 cup finely chopped onions

2 tbsp extra-virgin olive oil

2 - 3 cloves garlic, minced

3 cups cooked quinoa

1 cup cooked chickpeas

1/2 tsp sea salt or Herbamare

2 pinches ground cumin

1/8 tsp black pepper

1   Steam the spinach for 30 seconds, squeeze out the juice, chop and reserve.

2   In a large skillet, sauté the onions in the oil for about 5 minutes.

3   Add the garlic and sauté another 2 - 3 minutes.

4   Lower the heat, add the spinach, quinoa, chickpeas, salt, cumin and pepper, mix well, cover and simmer until heated through.

5   Adjust seasoning and serve.

VARIATIONS:

1. The spinach can be chopped and used raw.

2. The spinach can be substituted with any other leafy green or lightly steamed vegetables of your choice.

HOMEMADE PATTY SHELLS

Bought patty shells are crisp, light, fluffy and puffy; that's why the French call them *vol-au-vents*, but they are loaded with bad fat. Why not make your own; it's a kind of a fun thing to do, if you are lucky enough to have time to play around in your kitchen (like when you made sand pies when you were three or four). All you need is sliced whole-meal bread and ramekins (see Helpful Hint below). Use one slice of bread for one patty shell.

1 Preheat oven to 350° F.

2 Trim the crust of each slice of bread.

3 With a rolling pin, roll out each slice to make it soft and bigger.

4 Brush each slice lightly with extra-virgin olive oil.

5 Lightly grease the ramekins, and press each slice into one ramekin.

6 Bake for 10 minutes, or until lightly browned.

7 Fill with your choice of a suitable filling (see **Appetizers**, page 245), and serve hot.

HELPFUL HINT:

A ramekin is a round, porcelain or earthenware baking dish (3 - 4 inches in diameter), which resembles a miniature soufflé dish.

BASIC WHITE RICE

You may have found out already that I have declared war on white rice. Nevertheless, I often eat rice, but it's always brown. Here is one recipe that will never fail you, and it's one way to wean you off the white stuff; it works well for me.

1 Take one or a few mugs you may have hanging around the house and that you don't know what to do with. I mean the ones bought at an airport souvenir shop, with the maudlin inscriptions like: "We love grandma", or, "To the greatest dad".

2 Fill each mug 3/4 full with raw, unwashed white rice, and stick all your various pens, pencils, and scissors into them. Distribute the mugs throughout the house, preferably near your telephone or telephones.

3 The only down- side to this recipe is the fact that you no longer have an excuse not to take telephone messages, because you do not have a pen or pencil nearby.

"North Americans on the SAD (Standard American Diet)
are overfed and undernourished"

"SHANGRI-LA" - OUR YEARLY GET-AWAY

"Shangri-La" was for 12 years our yearly, 2-weeks-Florida-Winter-Get-Away. Don't get the wrong idea; it was neither a fancy-schmancy pampering spa nor, as the name would suggest, an Asian - transcendental kind of place. Sprawled on acres and acres of magnificent typically Floridian natural habitat, it offered each guest a personally - tailored and supervised health program, according to each one's particular needs and goal for being there. You could stay a minimum of one week, or all winter. You had the option to eat three all-raw vegan meals each day in the large, airy dining room, looking out on the most magnificent, humongous tropical plants; or to do a water fast from three to thirty days. In that case, your nourishment would be an unlimited amount of distilled water any time.

The meals consisted of the same kind of food for breakfast, lunch and supper. There was an abundance of fresh fruits and vegetables; and a few raw nuts and seeds were added at lunch or supper time.

We were among the 'lucky' guests, who came merely to relax, detoxify, rejuvenate, regenerate and lose weight. But it was my first experience to come face to face with those that came because they were very sick and had been suffering for a long time without getting cured by their medical treatments. To witness the slow progression from illness, often chronic and life-threatening, to vibrant health in a matter of days or weeks, left a deep and lasting impression on me. It was a defining moment in understanding the progressive process from health to illness, and how it can be reversed by purely natural means without the risk of any side effects.

My husband, incidentally, water-fasted every year for about 10-12 days, losing between 10-12 pounds each time. It didn't matter that over the next year he faithfully gained it all back, as this gave us the opportunity to return yearly in order to again de-toxify, rejuvenate and de-stress and, at the same time, touch base with friends from all over the world who had become dear to us. My loyal American friend, Margaret Eaton, still sends me the only Valentine cards I get and keeps me posted about her interesting life and travels. She presented me with my first ever 'healthy' cookbook, entitled "The Cookbook for People Who Love Animals". She just shared a milestone in her life with me as she completed the FIVE POINTS OF LIFE marathon in Gainsville, Florida, in seven hours and seven minutes, winning a medal and a trophy.

But more than anything, it was the brilliant almost-nightly lectures by the Health Director, Dr. Frank Sabatino, which set the stage for my converting to a healthier lifestyle. It was a total and much needed brainwash lasting to this day. This was in the late 70's, when a whole and natural diet was generally considered somewhat offbeat, but I was determined not to become another crippling osteoarthritis statistic.

Last but not least, it was in Shangri-La where I learned about the "American Natural Hygiene Society", and when I returned to Toronto, I promptly joined the "Canadian Natural Hygiene Society", which brought me personally in touch with those people who followed a vegetarian lifestyle. The bi-monthly lectures by prominent Health Professionals from North America and beyond, became my ticket to the way of whole health (see **Bibliography**, page 257).

Shangri-La does not exist anymore, but its aura and lessons will remain with me as long as God allows me to keep my memories.

PASTA

WHEN ALL ELSE FAILS

Since I have furnished an introduction to each of my food sections, I am told it is only proper to do the same for pasta. But what is there to say about pasta? Doesn't everyone love pasta (the way I do?) After all, it's such a cuddly comfort food, and it's always patiently waiting for you in your cupboard (if you included it in your shopping list!) With a little bit of imagination and pizzaz, anyone can make absolutely delectable pasta dishes in no time at all. For upgrading your grainy nutrient-quotient, try to choose pasta made from wholegrain or whole meal flours.

GET OFF THE YO-YO DIETS AND GET REAL!

The thought of dieting will make us cringe, and leads us quickly to overeat and binge.
"Eat, drink and be merry" is what we say; "tomorrow we'll diet" and with hunger pangs will pay.
But you should know there's a better way; eat whole and natural food ! I say.

Forget about pizza or a chunk of meat, fruits and veggies should be your daily feed;
Nuts, beans and grains you also need, and you'll find a healthier life you'll lead.
When you eat grains for that extra kick, your yo-yo dieting you'll be able to lick.

The white sugar monster, no more a temptation, as you acquire a new realization;
Your cravings will be a thing of the past, as your new lifestyle will forever last.
Your food will be fuelled with high octane, as you'll be cruising in the slow lane.

And when your body will be well-fed, the pounds on you will slowly shed.
Then as you let go of all junk food, your brain will reward you with a good mood.
Don't take my word for it 'cause it's in rhyme, try it yourself - but give it some time!

GOOD OLD-FASHIONED SPAGHETTI

This pasta is indeed 'old-fashioned', and I know you don't have all day to cook, and probably have a hundred other things to do today, but this is basic, good food and very satisfying and comforting to eat.

Serves 8

1 (16 oz) package spaghetti (wholegrain)

3 medium onions, chopped

1 medium carrot, chopped

1 stalk celery, chopped

3 cloves garlic, chopped

1 cup chopped mushrooms

2 tbsp extra-virgin olive oil

1/2 cup chopped sweet red pepper

1 cup firm tofu, mashed

1 (28 - oz) can plum tomatoes

1 (8 - oz) can tomato paste

1 tsp dried oregano

1/2 tsp sea salt or Herbamare

Black pepper to taste

1 1/2 cups **Kombu-Shiitake Stock** (see page 105) or **Vegetable Stock** (see page 104) or water

1/8 cup chopped flat-leaf parsley or basil

1 Cook the pasta according to package directions, drain and reserve.

2 In a large saucepan, sauté the onions, carrot, celery, garlic and mushrooms in oil for 5 - 6 minutes.

3 Add the red pepper and tofu, and sauté for 5 minutes.

4 Add the tomatoes and the tomato paste, mix well and bring to a boil.

5 Add the oregano, salt, pepper and half the water or stock, and let boil for 2 minutes.

6 Reduce the heat and simmer for 45 minutes, stirring occasionally.

7 Add the remaining water or stock, stir, and simmer another 45 minutes, stirring occasionally.

8 Add the pasta and the parsley or basil, adjust seasoning, mix well, heat through and serve.

ELBOWS, SPINACH 'N' CHICKPEAS

This is a great main course pasta dish, laced as it is with fragments of greens and legumes. It can also serve as a party-buffet dish.

Serves 4

1 (8 oz) package spelt elbows

1 tbsp extra-virgin olive oil

2 cloves garlic, minced

1 cup packed chopped baby spinach

1 (16 oz) can diced tomatoes, with juice

1 cup cooked until baby-soft chickpeas or from a can and drained

1/8 cup chopped basil or 1/2 - 1 tsp dried basil

Black pepper to taste

Sea salt or Herbamare to taste

1 Cook elbows according to package instructions, drain and reserve.

2 In a large saucepan, sauté the garlic in oil for 1 minute.

3 Add the spinach, tomatoes and juice, and bring to a boil.

4 Lower heat and simmer, uncovered, for about 10 minutes.

5 Stir in the chickpeas, cover and simmer for another 5 minutes.

6 Add the pasta, basil, pepper and salt, and stir gently.

7 Cover until heated through and serve.

VARIATIONS:

1. The baby spinach can be substituted with regular spinach, or any other leafy greens of your choice.

2. The elbows can be substituted with other pasta of a similar size.

LINGUINE WITH MUSHROOMS

This dish is really quick and easy to prepare and will please all pasta lovers. The fresh shiitakes add a rich, soothing, feel-good flavour to the pasta. Served as an appetizer, it is ever so elegant and filling (so you don't need to knock yourself out for the rest of the meal).

Serves 3-4 as a main dish or 6-8 as an appetizer

8 oz linguine

1 1/3 cups chopped shiitake mushrooms (1/2 - inch pieces)

3 cloves garlic, minced

1 tbsp extra-virgin olive oil

1 tbsp umeboshi vinegar

1/8 cup finely sliced green onions

Sea salt or Herbamare to taste

Black pepper to taste

1/8 cup chopped basil or 2 tsp dried

1 Cook the pasta according to package directions, drain and reserve the cooking liquid.

2 In a large saucepan, sauté the mushrooms and garlic in the oil for about 6 - 8 minutes, stirring occasionally.

3 Lower the heat, add the pasta, umeboshi vinegar, green onions, salt, pepper and basil, and toss well.

4 Add from the cooking liquid just enough to have the desired saucy moisture.

5 Cover, heat through and serve.

───── ✿ ─────

GREEN VARIATION:
1/2 cup packed finely sliced, lightly steamed kale can be added at step 3.

SUZANNE'S NOODLE BAKE

This recipe was inspired by Suzanne Adams, whom I met for the first time at *True North Health Education Center* in California, in July 2005. It just so happens that upon meeting her there for the first time I found her to be the nicest, most put-together and helpful woman, with an absolutely simple, down-to-earth charm. She was doing a 15-day-water-fast, while I was on fruits and vegetables. It turned out that we also share a dear friend, Esther Lipschitz, who, together with her exemplary husband Morty, carries on the vegan tradition in Israel, where Esther was born.

Serves 6-8

2 cups **Béchamel Sauce** (see page 111)

1 (16 oz) package broad noodles

2 small eggplant, peeled and chopped (1/2 - inch pieces)

1 tbsp extra-virgin olive oil

1 cup chopped onions

2 cloves garlic, minced

1 (28 oz) can tomatoes

Sea salt or Herbamare to taste

Black pepper to taste

8 thick large slices of tomato

1/8 cup chopped basil

1 Preheat oven to 350° F.

2 Cook the noodles, strain and reserve the pasta and the cooking water.

3 Prepare a double portion (2 cups) béchamel sauce, using reserved pasta cooking water as the liquid for the recipe.

4 In a large saucepan, sauté the eggplant, onions and garlic in oil until the onions are translucent, stirring occasionally (4 - 6 minutes).

5 Add the tomatoes with their juice, and simmer for 5 minutes.

6 Add the noodles, salt and pepper, mix well, and adjust seasoning.

7 Transfer this mixture to a 13 x 9 x 2 - inch ovenproof baking dish.

8 Carefully pour the béchamel sauce over the noodles and arrange the tomato slices on top.

9 Garnish with the basil, and bake uncovered for 25 - 30 minutes.

ANGEL HAIR SUPREME

We all have our angels, whether we know them or not. I am reminded of a *Shevuos Shir* (holiday lecture) by Rabbi Feuer in Monsey. He told us, among other fascinating stories, that angels have the distinct quality to totally focus on one task only; they cannot do otherwise. They also have no ego and, therefore, no stress. Perhaps some of us think that such an existence would be boring and without challenges. But let me tell you! Some days I wouldn't mind just sitting on a fluffy cloud, totally stress-free and minus my ego, observing our mad, multi-tasking world. Why is it that many of us find it so difficult to focus on one task only at any given time? Why can we hardly ever "be fully in the moment"?

Back to earth! This is my favourite pasta recipe. It is easy and simple to prepare, but oh tastes so yummy!

Serves 3-4

1 (8 oz) package Angel Hair pasta (spelt)

2 tsp extra-virgin olive oil

2 cloves garlic, minced

1/4 cup sliced green onions

3 large tomatoes, parboiled, peeled and diced

3/4 tsp sea salt or Herbamare

Black pepper to taste (optional)

2 tbsp chopped basil

1 Cook the Angel Hair according to package directions, drain and reserve.

2 In a large skillet, sauté the garlic and green onions in the oil for 1 minute.

3 Add the tomatoes, stir, and cook for 2 - 3 minutes.

4 Add the Angel Hair, salt, pepper and basil, stir, cover, and heat through.

5 Serve immediately.

VARIATIONS:

1. Spaghetti, fettuccine or linguini can be substituted for the Angel Hair.
2. Regular onions can be substituted for the green onions at Step 2.
3. For a more Primavera version, strips of cucumber or red pepper can be added at step 3.
4. Small tofu squares can be added at Step 2, to proteinize this dish.
5. This dish can also turn into a scrumptious party salad. Simply add your favourite salad dressing and serve at room temperature.

GREEN LOKSHIN KUGEL

For the health-conscious and the lean 'n' green crowd, here's a new spin on the old Shabbos kugel.

Serves 10-15

1 (16 oz) package broad whole grain noodles

2 1/4 cups packed spinach

4 organic eggs, well beaten

1 1/2 tbsp extra-virgin olive oil

3/4 cup chopped onions

2 cloves garlic, minced

1/8 tsp black pepper, or to taste

1/2 tsp sea salt or Herbamare

Pinch ground nutmeg

2 tbsp oat bran

Unhulled sesame seeds for garnish (optional)

1 Preheat oven to 350° F.

2 Cook noodles according to package instructions, drain and reserve.

3 Steam spinach for 30 seconds, squeeze out all the liquid, and chop coarse.

4 Sauté onions and garlic in oil about 5 minutes and cool slightly.

5 In a large mixing bowl, place the noodles, spinach and sautéed onions, and mix well.

6 In a medium bowl, combine the beaten eggs with pepper, salt, nutmeg and oat bran.

7 Add the egg mixture to the noodle-spinach bowl, mix well, and pour into a greased 13 x 9 x 2 - inch baking pan.

8 Garnish liberally with sesame seeds, if used.

9 Bake uncovered for 30 minutes and serve hot or at room temperature.

LIFE WITH BIG BOY

When I got married, I would have liked, besides children, also a dog. But by the time I had the courage to ask for one, three-fifths of our family vetoed it outright. The only other animal-lover was our youngest son, Michael. The dogs followed him home from school. The cool hippy cats of the 60's assembled every Friday afternoon on our Viewmount Avenue doorstep, where they were treated to gourmet fish salad, which had been destined for our Shabbos table. It was replete with fresh-squeezed lemon juice, home-made mayonnaise, fresh dill and parsley and imported capers. In our backyard, he had squirrels nibbling on the finest assortment of roasted nuts. It was then that I decided to look for a house pet, and we chose two quiet, unassuming and non-threatening goldfish. The idea behind this was that the children would be responsible for the care of these fish. But once the novelty wore off I became the sole provider. Whether from anorexia or bulimia, one of them was always floating belly-up in the tank in the morning. For a while, I kept supplying a new mate for the lonely survivor, but I got tired of their deadly game and the responsibility of running a fishy hospice all by myself.

Next we bought a very compatible looking couple of turtles and settled them in on our dining room window sill. That also proved a disaster from day one. I was jealous of them, either when they stayed under water till twelve noon on a rainy day, or when they sat on their little rock, contentedly sunning themselves; much like elderly arthritic couples do on a Miami beach. However, "Mr. and Mrs. Turtell" ended up literally bored to death, which reaffirmed my theory that a life totally devoid of any stress can also kill.

Then one day I saw the cutest little budgie at Woolworths and on a sudden whim I bought it. There was an immediate bonding between us; it was love at first sight.

When I brought the budgie home we called him "Big Boy", which may be saying something about the pecking order in our family. Again, no one volunteered to take care of his needs. But that was okay with me, as it gave me the opportunity to cultivate a seven-year, mutually-loving and totally stress-free relationship.

In retrospect, Big Boy displayed many personality traits which resonated with my own. He was vain. He would never tire of looking in his little mirror. The difference between us was that he needed no makeup. He had the softest, silkiest, powder-blue feathers, and for jewelry he wore a permanent necklace of the tiniest black and white feathery beads around his little neck. But, unlike me, he had a strong self identity. He knew who he was and what he wanted and did not want. He was never bothered by procrastination or having guilt feelings and stuff like that.

He was very clean, not withstanding the fact that he adamantly refused to take a bath; and a shower was out of the question as far as I was concerned.

He was a morning person like me. At the dawn of each new day Big Boy exuded an air of cheerful happiness. This was manifested by frenetic chirpings, which gave me the energy to face before-school breakfast time with three high-spirited youngsters. Each morning, when our children had gone to school, Big Boy would come out of his cage to have quality time with me. He established the following ritual: after I opened the cage he would hop onto the kitchen table, take a few bits of my weight-watchers cottage cheese from my plate, give me two pecks on my lips and return blissfully to the security of his home, where he would not leave again until the next morning. No amount of coaxing or open-door policy would make Big Boy ever come out of his cage except when the two of us were alone in the early morning hours.

Like mine, his energy level would distinctly wane at around 5 P.M., with the difference that he could afford to retire at that time for a long, quiet evening at home, whereas my day was just beginning to peak with the demands of my lively family. Not another sound came from Big Boy's cage for the rest of the evening, as he turned inward to meditate and prepare for a peaceful night.

Big Boy was a strict vegetarian long before I embraced that lifestyle. His vegan diet was of the simplest nature. Totally undemanding, he ate his millet uncooked, and took his daily liquid requirements from one celery leaf. This was a lot easier to schlepp home than an assortment of large, economy-size cans of High "C" fruit juices. In a sense, Big Boy was my first guinea pig, as I soon realized that his health, happiness, longevity and beautiful, shining feathers were the result of his vegan lifestyle.

But what bound us together more than anything else was our love of music. In those days of my belated journey through a liberal art's degree, we both listened passionately to a complete menu of operas, symphonies and concerti, ranging from early Baroque to the middle of the twentieth century; for that was my homework. We had our favorites. Vivaldi was for a measured, up-beat and charming baroque treat, while Bach was for a more mathematically structured and monumentally acoustic delight. But it was Mozart who transcended all cultural boundaries. We both developed a severe case of Mozartitis Chronica as we became obsessed with listening to anything Mozartian that would come our way, either over the CBC, FM radio, or via my 33 1/3 record collection. Mozart suited all our moods and all our seasons. Once, when listening to The Magic Flute, Big Boy instinctively knew that the voice coming from the radio was, like himself, a feathered creature - and he went berserk. When Papageno sang his dramatic aria about the longing for a suitable mate, Big Boy ecstatically joined him, screeching at the top of his unrehearsed lungs, and I shall never ever forget that haunting duet.

Big Boy was the perfect companion. He was grateful, loyal, always cheerful, beautiful to look at and totally undemanding.

Every morning at l0:30, Big Boy had his social hour on the dining room window sill. At that time he would cavort with a gang of sparrows having their coffee break on the high wires outside. Docile, gentle little Big Boy would then become transformed into a somersaulting, hysterically screeching and obnoxious creature. Peer pressure is something every parent has to cope with at some time, and it was pitiful to watch how Big Boy's attention-getting social overtures were totally ignored by those 'vilde chayes' (wild animals) outside. As a result, feathers were flying all over our dining room, and each time my cleaning lady came I had to stay home the whole day to make sure she would not strangle him.

Once in a while Big Boy's nails needed cutting. But whenever I approached the cage with my scissors, his nervous flutterings would make him lose quite a few feathers, which were none in my cap. It seems that I had overestimated his confidence in me. Finally, it became too much of a hassle for me, and I decided to take him to a vet to have his nails clipped. I had to leave him there for a few hours and upon my return I was unceremoniously informed that Big Boy was a girl. I should have known all along that something was "amiss" because Big Boy always behaved so perfectly lady-like. It was certainly not her fault that early in life we imposed the masculine gender on her.

Michael never became quite as enamoured with Big Boy as did his mother. On his return from camp one summer, he was accompanied, besides a trunk full of dirty and torn clothes, by two frogs and a garden snake, which were certainly more challenging than lady-like Big Boy.

While on one of my lengthy trips to Israel, Big Boy, having been farmed out to friends, died. The cause was surely a broken heart (on his-her high-fiber-no-fat diet he-she had neither high blood pressure nor clogged arteries). Michael arranged a private, dignified memorial service in our backyard under the shade of my beloved weeping willow tree, near the always neglected bed of geraniums.

LEGUMES

&

TOFU

LEGUME AND TOFU RECIPES

LEGUMES

THE PROTEIN FOOD OF VEGETARIANS AND VEGANS

The proverbial question most asked of vegetarians and vegans is: "Where do you get your protein from?" People from Western countries seem to have a distorted notion when it comes to defining dietary protein. They tend to think of protein consumption only in terms of meat, fowl, fish, eggs and dairy products. They apparently believe the TV commercials, sponsored by the Dairy Industry, showing luscious mermaids cavorting in a sea of bubbly, cool milk, totally osteoporosis-free. What they do not know or realize is that animal proteins, when eaten habitually, are sooner or later associated with kidney failure, gout, damage to arteries with resulting heart disease, osteoporosis, etc; all stemming from calcium loss (and no amount of drinking milk or bathing in it can prevent these processes).

Legumes, on the other hand, are a great source of quality protein as well as complex carbohydrates. They are rich in thiamine, niacin, B6, and folic acid as well as in calcium, iron, phosphorus and potassium. They are heart-smart because they are cholesterol-free. They have a higher protein content than milk, eggs, meat or fish and are an excellent source of dietary fibre. Unlike other carbohydrates, such as bread, cereals, potatoes and pasta, beans don't increase blood sugar levels for diabetics. Legumes are also known to protect against various forms of cancer.

Split peas, lentils, adzuki beans, baby limas, chickpeas and all white beans are the easiest beans to digest, provided they are properly cooked. For the purpose of good digestion, it is recommended to use the sea vegetable kombu in the cooking of all beans (see **Sea Vegetables - *Mining Precious Trace Minerals***, page 27)

Adzuki beans are the most practical little fellows to have around the kitchen. They don't need soaking overnight, and cook faster than most other beans. They can enhance any main course, or salad. If you cook large quantities and store them in portions in the freezer, you are prepared for frantic days.

TO COOK LEGUMES:

1. Place beans on a large plate, sort and discard any damaged or discoloured pieces.

2. Wash beans thoroughly.

3. Soak beans overnight with a ratio of 4 cups of water to 1 cup of beans.

4. Drain the beans, discard the soak water and rinse thoroughly.

5. If for any reason you have not soaked your beans overnight, you can use the QUICK-SOAK METHOD: Place the washed beans in a suitable saucepan, add two cups water to one cup of beans, and bring to a boil. Turn off heat, cover and let stand for one hour. Drain, rinse and proceed as per instructions in the recipe.

6. In a suitable pot or saucepan, add the beans, the pre-soaked kombu and the required amount of water, and bring to a boil. Do not salt the beans at this time, as this will make them tough.

7. Reduce the heat, cover and cook on low heat for the required time. Skim off any foam that develops on top and discard; (the older the beans are the longer it will take until they are done).

8. Do not discard the kombu! It is a precious nutritional food full of trace minerals; use it along with the beans!

HELPFUL HINTS:

1. Legumes by themselves lack a certain amino acid and so do the grains. Therefore, when these two food groups are combined they constitute a complete protein. However, it is not necessary to combine them always at the same meal; it can be done at various meals within 24 hours.

2. Legumes can be made into soups, salads, stews, casseroles, patties, sauces, vegetarian liver, dips and patés.

3. To proteinize almost any salad, cooked beans can be added in modest quantities. I often add cooked adzuki beans or chickpeas (always stored in my freezer) to my salads.

4. Cooked chickpeas (garbanzo beans) add variety and nutrition to many dishes. However, they may take from 1 3/4 - 2 1/2 hours to cook to desired softness. I cook large quantities and store them in portions in the freezer. I add them cooked and defrosted to salads, cooked vegetable soups and stir-fries.

SAUCY LENTILS

This is a very tasty and succulent legume dish, especially when served over rice or other grains.

Serves 4-6 as a main dish, or 6-8 as a side dish

4 cups water

1 cup lentils

1/2 cup coarsely grated carrots

3/4 cup chopped onions

1/2 cup chopped yams (1/4 - inch pieces)

2 cloves garlic, minced

1/2 cup chopped celery (1/4 - inch pieces)

2 bay leaves

1 1/2 - inch piece ginger, grated

1/2 tsp sea salt or Herbamare

1/4 tsp black pepper

1 tsp ground cumin

1 tsp dried marjoram

1 tbsp organic soy sauce

1 cup canned tomato sauce

1. In a medium pot, place the water, lentils, carrots, onions, yams, garlic, celery, bay leaves and ginger, cover and bring to a boil.

2. Cook on medium-low heat for 30 minutes.

3. Add salt, pepper, cumin, marjoram, soy sauce and tomato sauce and simmer another 30 minutes.

4. Remove bay leaves, adjust seasoning, and serve.

———— ❧ ————

SPICY VARIATION:
You may substitute the marjoram with ground curry or ground coriander.

SPICY DAHL

This dish has real pizzazz and goes well with steamed rice as a main course. It's a most pleasant and dahl-lightful way to eat legumes.

Serves 4

1 cup yellow split peas, soaked overnight

2 cups water

1 large bay leaf

1/2 cup finely chopped onions

1 tbsp extra-virgin olive oil

1/2 cup sliced sweet red pepper (1/4 - inch pieces)

1/8 tsp ground cumin

1/4 tsp grated ginger

1/8 tsp ground coriander

1/8 tsp ground turmeric

Pinch ground curry

1/4 tsp sea salt or Herbamare, or to taste

1 Drain the peas, place in a medium saucepan with the water and the bay leaf; cover, bring to a boil and cook on medium heat for 30 minutes.

2 In a small skillet, sauté the onions in oil until translucent, about 5 minutes.

3 Add red pepper and sauté for another minute.

4 Add the cumin, ginger, coriander, turmeric, curry and salt, and mix well.

5 Add this mixture to the peas, and continue to cook for another 30 minutes, or until dahl thickens and is the consistency you like.

6 Discard bay leaf, adjust seasoning and serve.

———————— 🐝 ————————

GRAINY VARIATION TO GO WITH THE DAHL:

If you are in a time crunch, or for variety, you may substitute quinoa or millet for the rice - it cooks in less time than rice, or get in the fast lane and use couscous!

ANGELA'S CLASSIC BAKED BEAN CASSEROLE

This savoury dish for life in the slow lane and cooked in 'Adagio' tempo was given to me by one of my computer angels, Angela Roberge, who for more than a year drove a few times a week from Aurora to Toronto through the Ontario landscape and snowscape. Her sense of humour, combined with some of mine, gave us many fun hours together.

Serves 4

1 cup navy beans, soaked overnight

3 cups water

1/2 cup chopped onions

1 tbsp extra-virgin olive oil

1/4 cup canned tomato paste

1/8 cup pure maple syrup

2 tbsp organic soy sauce

1 tsp stone-ground mustard

1/8 tsp black pepper

1/2 tsp sea salt or Herbamare

1 tsp apple cider vinegar

1 Preheat oven to 325° F

2 Drain beans and place in a medium saucepan.

3 Add water, cook about 45 minutes or until soft, drain, and reserve the cooking water.

4 In a large skillet, sauté the onions in oil until translucent.

5 In a one-quart casserole dish, stir together the cooked beans, onions, tomato paste, maple syrup, soy sauce, mustard, pepper, salt and vinegar, adjust seasoning, and add enough of the cooking water to cover the beans.

6 Bake, covered, for 2 - 3 hours, or until the beans have turned dark brown. (Check the beans once in a while and, should they become dry, add from the cooking water to keep moist.)

Lima Bean Casserole

This casserole is a very tasty choice as a vegetarian main course, and is easy to prepare.

Serves 6

1 cup baby lima beans, soaked overnight
3 cups water
1 cup chopped onions
1 tbsp extra-virgin olive oil
1 (28 oz.) can tomatoes
1 tbsp organic soy sauce
1/2 tsp ground cumin
1 tsp stone-ground mustard
1/2 tsp dried marjoram or dried basil
Sea salt or Herbamare to taste
Black pepper to taste
1/2 cup whole wheat breadcrumbs

1   Drain beans, rinse, and place in a medium saucepan.

2   Add water and cook for 1 - 1 1/2 hours, or until soft. Drain.

3   Preheat oven to 350° F.

4   In a large skillet, sauté onions in oil about 5 minutes.

5   Add the tomatoes, soy sauce, cumin, mustard, marjoram or basil, salt and pepper, and mix well.

6   Add the beans, toss well and adjust seasoning.

7   Place the above mixture in an ovenproof (2 - quart) casserole dish, sprinkle the breadcrumbs over the top, and bake, uncovered, for 45 minutes.

"The more animal protein we eat, the more calcium we will lose."

CHICKPEA PATTIES

These patties are a practical protein stand-by, and can be eaten hot, at room temperature, or cold. They also make substantial sandwich fillers.

Yields 10 patties, 2 1/2 - inches diameter

1 tbsp extra-virgin olive oil

1 cup finely chopped onions

1/3 cup finely diced carrots

1/2 cup finely diced celery

3/4 cup finely diced sweet red pepper

2 tbsp chopped flat-leaf parsley

1/4 tsp garlic powder

1/8 tsp ground cumin

1 1/2 - 2 tbsp organic soy sauce

1 cup cooked chickpeas

1/8 cup tahini

1   Preheat oven to 350° F.

2   Cover a medium baking pan with parchment paper, and reserve.

3   In a large skillet, heat oil and add the onions, carrots, celery, red pepper and parsley, and sauté for 7 - 8 minutes.

4   Add the garlic powder, cumin and soy sauce, mix all together and sauté another 30 seconds.

5   Place the chickpeas in a food processor with the tahini, and process until mashed. (You may need to scrape the sides of the bowl a few times.)

6   In a large bowl, combine the vegetables in the skillet with the chickpea mixture, and adjust seasoning.

7   Form patties (2 1/2 inches in diameter), place on the baking pan, bake 12 - 15 minutes on one side, turn them over and bake 10 - 12 minutes on the other side.

HELPFUL HINT:
These patties can be frozen in individual portions.

PAN-FRIED LENTIL PATTIES

These patties are delicious, but they are not "fast food" stuff. If you have the time, like to cook good food, and love to eat it, this is for you! It's well worth the effort in terms of preparing a healthful dish, which can be a main course, sandwich filler, or a snack.

Yields 8 patties

1/2 cup lentils
1 1/4 cups tomato juice
2 dried shiitake mushrooms
1/8 cup tahini
1/8 cup chopped onions
1/8 cup finely diced celery
1 clove garlic, minced
4 tsp extra-virgin olive oil
1/4 tsp sea salt or Herbamare
1/8 tsp black pepper
1/8 tsp ground cumin
1/8 cup oat bran
1/8 cup whole spelt or whole wheat flour
1/2 tsp stone-ground mustard
1 tsp organic soy sauce

1   In a medium pot, bring lentils and tomato juice to a boil. Cook, covered, for about 45 minutes, or until lentils are soft.

2   Place shiitakes in a small pot with water to cover, bring to a boil and cook for 10 minutes.

3   Drain the shiitakes and cool and reserve the water.

4   Mix the tahini with enough mushroom water to make a paste, and reserve.

5   Slice the shiitakes into 1/4 - inch pieces, discarding only the hard ends of the stems.

6   Sauté shiitakes, onions, celery and garlic in oil for about 8 minutes.

7   Add salt, pepper and cumin, and stir.

8   In a large bowl, mix together the cooked lentils, sautéed vegetables, tahini, oat bran, flour, mustard, and soy sauce and adjust seasoning.

HELPFUL HINT:
These patties can be frozen in individual portions.

9   Shape patties into 2 1/2 - inch size. (If the mixture is too soft to hold, add a bit of flour or oat bran.)

10 Pan-fry the patties in shallow oil until golden brown on both sides.

PIQUANT CHICKPEA SALAD

This salad makes a great side dish and is compatible with most main-course choices.

Yields 1 cup, serves 3-4 as a side dish

1/2 cup raw chickpeas, soaked overnight and cooked until very soft

1/8 cup finely chopped sweet red pepper

1 tsp finely chopped purple onions

2 tbsp finely chopped green onions

1/4 cup chopped baby spinach

1 tbsp chopped flat-leaf or curly parsley

1/2 tsp garlic powder

2 pinches ground paprika

Pinch ground cumin

1 - 2 tsp flaxseed oil

2 tsp umeboshi vinegar

2 tsp apple cider vinegar

1 In a medium bowl, combine the chickpeas, red pepper, purple and green onions, spinach, parsley, and toss.

2 In another small bowl, whisk the garlic powder, paprika, cumin, flaxseed oil and vinegars.

3 Pour over the chickpeas, toss until all is well mixed, and adjust seasoning.

4 If time permits, marinate this salad for 1/2 - 1 hour, and serve at room temperature

HEALTHFUL HINT:

Be Kitchen-Smart! Cook extra chickpeas to have on hand to add to salads, soups, grains, pasta, etc...

Pinto Bean Salad

This frisky and succulent salad is chok full o' protein and goes well with almost anything else on your menu. Nutritionally speaking, it will perk up a main-course grain dish, adding sugar-free 'brownie points' to your protein account.

Serves 3-4

1/4 tsp stone-ground mustard

1 tsp umeboshi vinegar

1 tsp brown rice vinegar or apple cider vinegar

2 tsp flaxseed oil

1/2 tsp sea salt or Herbamare, or to taste

1/8 tsp black pepper

1/8 tsp ground cumin

A few pinches dried marjoram

2 tbsp finely chopped onions

2 tbsp finely chopped celery

2 tbsp finely grated carrot

2 tbsp finely chopped sweet red pepper

1 tbsp chopped flat-leaf or curly parsley

1 cup cooked pinto beans

1 In a medium bowl, whisk together the mustard, vinegars, oil, salt, pepper, cumin and marjoram.

2 Add the onions, celery, carrot, red pepper, parsley and pinto beans, and toss together gently but thoroughly.

3 If time permits, marinate this salad for 1/2 - 1 hour, or overnight, and serve at room temperature.

VARIATIONS:

1. In a pinch, canned beans may be substituted for the freshly cooked ones. Discard the liquid and rinse the beans well!

2. The pinto beans can be substituted with any other beans of your choice.

3. You may substitute your favourite fresh herbs!

CHOPPED LIVER BUT NOT LIVER

Chopped liver move over or go back to your take-out!! This is the real thing. This chock full o' plant protein paté looks like chopped liver and tastes like it, but that's where the similarity ends. It can be served as an appetizer (see below), sandwich spread, a dip with raw veggies, a snack on crackers or rice cakes, or rolled up in a small lettuce leaf as finger food.

Yields about 4 cups

1 1/2 cups coarsely chopped onions

3 tbsp extra-virgin olive oil

4 cloves garlic, minced

2/3 cup raw organic walnuts

1 cup green split peas, soaked overnight and cooked

3/4 cup chickpeas, soaked overnight and cooked

1/4 tsp ground cumin, or to taste

3 pinches black pepper

Sea salt or Herbamare to taste

1 Sauté onions in oil until well browned.

2 Add the garlic and cook 2 - 3 minutes.

3 Place the walnuts into a food processor and process into coarse meal.

4 Gradually add half the peas and half the chickpeas and process until mashed.

5 Add the sautéed onions, cumin, pepper, salt and the rest of the split peas and chickpeas, and process all until smooth.

6 If the mixture is too thick or dry, a few drops of liquid may be added.

7 Adjust seasoning. (This liver needs really strong flavouring to compete with the other "liver".)

HELPFUL HINT:

It keeps well in the refrigerator for 3 days and freezes well in tightly covered containers.

APPETIZER:

Place a dollop of "liver", 1/3 - 1/2 cup, on a lettuce leaf on individual plates, and garnish with tomato wedges and parsley sprigs, and stick one or two cocktail pretzels on top, if on hand. Since we also eat with our eyes, "Edible Art" makes for happy, satisfied eaters.

PEASFUL HUMMUS

I have substituted the traditional chickpeas with yellow split peas so as to get a very easy-to-prepare, smooth-textured end product. The split peas cook much faster than chickpeas. This is a zesty and versatile dip to start a meal or to snack on, and it's great with veggie sticks or crackers.

Yields 2 cups

1 cup yellow split peas, soaked overnight in 3 cups water

1/4 tsp garlic powder

1 1/2 tbsp lemon juice

2 tsp umeboshi vinegar

1/4 tsp ground cumin

1/2 tsp ground coriander

1 tsp sea salt or Herbamare, or to taste

1/4 cup tahini

1/4 cup finely chopped flat-leaf parsley

1 Drain the peas, place in a medium saucepan, cover with fresh water and cook for 45 minutes, or until very soft (save the cooking liquid for stock).

2 Place the peas in a food processor, add the garlic powder, lemon juice, vinegar, cumin, coriander, salt, and tahini, and process until smooth.

3 Transfer to a bowl, adjust seasoning and mix in the parsley.

4 Refrigerate in an airtight container; (will keep for 5 days).

HELPFUL HINT:
This dish can be frozen, and stored in sizeable portions.

"No one diet is right for everyone all the time."
- Robert S. Mendelsohn, MD

WHY I BUY CORN WHEN IN ISRAEL

Whenever I go to the supermarket in Israel I think of my first Hebrew teacher in Germany. This story is not about him, however, but about me having forgotten most of the *ivrit* (modern Hebrew) that he so diligently and enthusiastically taught me. It has taken me almost a lifetime to rate my self-esteem in the middle range of the scale, yet whenever I enter a supermarket in Israel, it plummets to near zero. Usually an assertive person, here I maintain a low profile. Grabbing a buggy, I saunter through the aisles as inconspicuously as possible, hoping I look as if I know what I am buying.

For reasons of my own, I am an avid supermarket label reader, at least in Canada. In Israel, though, I have to rely on guesswork, and that has not always been a positive experience. I still remember the time I brought home laundry bleach instead of vinegar. Luckily, I have since learned the difference between *chometz* (vinegar) and *economica* (Javex). Being an intuitive person, I try to divine the difference between barley and wheat kernels, but for some reason my intuition fails me completely in an Israeli supermarket.

I nevertheless hang in there, since I am not one to give up easily and am a firm believer in asking for help when needed. So I look for approachable human beings - people who seem kind and don't appear to be in too much of a hurry. The logical choice, of course, is English-speaking customers. They can be from any English-speaking country: England, North America, South Africa, Australia - they all look good to me. The only trouble is that what makes them desirable is precisely what intimidates me about them. They appear so totally in control, relaxed and self-assured - qualities that come from having taken the trouble to attend an excellent *ulpan* (Hebrew course) to learn Hebrew. Thanks, but no thanks! I'm not going to risk having my self-esteem slide further down the scale. To approach a youngster seems like a good idea. He or she probably respects me, putting me in the grandmother class. But, wait a minute, what is he/she doing out of school in the middle of the day? I cannot encourage such behaviour. As a last resort, I approach a young employee who is making a vain attempt to rearrange the shelves. I hope he's completed the grade in high school that included English. I ask him politely if he could kindly tell me where I can find bottled spring water. But he looks right through me as if I'm transparent; customer relations was evidently not part of his training.

Fortunately, however, I am never at a complete loss. Problem-solving is one of my hobbies, and so I end up buying quite a few cans of corn as I can be sure from the picture what it is. It's not that I really need all those cans of corn, but when you've been seen stalking the aisles for one-and-a-half hours, you don't want to be caught checking out with just one can of corn. And they do come in handy when our *Sabra* (Israeli-born) grandchildren come over for supper; they have a passion for corn. May they eat it until one-hundred-and-twenty, or until *Moshiach* (the Messiah) comes - whichever comes first.

When checking out my ten bottles of spring water, the girl at the check-out counter asked in her best school English, "Are you preparing for the war?" With this parting and comforting thought I traipsed home, all the while having the specter of a scud war weighing heavily on my shoulders.

TOFU

THE JOY AND PLOY OF SOY

What vegetarians have always known is now being explained by scientific research and advocated as new discoveries; mainly that there are great health benefits to switching your diet from animal protein (meat and dairy) to vegetable sources of protein, such as soy beans and all other beans and whole grains.

Tofu is a cholesterol-free alternative to animal protein food and is relatively low in calories and saturated fat. It is a good source of iron and phosphorus, B vitamins and the antioxidant vitamin E. When coagulated with magnesium chloride, or calcium sulfate, tofu is a rich source of calcium. Innumerable scientific studies have concluded that eating tofu may help reduce menopausal symptoms, lower bad cholesterol thus protecting the heart, prevent osteoporosis by strengthening bones, and can inhibit cancers of the breast, prostate, colon, lung and skin. One cup of tofu has more calcium than two cups of milk. Dairy cheese, in contrast to tofu, is full of saturated animal fat, which is known to raise blood cholesterol, and it is also the cause of many respiratory problems, as it puts phlegm on the chest.

Tofu, which has no flavour of its own, is an extremely versatile food. It will take on any flavour it is combined with, and can be roasted, fried, steamed, baked, broiled, scrambled and used in desserts and baked goods. When cut into tiny cubes, it can be added to soups, and all main course dishes, for an extra boost of protein.

Having said all the above, at the same time I have to put a damper on tofu, if it is eaten too often. Like with everything else in life, moderation is always the best and most health-promoting way to go. Tofu, being a processed food, should be eaten no more than two times a week. As a matter of fact, Dr. Joel Fuhrman, in his latest book: "*Eat to Live*", recommends eating a variety of all beans daily, which give the same beneficial effect as tofu does in terms of protein and other nutritional requirements (see **Bibliography**, page 257).

Nothing in life is categorical, and that applies to health food as well. There are pros and cons for certain foods and we need to learn how to strike a balance between the two. As tofu has gained popularity, numerous prepared soy products have popped up on the market. Ready-to-eat deli slices, hot dogs, stews, desserts, faux cheeses, spreads - you name it - get our diet-conscious attention when shopping. These foods are processed, filled with additives and 'flavour enhancers', **and should be avoided at all costs**.

TOFONY SCRAMBLED EGGS

Served on whole grain toast with a salad, this makes a substantial lunch, and can also complement a grainy supper.

Serves 1-2

2 tsp extra-virgin olive oil

1/2 cup finely chopped onions

10 oz. medium firm tofu, mashed

1/4 tsp garlic powder

1/4 tsp ground paprika

1/8 tsp sea salt or Herbamare

1/8 tsp black pepper

1 tbsp finely chopped flat-leaf parsley

1 In a medium skillet, heat oil and sauté onions for 3 minutes.

2 Add the tofu, garlic powder, paprika, salt and pepper, and stir until edges of tofu become brown (about 5 - 6 minutes).

3 Add parsley and serve immediately.

"An ounce of prevention is better than a pound of medical prescriptions."

BAKED TOFU

Here's the answer to all the whining "I-don't-know-what-to-do-with-tofu" crowd. Many tofu recipes ask you to marinate the tofu overnight, but I find the method below simpler and quicker and the taste is just fine for us.

Serves 4

1 cup water

3 tbsp white spelt flour

1 tsp onion powder

1 tsp garlic powder

1/2 tsp ground ginger

3 tbsp organic soy sauce

1 block firm tofu (about 250 grams), cut into 8 equal slices.

1 Preheat oven to 350° F.

2 In a saucepan, combine the water, flour, onion and garlic powders, ginger and soy sauce and bring to a boil, stirring continuously until sauce is thickened.

3 Pat the tofu slices dry and place into a 13 x 9 x 2 baking pan; do not overlap.

4 Pour the sauce over the tofu and bake 30 - 40 minutes until lightly browned on top.

5 Serve hot or at room temperature.

HELPFUL HINT:

Leftover slices make excellent sandwich fillers, or can be diced and added to soups, stir-fries, stews, grains or pasta.

VARIATION:

If you like more crispness, after Step 4, broil the tofu for a few minutes!

PAN-GLAZED TOFU

I have tried my culinary skills at fusion cooking, which seems to be all the rage nowadays. But unfortunately my *Ashkenazy* genes always get the better of my taste buds. Somehow, sushi meshi, spicy peanut sauce, toasted sesame oil, coconut milk, Thai chili and teriyaki are just too yucky for me. Here is my version and, if you wish more Asian and healthy flavours, use freshly grated ginger instead of the ginger powder and, for more anti-viral health, use fresh garlic instead of the garlic powder.

Serves 2-3

1/2 package (250 grams) firm tofu

1 1/2 tbsp **Kombu-Shiitake Stock** (see page 105) or water

2 tbsp organic soy sauce

1 thinly sliced green onion

1/4 tsp garlic powder or 1 clove garlic, minced

1 tsp fresh grated ginger or 1/8 tsp ginger powder

1/2 tsp ground paprika

1 tsp arrowroot powder, with just enough water to make a paste

1 Drain tofu, pat dry and slice into 3/4 x 1 - inch cubes.

2 In a medium skillet, place the stock or water, soy sauce, green onion, garlic, ginger, paprika and arrowroot paste.

3 Bring to a boil while stirring constantly until sauce has thickened and bubbles.

4 Add the tofu, cover, reduce heat to low, and simmer 8 - 10 minutes.

5 Adjust seasoning and serve immediately.

HELPFUL HINT:
The arrow root powder may be substituted with an equal amount of flour.

TOFU CACCIATORE

This is a wonderful side dish. It's real yummy served over carbs like: rice, other grains, mashed potatoes, or on a thick slice of whole meal bread.

Serves 4

1/2 package (250 grams), medium firm or firm tofu cut into 1/2 - inch cubes

Enough white spelt flour or arrowroot powder to coat tofu

2 tbsp extra-virgin olive oil, divided

1/2 cup sliced onions

2 cloves garlic, minced

1/2 cup diced carrots (1/4 - inch pieces)

1/2 cup sliced celery (1/4 - inch pieces)

1 cup diced sweet red pepper

1 1/2 cup coarsely chopped mushrooms (1/4 - inch pieces)

2 bay leaves

1 cup tomato sauce or crushed tomatoes

1/2 tsp sea salt or Herbamare

1/4 cup chopped flat-leaf parsley or 1/8 cup chopped basil

1 Dredge tofu in arrowroot powder.

2 In a large saucepan, heat 1 tablespoon of oil and sauté tofu until brown on all sides, (about 7 minutes), remove from pan, and reserve.

3 Add remaining oil to saucepan and cook onions and garlic for about 5 minutes.

4 Add carrots, celery, red pepper, mushrooms, bay leaves and tomato sauce, cover, and simmer for about 20 minutes.

5 Remove bay leaves, add reserved tofu, salt, parsley or basil, mix well, cover to heat through and serve.

TOFU SPONGE

This is no-fuss gourmet stuff; just don't tell anybody what it is!

1 Freeze any quantity of leftover firm tofu in a plastic bag.

2 When needed, remove from freezer, defrost and thoroughly squeeze out all the water.

3 Cut the tofu into 1/2- inch x 1 - inch cubes, and add to any hot soup for a few minutes. The pieces will resemble tiny sponges and will absorb the flavour of your soup, provided your soup is flavourful in the first place.

LIFE WITHOUT A DISHWASHER

I am "dishwasher-safe", not because I come with that now all-too-familiar label, but because I don't have a dishwasher. Don't get me wrong, I'm happy for all those who can make their kitchen life easier with a dishwasher or, for that matter, with six dishwashers.

The reasons I don't have a dishwasher are not ideological but purely practical. Number one: I don't have greasy dishes, and I don't have to serve a large family at this point in time any more. Number two: Loading and unloading a dishwasher is a strain on my back, which is something I can do without. Not for nothing did I spend half of my life in the waiting room of my chiropractor. Meanwhile, I have learned Tai Chi, which is a graceful, beautiful and energizing ancient form of exercise in slow motion, and, once mastered is a great help to get through life without having to bend ones back. So, when all is said and done, I will bend over backwards not to have to bend over forwards. Number three: washing dishes, pots and pans gives me the opportunity, not easily available in this noisy, electronic world, to tune out some of the distracting "chatter", to be alone with my thoughts and become introspective.

On Friday evenings, when we often share our *Shabbos* (Sabbath) table with friends and neighbours, I have a non-wired, real-live dishwasher in the form of a very nice woman who comes in to do the dishes.

Shabbos lunch was a problem, and the way I solved it was to convince my husband that it was okay to use gorgeously-patterned paper plates with matching napkins. The lack of elegance which comes from not eating on real china is off-set by the *naches* (pleasure) derived from being able to throw all the plates into the garbage.

P.S. If you want to make yourself a cup of coffee or tea when you're visiting your kids but can't find a cup, just look in the dishwasher!

NUTS
&
SEEDS

NUT AND SEED RECIPES

NUTS & SEEDS

IT'S OK TO GO NUTS!

Yes, it's okay to "go nuts" but, because they are such a concentrated food, moderation in eating nuts is advised, and some nutritional knowledge is helpful as to how to go nuts in the best and healthiest way.

Nuts and seeds are packed with vitamins and minerals our bodies need to stay healthy. They are chuck full of potassium, calcium, selenium, the powerful antioxidant vitamin E, magnesium; a deficiency of which is associated with increased heart disease, and folic acid; one of the B vitamins often lacking in the American SAD (Standard American Diet).

Many people think that because nuts contain a lot of fat they are fattening. But the fat contained in nuts and seeds are the monounsaturated ones, which are absolutely essential to our health, especially our heart health. They may also help to prevent diabetes. Substituting nuts and seeds for cheeses and highly saturated fatty dressings will considerably help to reduce LDL cholesterol levels and their dire consequences.

Yes, it's true that people who snack on nuts and seeds between or after their daily carnivorous meals may well be overdoing it on consuming fat, but vegetarians cannot do better health-and-calorie-wise, since nuts and seeds are one of the most nutrient-dense foods they can eat. Only a small amount of nuts and seeds are needed to meet protein requirements; one to two ounces eaten a few times daily is enough for most people.

Nuts and seeds can be eaten plain or in combination with other foods. Chopped or coarsely ground, nuts are a crunchy and elegant topping on salads, fruit and all kinds of desserts.

Since some people find nuts difficult to digest in their concentrated form, soaking them overnight or even as long as 24 hours, thus bringing them to a semi-sprouted state, will make them more digestible for good protein assimilation. In whatever state they are, nuts and seeds should always be kept in the fridge or freezer to avoid rancidity. If and when they taste rancid, they need to be discarded.

Whether to eat nuts only in their raw state or roast them is a nutty and controversial matter. Some hold that they must be roasted before eating to release certain fatty acids and kill any mould, while others are as vehement about never roasting them so as not to lose their precious enzymes. In any case, do not buy nuts and seeds already roasted; the refined oil being used is a no-no.

Personally, I take the middle road and roast them on a baking sheet in a low oven for as short a time as possible.

FLAX YOUR MUSCLES WITH FLAX APPEAL!

Flax seeds are in a class by themselves. The flax plant has always been associated with linen and other such products, but apparently the many nutritional properties of its seeds have not been known or have been overlooked. Like oat bran, flaxseed is rich in cholesterol-reducing soluble fibre so beneficial to our cardiovascular system. Each seed packs a punch, being loaded with fibre, lignans, protein, vitamins and omega 3 and omega 6 fatty acids, which are the stuff we absolutely need to maintain whole health.

Flaxseeds may well prove to be an easy-to-handle, readily-available miracle food. They have no glamour but supposedly contain twenty-seven anti-cancer compounds and could possibly be able to reduce the growth of breast cancer tumors. I would want to be friends with them. They may also reduce the risk of adult-onset diabetes. Their fatty acids are similar to those found in fish oil; as a matter of fact, eating about one tablespoon of flaxseeds two times a week would be equivalent to one portion of fish. As if that wasn't enough, the linolenic acid flaxseed contains could also be a potential weapon against asthma, arthritis and psoriasis.

HELPFUL AND HEALTHFUL HINTS:

1. Flax seeds go rancid very quickly, so if possible buy them loose, or make sure the packaged ones are fresh. For best results, grind them fresh as needed in a coffee or nut grinder and store them in the fridge or freezer.

2. Ground flaxseed can be sprinkled on fruits, fruit and vegetable salads, cereals, and/or mixed into any juices or shakes. In their whole form, flax seeds can be used in baking cakes, muffins and breads.

3. Vegans can also eat their cake and have it too. In any cake, three tablespoons of ground flax seeds and one tablespoon water can be substituted for one egg (let sit for two minutes before use).

4. Flaxseed oil is the best thing that can happen to your salads and your health. I use it exclusively for all my salads, which gives me the minimum daily requirement for omega 3 EFA's. However, flaxseed oil must not be heated, and therefore cannot be used in cooking or baking. When buying flaxseed oil, always check the expiration date and always keep the oil in the refrigerator.

5. To get the greatest nutritional benefit from flax seeds, they need to be eaten ground, not whole.

6. Whole flax seeds are unsurpassed as a natural laxative. And, if taken for this purpose, they have to remain whole and not be ground. (One or two tablespoons can be taken whenever the need arises, washed down with plenty of water).

NUTTY-EDITH TRAVEL MIX

I always carry some of this mix with me, whether I'm gallivanting around town in my car, or flying 30,000 feet in the air. While other passengers eat their inedible-looking stuff that masquerades for real food, I eat my home-made sandwich, ask for hot water, to which I add my grain coffee and munch on my travel mix for dessert.

Yields 2 cups
1/2 cup raw organic almonds

1/4 cup raw organic hazelnuts

1/4 cup raw organic cashews

1/4 cup raw organic walnuts

1/4 cup sunflower seeds

1/4 cup organic Thompson raisins or dried organic currents

1 Preheat oven to 275° F.

2 Roast almonds and hazelnuts together in a 275 degree oven for 12 - 15 minutes, or until they give off a nutty fragrance, and transfer to a large bowl.

3 Roast the cashews and walnuts for 8 - 10 minutes and add to the bowl.

4 Let the ingredients cool down, add the sunflower seeds and raisins, and mix everything thoroughly together (best done with your hands).

5 Store in a tightly-covered container in the refrigerator or freezer.

HELPFUL HINTS:

1. While roasting your nuts and seeds, do not stray too far from your oven and do not get caught up in a gossipy phone conversation. Nuts and seeds love hot weather and have a nasty habit of wanting to burn, and so does gossip.

2. Make sure all your nuts and seeds are fresh and unsalted when you buy them, preferably loose and not packaged.

HEALTHFUL HINTS:

1. Due to their high fat content, quantities of nuts and seeds eaten should not exceed 1 - 2 ounces at one time.

2. For the utmost nutritive benefit, please refer to the **Food Combining Chart** (see page 251).

NUTTY-EDITH CRUNCH

This roasty-toasty, home-made mix is a staple in my fridge. I'm really nuts about it. Almonds and other nuts are a protein powerhouse and are also packed with calcium, magnesium, fiber, potassium and vitamins. A few sprinkles of this recipe will transform any plain dish into crunchy elegance.

Yields 1 cup

1/4 cup raw organic almonds
1/4 cup raw organic hazelnuts
1/4 cup raw organic cashews
1/4 cup raw organic walnuts

1 Roast almonds and hazelnuts together in a 275° oven for 12 - 15 minutes or until they give off a nutty fragrance, and reserve.

2 Roast the cashews and walnuts together for about 10 - 12 minutes.

3 In a food processor or nut mill, with an on-off pulsing motion, process the almonds and hazelnuts together until they are partly ground and partly chopped, and transfer to a large bowl.

4 Process the cashews and walnuts together as above. Add to the bowl and mix all the ingredients together.

5 Store in a tightly covered container in the refrigerator or freezer.

HEALTHFUL HINTS:

1. Use only unsalted nuts. Purchase them preferably loose and not in a package, where they may have gone rancid and may also contain little critters, which are not recommended on our diet.

2. This mix can be sprinkled on any and all sweet treats, such as: fruit mousses, fruit salads, apple sauce, Rice Dream (non-dairy frozen dessert), sorbet, hot and cold cereals, etc.

"I'm not really a health nut, but I'm nuts about health."

GOMASIO

This is a condiment made from unhulled sesame seeds and sea salt or Herbamare. Kept in a shaker, it can be sprinkled on any and all foods which are enhanced by a salty flavour. It is particularly tasty when sprinkled over steamed greens, and is a far more health-promoting seasoning than iodized table salt, because it balances (alkalinizes) the acidity of foods without damaging the kidneys.

Yields 1/4 cup   1/2 cup unhulled sesame seeds

1/2 tsp sea salt or Herbamare

1   Roast sea salt or Herbamare in a dry frying pan on low heat for 5 - 6 minutes.

2   Add the sesame seeds and keep roasting, stirring occasionally. When the seeds give off a nutty aroma, or crumble when rubbed between two fingers, they are ready.

3   While still warm, grind in a nut mill or coffee mill, keeping about 1/4 of the seeds whole. (If you are a true health-nut, and not a faux one like me, you will undoubtedly be grinding the sesame seeds into Gomasio by hand with a suribachi).

DR. ROSENTHAL'S NUTS 'N' SEEDS MIX

This is one raw deal that's worth eating or drinking. Dr. Rosenthal is a naturopathic doctor in Jerusalem, who is a firm believer in and strict follower of an all-raw-food-diet. He prescribes this formula to all his clients including Yours Truly. The nuts and seeds, being ground and mixed into a liquid, make digestion and absorption much easier than snacking on them whole between or after meals. Each morning, this is part of my "Rise 'N' Shine" breakfast, as I add 1 1/2 tablespoons of this mix to my vegetable juice.

Yields about 2 3/4 cups

1/2 cup almonds

1/4 cup hazelnuts

1/4 cup walnuts

1/2 cup sesame seeds

1/2 cup flaxseeds

1/2 cup sunflower seeds

1/4 cup dried nettle leaves (optional), but very important for blood-building

1   Grind each type of nuts separately in a nut grinder or processor and place in a large bowl.

2   Grind each type of seeds in a nut grinder or coffee mill separately and add to the bowl.

3   Pulverize the nettle leaves and add to the bowl.

4   Mix everything thoroughly together and keep refrigerated in an air-tight container.

HEALTHFUL HINTS:

1. All nuts and seeds should be fresh, unsalted and unroasted.

2. Dried nettle leaves are curative for minor ailments and, according to Dr. Rosenthal, an important ingredient in this mix. He treats people with low blood count and blood poisoning with this mineral-rich plant.

3. To make a protein drink, add 1 - 2 tablespoons of this recipe to a fruit or vegetable juice, or any other suitable liquid, and mix well. Drink as soon as possible - do not store the drink once it is mixed!

NUTTY- EDITH POEM

Let's wrap up all the nuts and seeds
In a package that poetic reads;
Number one, they are a foil to meat
And for protein a much better feed.

They're much easier for you to digest,
'Cause little energy you need invest.
They're an easy food for breakfast or lunch,
Combined with a salad they add a crunchy punch.

They travel easy as a healthy potion
Over borders, with no gel or lotion;
And if you're tired of the endless poetic
While Nutty Edith is getting frenetic,
Go to the chapter for Guilt-Free Pleasures
And prepare yourself some healthful treasures.

DRIVING MOTHER NUTS

Mummy, where does the Shabbos go when we make havdalah?
Remind me to ask him next week.

Mummy, are challes lonely during the week?
No, they have lots of old friends. Go to Sleep!

Mummy, how are gefillte fish born?
Every Thursday evening in your grandmother's parve pot.

Mummy, is there kosher dog food?
Who cares, we don't have a dog.

Mummy, do matzos like to be so thin?
I don't know, but I'm jealous. Go to sleep!

Mummy, do ice cubes ever catch cold?
No, they take mega doses of vitamin C. Go to sleep!

Mummy, are pickles sour 'cause they have so many warts?
Don't worry, we'll take them to our skin doctor next time we go. Go to sleep!

Mummy, why didn't Hashem make eggs square?
Because this way it's easier for you to roll 'em off the table when I turn my back. Go to sleep now!

Mummy, is my teacher stupid?
Yes, but you are not supposed to know.

Mummy, does God know what I want for Chanukah?
He knows, and I hope He keeps it a secret from me.

Mummy, is it true that I am very smart?
Yes, but you are not supposed to know.

Mummy, what do you do at your weekly meetings with all those ladies?
That's not important for you to know, you are supposed to be asleep. Just wait till your father
comes home!

Mummy, if it's not important, how come you spend hours on the phone discussing your projects
while our dinner burns to a crisp?
That's no way to talk. Don't get fresh with me!! Just wait till your father comes home!

Mummy, how come you always like our cottage cheese fresh; what's the difference between
cheese and me?

Cheese doesn't ask questions and doesn't talk back and I can put it in the refrigerator and close
the door. Will you go to sleep now and stop driving me nuts!

Mummy, do you want me to shut up and go to sleep now?
Definitely!! no! yes! I mean, it might be a good idea.

Mummy, why can't you ever make up your mind and be decisive?

FISH
&
EGGS

FISH AND EGG RECIPES

FISH

To Fish or not to Fish

I would like to explain why I included a few fish recipes in this book. Friday evenings is the time when we socialize at home and share our *Shabbos* (Sabbath) table with friends and neighbours. As a matter of fact, it is to their credit that they, over the years, have contributed tremendously to this book by rating and evaluating many of my appetizers and main course dishes. The reason I serve fish on Friday evenings is that I was not prepared to impose a totally vegan way of eating on our guests and their "*neshama yesera*" (shabbos soul). Why should they sit there drooling in thoughts over chopped liver, chicken soup with fat rings floating on top and humongous fluffy *knaidel*, honey-glazed chicken, swimming in a raisin-ketchup sauce, *lockshin* kugel glistening with 'bad oil', etc., while forced to eat what we consider healthy food.

Most of the sources which guide me in my dietary way of life consider fish *verboten* since they are vegans in the strictest sense, but I have to assume that most of my readers are not. Here's my dilemma. On the one hand, I feel obligated in the context of this book to inform you of the latest "scientific" findings and on the other hand, I have no pat answers for the fishy controversies that continue to rage.

There are compelling reasons on both sides of the divide and poor me is somehow forced into the middle. I am willing to impart to you what I have learned in my extensive research on this topic, but then you are on your own. I would like to go angling for Omega 3's, but I'm not prepared to keep fishing in murky waters.

Fish is rich in essential fatty acids (EFA's), also called omega 3's, which are essential to our health and which our bodies cannot produce on their own. Therefore, the theory has long been held and supported by many scientific studies that eating fish can lower cholesterol and triglycerides, alleviate rheumatoid arthritis and other auto-immune disorders. It may also reduce inflammatory processes in blood vessels, thus avoiding blood clotting that can lead to heart attacks.

A new study has recently been conducted which associates taking fish oil capsules with a reduction in Alzheimers symptoms (apparently the senior mice did very well on memory tests). Another study concluded that eating fish once a week may lower the risk of Alzheimer's by 60%, compared to those who rarely or never eat fish. The same researchers also found that people who have diets heavy in saturated fats run a double risk of getting Alzheimer's.

All that sounds real good, but apparently not all is well in Fishland and not all fish are born equal. Many of them must be going through a severe identity crisis at this time, being tagged as dangerous species. Numerous scientific studies have now concluded that many fish are saturated with pollutants, toxins and heavy metals. The PCB's, mercury, lead, DDT and dioxin cannot be destroyed by cooking or freezing. So now, when facing the fish counter at the store, you have to make the decision between 'farmed' fish and (wildly-expensive) 'wild' fish; you really need to look into their 'yichus' (family background).

So which fish is safe to eat and which is not? And how much or how little can we afford health-wise? Some government agencies, having set new guidelines for consuming fish safely, advise eating fish not more than once or twice a week. Pregnant women, women of child-bearing age, and children should eat no more than once a month of certain species, especially tuna fish. Low mercury options seem to include salmon, (the wildly expensive 'Pacific Wild' salmon being the best health-wise and taste-wise), mackerel, herring and sardines. These are also the good sources for obtaining the omega 3 EFA's so essential to our health.

The question begs itself; is there a way to eat healthy and be totally safe in light of the above flip-flop controversies? The answer is, yes there is, for anyone willing to go that way. We can get all our needs for EFA's met with a strictly vegetarian or vegan diet, which includes raw nuts and seeds (especially flaxseed). As to proteins and other essential nutrients, we can get all those from fruits, vegetables, grains and legumes, provided we eat enough quantities of them and in the right proportions. Such a diet has the added advantage of supplying us with the EFA's in the right ratio of omega 3's to omega 6's. North Americans on the SAD (Standard American Diet) consume 10 - 20 times more omega 6 EFA's than they need, which supposedly makes it difficult to maintain whole health in the long run.

PIQUANT FISH SALAD

Fish salad is to *Yekkes* (German Jews) what *gefillte* fish is to Eastern European Jews. It was a hallowed delicacy, the kind of dish that was noshed on with crackers on Friday afternoons, to usher in the inimitable taste of *Shabbos*. When he was growing up, our youngest son the animal lover used to feed it to all the stray hippy-cats of the Sixties on our Viewmount Avenue front doorstep every Friday afternoon. They couldn't get enough of it. When he insisted on adding capers and parsley for garnish, I stopped the whole operation and told him to tell them to hang out somewhere else on Friday afternoons. This succulent, delicious salad is light and a great protein meal or snack with crackers or rice cakes, and it lends itself perfectly to an elegant seafood appetizer (see below).

Serves 4

1 cup water

1/2 cup diced onions

2 bay leaves

1/2 tsp sea salt or Herbamare

4 medium fillets (haddock, halibut, orange roughy, turbot, tilapia (St. Peters), or any other fish that is not too delicate and has no small bones)

1 tbsp umeboshi vinegar

2-3 tbsp **Nayomaise** (see page 119)

2 tbsp finely chopped dill or flat-leaf parsley

1 In a wide saucepan, bring water, onions, bay leaves and salt to a boil.

2 Lower heat and simmer 8 - 10 minutes.

3 Add the fillets, careful not to overlap them too much, cover and simmer the fish for 6 - 8 minutes. The fish is done when it flakes easily with a fork.

4 Lift out the fish with a spatula into a bowl and cool.

5 Discard the bay leaves and reserve the stock.

6 Add the umeboshi vinegar, Nayomaise, dill or parsley to the bowl, gently toss and adjust seasoning. You may add some fish stock until you have the desired consistency.

APPETIZER:

1. Place a 1/3 - 1/2 cup of the fish salad on a lettuce leaf and decorate with tomato wedges, capers, a dollop of Nayomaise, and a sprig of parsley or dill.

> **HELPFUL HINT:**
> Keeps for 4 - 5 days refrigerated in a tightly-covered jar.
> FOR PESACH: Substitute salt for the umeboshi vinegar and Pesach mayonnaise for the Nayomaise.

2. Cut unpeeled cucumber slices into 1/4 - inch pieces on the diagonal, place a generous portion of fish salad on top and decorate.

3. If you want to be extra-elegant, serve this salad in your crystal (or glass) stemware, and decorate, adding two tiny cocktail pretzels to each portion.

4. If you want to be extra non-elegant, use throw-away dishes and clutter up the universe.

MINCED 'N' BAKED FISH PATTIES

These patties are ever so handy for health-conscious, time-pressured 21st-century cooks. Not meant to replace the traditional and hallowed *Gefillte* Fish, they are a different kettle of fish. They are great as a main course, sliced as a sandwich filler, wrapped into a romaine leaf as a quick and savoury protein snack, or served as an appetizer.

Yields about 8 patties, 2 1/2 - 3 inches in diameter

1 pound whitefish, minced

1/4 cup coarsely grated carrots

1/4 cup finely chopped celery

1/4 cup finely chopped sweet red pepper

1/2 cup finely diced onions

1/4 cup finely chopped flat-leaf parsley

1/2 tsp garlic powder

1 tsp sea salt or Herbamare

1/4 tsp black pepper

1/2 tsp grated ginger or 1/4 tsp powdered

1 tbsp Nasoya Nayonaise (optional)

1 tbsp water

Enough tomato sauce to coat the patties

2 tsp unhulled sesame seeds

1 Preheat oven to 350° F.

2 Line a baking sheet with parchment paper and reserve.

3 In an electric mixer or a food processor, place the whitefish, carrots, celery, red pepper, onions, parsley, garlic powder, salt, pepper, ginger, Nasoya Nayonaise and water, and mix well.

4 Adjust seasoning, form into patties and transfer to the baking sheet.

5 Coat with tomato sauce and sesame seeds, bake for 20 - 25 minutes, turn off the oven and let them sit another 10 minutes just to socialize in the warm weather.

PINK VARIATION:

Minced salmon can be substituted for the whitefish; in that case substitute Nasoya Nayonaise for the tomato sauce on top.

HELPFUL HINTS:

1. If the mixture is too sticky, wet your hands with cold water while forming the patties at step 4.

2. If pressed for time, skip the tomato sauce and garnish with paprika and sesame seeds.

HERRING SALAD (HERING SALAT)

The only defense I have to include this salad here is that it is a nostalgic throw-back to my childhood, when this salad was served every week on *Shabbos* at the *seuda shlishit* (3rd Sabbath meal).

I dedicate this recipe in memory of one of our very favourite cousins, Liesl Rosenbluth, *Zichronah Livrocho* (of blessed memory), who was such a specially good person and so much fun to be with. I called her in Jerusalem a few years ago and asked her to help me reconstruct this *yekkishe* recipe, which was of course also part of her culinary heritage.

The mauve colour of this salad adds lovely eye appeal, and certainly beets to a different drummer. It is my fervent hope that you will do as I do and make this salad on very rare occasions only because of its high salt content. This colourful presentation makes also for a very attractive, eye - appealing, succulent appetizer (see following page).

Yields 3 cups

1 Matjes herring, sliced (1/4 - inch pieces)

1/2 cup boiled peeled and chopped beets (1/4 - inch pieces)

1/2 cup boiled peeled and diced potatoes (1/4 - inch cubes)

1/3 cup finely chopped sour pickles

1/3 cup finely diced purple or white onions

1/2 cup peeled and chopped apple (1/4 - inch pieces)

2 pinches black pepper

3 tbsp Nasoya Nayonaise

2 tsp apple cider vinegar or umeboshi vinegar

1/4 cup water

1 If you buy a whole herring, drain off all the oil, cut in 1/2 lengthwise, soak a few hours in water to reduce saltiness, and then cut into 1/4 - inch pieces.

If you buy the herring already sliced in a jar, drain off the oil, taste for saltiness and, if need be, soak as above and then cut into 1/4 - inch pieces.

2 In a large bowl, mix the herring, beets, potatoes, pickles, onions, apples and pepper.

3 In a small bowl, emulsify the Nayonaise with the vinegar and 1/4 cup water, add to the large bowl, mix everything together, and adjust seasoning.

4 To meld the flavours, let the salad rest for a 1/2 hour or more, always keeping it refrigerated.

continued

HELPFUL HINTS:

1. It is up to your discretion as to how salty you want the herring to be. You can adjust the taste according to how long you will soak same. True herring lovers may want to use the herring as is, without soaking it first, but that makes it a very wicked dish healthwise.
2. Serve on crackers or rice cakes as a succulent savory snack, or use as a sandwich filler.
3. Serve as a main course, about 3/4 - 1 cup per person.
4. For buffet-style party fare, serve in an attractive crystal bowl and garnish with parsley. If you don't have a crystal bowl, serve this salad in whatever you have, or use a plastic throw-a-way dish and clutter up the universe!

HEALTHFUL HINT:

If you are vegan, or if you wish to cut down on salt - which has been called the Silent Killer - check the **Colour-Me-Purple Salad** (see page 83) and try this non-fishy but similar-tasting salad.

MOUTH-WATERING APPETIZER:

Pile 1/3 - 1/2 cup of this salad onto a large salad leaf on individual plates, and garnish with parsley. If you serve this appetizer, you'd better be prepared to serve a big meal afterwards, because its saltiness will stimulate big appetites!

PÂTÉ DE PETITS POISSONS

This haute-cuisine-sounding dish is made with sardines. Yes, those tiny critters that are always packed so neatly and that some people would only eat on a camping trip. They supply us with the omega-3 essential fatty acids that our bodies cannot produce, and vitamin E that can improve our brain power, besides its other health benefits. Considering today's toxic and polluted environment, we ought to pay greater respect to these little ones, who may be too small to absorb a lot of toxins and thus have an advantage over some mighty bigger fish out there.

Spread this pâté on bread, crackers or rice cakes or use as an appetizer (see below).

Yields 1/2 cup

1 (100 - gram) tin of the finest sardines

2 tbsp finely chopped purple onions

1 tbsp finely chopped green onions

2 tbsp finely chopped flat-leaf parsley

2 tsp Nasoya Nayonaise

1 tsp umeboshi vinegar

2 tbsp freshly squeezed lemon juice

1 Drain the sardines of all juice or oil, and mash well.

2 Place sardines in a small bowl, add all remaining ingredients, mix well and adjust seasoning.

VARIATION:

One hard-cooked egg, finely chopped and a touch of mustard may be added.

APPETIZER:

Peel a cucumber and cut into 1/4 - inch slices on the diagonal. Pile this pâté generously on each slice and decorate with a bit of sweet red pepper or tomato and a sprig of fresh dill or parsley.

SUSIE'S BRIS

The other day, my husband called me from the office and chirped, "I am bringing you something home tonight from Susie's bris." (It was actually Susie's grandson's bris!)

I had visions of something "special". My favorite no-no food is lox and cream cheese on a bagel - a craving which, unfortunately, does not seem to diminish with time. Though ordinarily I would never bring this delicacy into my home, I dreamed of forgoing my rice and tofu that night and just pigging out on the unthinkable. Not just a plain bagel, but one covered liberally with poppy seeds. Not a pale version, but a bagel so tanned that it's almost burned. Not Philadelphia cream cheese, but its lighter, low-fat cousin. And not just any lox, but the finest, not-too-salty Nova Scotia, sliced paper-thin.

When my husband came home that night, I grabbed my little parcel from him. As I unwrapped the tiny cocktail napkin, a few pieces of dry, curled-up green and yellow pepper pieces fell into my hands. Devastated on the inside, but with a calm demeanor on the outside (most unusual for me), I marched into my kitchen, stir-fried my brown rice, veggies, and tofu, and tried to coax my mind into a state of healthy superiority.

EGGS

Eggspectations for Special Occasions

When it comes to eating eggs,
There are questions that it begs;
Do they come from happy hens,
Who roam freely without fence?
Is their food pure and organic?
Which would make their eggs dynamic;
Do they make their daily gains
Without genetically modified grains?
Does their menu have flaxseed,
A healthy omega-3 life to lead?
Are they full of antibiotic,
Hormones and steroids - quite idiotic?
Do they appear to be naturally happy,
Look puffed-up or scrawny and scrappy?

When chicks are exposed to natural light,
Their daily lives are surely more bright;
They don't have to engage in a vicious fight,
Or otherwise exert their pecking might;
Those hormonal chicks - they are real thugs,
But the chickens for my eggs don't do drugs!

CORNY EGG SALAD

The vegetables in this salad cut the richness of the eggs and add to your daily vitamin account. This makes a lovely lunch with rice cakes or crackers, and a succulent most attractive appetizer (see below).

*Serves 4
or more*

2 organic eggs, hard-cooked and coarsely chopped

1/4 cup canned corn niblets, or frozen corn, steamed

1/4 cup finely chopped celery

1/4 cup finely chopped sweet red pepper

1/8 cup finely sliced scallions

1 tsp chopped dill or 1/4 tsp dried

1/4 tsp sea salt or Herbamare or to taste

1/8 tsp ground paprika

A pinch black pepper

1 tbsp Nasoya Nayonaise or 1 tbsp flax seed oil

1/4 tsp stone-ground mustard

2 tbsp finely chopped flat-leaf parsley

1 Place all the ingredients in a medium bowl, mix well and adjust seasoning.

2 Serve at room temperature.

POPEYE VARIATION:

Add 1/4 cup finely chopped raw or barely steamed spinach. Since spinach should always be eaten together with a protein to avoid nutritional imbalance, this is one great way to eat it.

TOFONY VARIATION:

If you are an "absolutely-no-egg" person, you can still enjoy this salad by substituting 1/2 cup mashed tofu for the eggs.

AS AN APPETIZER:

On a medium lettuce leaf, place 1/4 cup Corny Egg Salad, and decorate with a parsley sprig and thin tomato wedges. If you have any cocktail pretzels around, stick one in the middle of each portion just for fun!

SAVOURY DEVILLED EGGS

Devilled eggs are nothing new but, by lacing them with spinach, I've added a new and colourful spin on an old recipe. Pile this on bread, or stuff it into emptied tomato cups, if you have the time and are inclined to fuss-and-please. It makes a mouth-watering perky appetizer (see below). By the way, the spinach haters will not suspect what the green stuff is in the dish if you don't blabber.

Serves 3-6
3 organic eggs, hard-cooked and shelled

1 cup packed steamed and finely chopped spinach

1 tbsp finely chopped purple onions

1 tbsp Nasoya Nayonaise

Dash umeboshi vinegar

Sea salt or Herbamare to taste

Black pepper to taste

Ground paprika and curly parsley for garnish

1 Cut the eggs in half and carefully scoop the yolks into a small bowl, making sure the whites remain intact.

2 Place the empty whites onto a serving plate or platter.

3 Mash the yolks with a fork, add the spinach, onions, mayonnaise, vinegar, salt and pepper and mix well.

4 Fill this mixture into the cooked whites and garnish with paprika and sprigs of parsley.

5 Serve chilled.

— 🦋 —

APPETIZER:

On each individual plate, place a lettuce leaf, add one or two halves of the egg, sprinkle with paprika and garnish with parsley.

UPSCALE APPETIZER VARIATION:

Drape a thin piece of smoked salmon, twisted, over each half egg and don't forget the parsley.

BASIC OMELETTE WITH ELEGANT VARIATIONS

Serves 1-2

2 organic eggs, beaten
1/8 tsp sea salt or Herbamare, or to taste
Black pepper to taste
1 tsp extra-virgin olive oil
Ground paprika for garnish

1 Season the eggs with salt and pepper.

2 In a suitable frying pan, heat the oil and add the egg mixture.

3 Turn down the heat and let it set for 1/2 a minute.

4 Tilt the pan sideways while lifting the edges of the omelette with a fork to spread the mixture evenly all around.

5 Cover the pan and cook the omelette for 2 - 4 minutes on low heat.

6 Lift the omelette onto a serving plate, fold in half, sprinkle with paprika and serve.

—— 🌿 ——

VARIATIONS:

To personalize your omelette and raise it to gourmet status, add any or all of the following, finely chopped, into your beaten egg mixture:

purple onions

green onions

tomatos

chives

spinach

dill

parsley

basil

sweet red pepper, etc.

CODDLED EGGS

This is surely the healthiest and most tasty way to eat an egg. You do not need butter or oil to cook the eggs, but you need a coddler. Egg coddlers are a real British thing. They are made from porcelain with a metal screw-on lid, and it is "Royal Worcester" who has been manufacturing these for over 100 years. They are often decorated with beautiful designs from nature, but the one I have has the characters from "The Tale of Peter Rabbit."

1   Break an egg into a small bowl to check for a bloodspot, transfer to the coddler, screw on the lid (no need to screw it on tightly) and reserve.

2   Boil about 2 3/4 cups water in a small saucepan and place the coddler into the saucepan when the water boils. For a soft-boiled egg, keep the water boiling for about 5 minutes. You may want to adjust the timing according to your own preference of how soft or hard you like your eggs.

3   Remove the coddler carefully from the saucepan (make sure you do not burn your hands), unscrew the top and enjoy your egg, which is eaten straight from the coddler.

"If you want to cuddle yourself - coddle your eggs."

AIM FOR THE TEN BIG 'C's WHENEVER YOU ARE IN YOUR KITCHEN!

Convictions

Committment

Calm

Caring

Cheerfulness

Consistency

Creativity

Cleanliness

Campaigns for anti-Clutter

BAKED GOODS,
DESSERTS
&
CHOCOLATE

BAKED GOODS, DESSERTS AND CHOCOLATE RECIPES

BAKED GOODS

WITHOUT THE WHITE SUGAR MONSTER

THE SOUR SIDE OF SUGAR

For me to rhyme is such a pleasure,
And therefore it's something I really treasure;
Since I always seem to have so much to say,
For me it's the quickest and easiest way.

In this section, you will find sweet-nothings confections,
And each time you'll be making some healthy connections;
It's all about goodies with sweet simplicity,
Without the sugar monster's unhealthy duplicity.

I want to tell you 'bout sugar from cane,
When used habitually it can affect your brain;
The white sugar monster has a quiet roar,
As he makes you crave that stuff more 'n more;
Which leads you always to be sugar-binged,
And you never suspect why you get un-hinged.

You can always substitute with a good grade of honey,
Which will each time be more worth your money;
Or, do as I do, use the syrup from maple,
Which is delicious and makes your health more stable.

If you switch to carbos that are more complexed,
Your body and mind may become more relaxed;
For sustaining your energy a longer time,
Eat fresh fruits and whole grains as it says in this rhyme!
As you become less and less addicted,
The symptoms you'll lose that kept you afflicted.

If you can quit the white sugar wagon,
You will have slayed this monster dragon;
It will make you an all-around person more able,
As your glycemic index becomes more stable;
Your appetite will increase for healthier food
And your brain will automatically gear into a better mood.

But no matter how much I will feed you my rhyme,
A transition period will always take time.
It will work if you always stop grabbing a candy,
Instead keep this book in a place that is handy;
It's where you will always find a good nosh
Without the sudden white-sugar rush.

SHORT PASTRY

This crust is tender and crisp and incredibly rich. Topped with apples or other fresh summer fruit and baked, it is a decadent gourmand's delight for very special occasions (see **European Apple Torte**, page 206).

Yields one 9-inch pastry crust

1 cup minus 2 tbsp whole spelt flour or whole wheat pastry flour

2 tbsp oat flour

1/8 tsp sea salt

1/4 cup unsalted butter, cold

2 tsp pure maple syrup

1 organic egg yolk

Ice water or freshly squeezed lemon juice

1   In a medium bowl, combine the flours and the salt.

2   Cut the butter into a few chunks, add to the bowl and, using a pastry cutter or 2 knives, work the butter into the flour until the flour has the consistency of small peas.

3   In a small bowl, combine the maple syrup with the egg yolk, add to the flour mixture and, with your hands, form a dough.

4   If necessary, add dropfuls of liquid, just enough to hold the dough together, and form into a ball.

5   The dough can be used immediately, kept in the fridge for a few days, or wrapped in wax paper and frozen.

VARIATIONS:

You may use white spelt flour instead of the whole spelt flour for a finer texture of dough, but then you may need to adjust the amount of flour a bit.

EUROPEAN APPLE TORTE

This is the kind of pastry that was the usual fare at Viennese coffeehouses, where the patrons spent many hours daily to read the newspaper, to socialize, to flirt, to argue politics, or, in order to combat their loneliness, just to watch others. And if they had a table by a window they could also watch the passers-by in the street. Of course, the tortes were always served with huge dollops of whipping cream. But that's where I draw the line; that is an absolute no-no for me, and maybe you shouldn't even think about it either!

Serves 12

For the Crust:
Use the **Short Pastry** recipe (see page 205)

For the Filling:
4 apples, (use the best baking apples you can find)
A few pinches ground cinnamon
Pure maple syrup, to taste

For the Topping:
2 organic eggs, separated
1 tbsp white spelt flour
1 tbsp pure maple syrup
1/2 tsp pure vanilla extract

1 Preheat oven to 350° F.

2 Pat the dough into a lightly buttered 10 - inch pie plate, or a spring form, making sure the sides are also covered with dough, and reserve.

3 Peel, quarter and core the apples, and cut each quarter into 3 - 4 slices length-wise.

4 Place the apple slices on the dough in an overlapping fashion, starting on the outside to end in the middle.

5 Sprinkle the apples with cinnamon, pour a thin stream of maple syrup over the apples, and bake for 20 minutes. Remove torte from oven.

6 Lower the oven to 325° F.

7 Prepare the topping; in a small bowl, whisk the egg yolks with the flour, maple syrup and vanilla.

8 Beat egg whites until stiff and gently fold into the yolk mixture.

9 Spread the topping mixture over the torte and bake for another 10 minutes or until topping is golden.

— ✤ —

VARIATION:

Peaches, plums, apricots, etc. can be substituted for the apples.

OLD FASHIONED TUTTI FRUTTI SPICE CAKE

This cake wins the Gold in my Olympian efforts to bake harmless. It is one of my favourites, laced with dried sweet fruits, which you can mix 'n' match to your taste. It has none of the damaging ingredients that bought cakes have and that can rob us of our health. I will sit down to a cup of hot grain coffee and a slice of this cake, sometimes even buttering it for a feeling of being extra pampered.

1/2 cup finely grated carrots

1/2 cup coarsely chopped organic prunes

1/2 cup dried organic finely chopped apricots

1/2 cup organic golden raisins

1 2/3 cups Rice Dream® non-dairy beverage

1/4 cup unsalted butter

1 1/2 tsp ground cinnamon

1/2 tsp ground nutmeg

1/8 tsp ground cloves

2 cups whole spelt or whole wheat flour

2 tsp aluminum-free baking powder

1 tsp baking soda

1/4 tsp sea salt

1/2 tsp ground ginger

1 Preheat oven to 375° F.

2 Place the carrots, prunes, apricots, raisins, Rice Dream® non-dairy beverage, butter and spices in a saucepan, cover, bring to a boil and simmer for 5 minutes.

3 Transfer to a bowl and cool.

4 Combine the dry ingredients in another bowl and stir well.

5 Add the dry ingredients to the cooled liquid mixture and stir until well mixed.

6 Pour into a well-greased and flour-dusted 9 - inch bundt pan and bake for about 45 minutes.

VARIATIONS:

1. If you are not a vegan and would like a lighter texture for this cake, add 1 beaten egg white at step #5.

2. Unsweetened apple juice or orange juice can be substituted for the Rice Dream® non-dairy beverage.

3. The dried fruits can be substituted with other dried fruits. I sometimes use 1/4 cup dried pears, 1/4 cup dried apricots, 1/4 cup dried dates and 1/4 cup dried prunes.

4. If you want more spice in your life, add ground cloves to taste.

TUTTI FRUTTI APPLE KUGEL

This succulent kugel can be served as a dessert, or as a side dish, warm or at room temperature, to any *Shabbos* (Sabbath) or *Yomtov* (holiday) main course, or as a great in-between snack. It has a yummy, natural sweetness which defies the white sugar monster, who has sinister designs on our health.

8 large baking apples, peeled, seeded and cut into 1 1/2 - inch chunks

3/4 cup organic golden raisins

1/2 cup coarsely chopped organic prunes

1/2 cup dried organic soaked and finely chopped apricots

1 orange, peeled and chopped fine

1 cup unsweetened fruit juice

1/2 cup water

2 tbsp freshly squeezed lemon juice

1 tsp lemon zest

1 tsp pure vanilla extract

3 cups oat flour

1 tsp ground cinnamon

1/4 tsp ground allspice

1 1/2 tsp baking soda

1 1/2 tbsp aluminum-free baking powder

1   Preheat oven to 350° F.

2   Place the first 10 ingredients into a saucepan, mix well, cover and bring to a boil.

3   Turn down heat and simmer for 15 - 25 minutes or until most of the liquid has been reduced.

4   Cool the apple mixture.

5   In a large mixing bowl, toss together the flour, spices, baking soda and baking powder and mix well.

6   Add the flour mixture to the apple mixture and stir well.

7   Pour into a 13 x 9 x 2 - inch greased baking pan, cover with parchment paper and then with foil, and bake for 30 minutes.

8   Remove the parchment paper and foil and bake another 20 - 25 minutes.

9   Serve warm or at room temperature.

HELPFUL HINT:

You can buy oat flour in a health food store, or make it yourself by processing rolled oats into flour in your blender or processor.

CHOCOLATE CAKE WITH A DIFFERENCE

Who says you can't have your cake and eat it too? "How is this cake different from all other cakes?" It has only health-promoting ingredients minus all the trans-fats, de-natured flours and the white sugar monster, which all contribute so greatly to the vast array of modern diseases and the ageing process. But that's not all; it tastes great in a sort of melt-in-your-mouth way, and the glaze on top adds the final touch for any closet chocoholic. Since you don't taste the carrots in the cake, you don't need to advertise them for the "I-hate-carrots" crowd. Although the glaze is not the real thing, it's the illusion that counts.

2 organic eggs

1/3 cup unrefined vegetable oil

3/4 cup pure maple syrup

1 cup finely grated carrots

1 cup finely grated apples

1/2 cup Rice Dream® non-dairy beverage

1 1/2 tsp pure vanilla extract

2 cups whole spelt or whole wheat flour

1/3 cup organic cocoa powder

2 tsp aluminum-free baking powder

3/4 tsp baking soda

Glaze:

1 tbsp organic cocoa powder, 1 tbsp pure maple syrup, 1 tsp water or liqueur

1   Preheat oven to 350º F.

2   In the large bowl of an electric mixer, cream the eggs, oil and maple syrup.

3   Add the carrots, apples, Rice Dream® non-dairy beverage and vanilla and mix.

4   In a medium bowl, combine the flour, cocoa, baking powder and baking soda, and mix.

5   On slow speed, gradually add the dry ingredients to the wet ones until well mixed.

6   Pour batter into a greased 10 - inch round spring-form or a 13 x 9 x 2 - inch baking pan, and bake for about 45 minutes or until cake tester comes out clean.

7   Cool thoroughly before unspringing and removing from pan.

8   For the glaze, combine cocoa with maple syrup and water or liqueur, and brush over the cake.

VARIATION:

If you like dark-brown choco-muffins, you may bake this recipe in 12 muffin tins and bake the remaining batter in a 9 - inch round Pyrex baking dish for an additional little cake; or use all the batter for more muffins.

FOR A SPLENDIFEROUS CHOCOHOLIC DESSERT:

Place a piece of this cake on individual dessert plates, add a dollop of vanilla and/or chocolate flavoured Rice Dream® non-dairy frozen dessert, dribble **30- Second Chocolate Sauce** (see page 239) over the top, and sprinkle with **Nutty-Edith Crunch** (see page 181) or **Homemade Chocolate Sprinkles** (see page 240).

APPLE - CARROT CAKE

This is a very substantial cake with lots of flavour and, because of its moist texture, it keeps fresh for a long time when refrigerated. You have the option of topping it with a lemon glaze when cooled, or sprinkling two tablespoons of sunflower seeds on top before baking.

2 cups unpeeled finely grated apples

2 cups finely grated carrots

3 organic eggs, beaten

1/2 cup pure maple syrup

1/2 cup Rice Dream® non-dairy beverage

1/2 cup unrefined vegetable oil

1/2 tsp pure vanilla extract

2 cups whole spelt or whole wheat flour

2 tsp aluminum-free baking powder

2 tsp baking soda

1/2 tsp sea salt

1 1/2 tsp ground allspice

3/4 cup organic golden raisins

2 tbsp sunflower seeds (optional)

1 Preheat oven to 350° F.

2 Grease a 13 x 9 x 2 - inch baking pan and reserve.

3 In a large bowl, place the apples, carrots, eggs, maple syrup, Rice Dream® non-dairy beverage, oil and vanilla extract and mix well.

4 In another bowl, place the flour, baking powder, baking soda, sea salt, allspice and raisins and combine.

5 Add the dry ingredients to the bowl with the wet ingredients, and mix well.

6 Pour batter into the prepared baking pan, top with sunflower seeds, if using, and bake for 45 minutes.

7 Remove from oven and cool in the pan.

Lemon Glaze:

1 tbsp arrowroot powder

1/2 cup water

1/4 cup freshly squeezed lemon juice

1 tbsp grated lemon zest

Sweetener to taste (I use 1/2 tsp stevia powder;
see **The Nutrilicious Pantry** page 17)

1 Mix the arrowroot powder with only enough water to form a thick paste.

2 In a small saucepan, combine water, lemon juice, and bring to a boil.

3 When the lemon juice mixture boils, add the arrowroot paste, stir continuously
until the glaze has thickened, and add sweetener to taste.

4 Remove from heat and when cool spread over the cake.

SWEET TREAT VARIATIONS:

1. Place one thick slice of cake under the broiler for a few minutes until just hot.

2. Remove, place on a plate and serve with a dollop of your favourite flavour of
Rice Dream® non-dairy frozen dessert on the side, or cover with **Ruby-Red
Applesauce** (see page 220) or **Strawberry Ambrosia** (see page 232).

"Cooking is fantasy - baking is reality."

OAT BRAN BANANA MUFFINS

These healthy muffins have it made. They are cholesterol-free, contain heart-healthy omega 3's, and taste so good.

Yields 12 muffins

2 tbsp ground flax seeds

1/4 cup unrefined vegetable oil

1/4 cup pure maple syrup

3 ripe bananas, mashed

1/4 cup Rice Dream® non-dairy beverage

1 cup whole spelt or whole wheat flour

1 tsp baking soda

1 1/2 tsp aluminum-free baking powder

1 1/4 tsp ground allspice

1 cup oat bran

1/2 cup organic golden raisins

Sunflower seeds for garnish, optional

1   Preheat oven to 375° F.

2   Lightly grease 12 muffin tins and reserve.

3   In a medium bowl, combine the ground flax seeds, oil, maple syrup, bananas and Rice Dream® non-dairy beverage and set aside.

4   In a large bowl, combine the flour, baking soda, baking powder, allspice, oat bran and raisins.

5   Pour the liquid mixture over the dry ingredients and stir just enough to blend.

6   Spoon batter into the muffin tins, sprinkle with sunflower seeds, if used, and bake for about 20 minutes, or until tester comes out clean.

HELPFUL HINT:
These muffins freeze well; make extras and treat your health-conscious friends to these untreated treats!

—— 🎋 ——

VARIATIONS:

1. If these muffins are too dense for you and you want a lighter product, add two extra tablespoons Rice Dream® non-dairy beverage at step 3.

2. For a more elaborate guilt-free treat to fill a sweet tooth, cut a muffin in half, place under the broiler for a few minutes, then cover with **Sweet Simplicity Ruby-Red Applesauce** (see page 220) or with **Strawberry Ambrosia** (see page 232).

CARROT SPICE MUFFINS

These wholesome, nutritious muffins travel with me in-and-out-of town. They are filling and quickly satisfy a sweet craving. They also make wonderful little gift-offerings for others; especially for those who appreciate healthful snacks and untreated treats.

Yields 1 dozen

Dry Ingredients:

2 cups whole spelt flour or whole wheat flour

1 tsp baking soda

1/2 tsp aluminum-free baking powder

1/8 tsp sea salt

1 tsp ground allspice, or 3/4 tsp ground cinnamon and 1/4 tsp ground nutmeg

1/2 tsp grated ginger or 1/8 tsp ground ginger

Wet Ingredients:

1/3 cup pure maple syrup

1 organic egg, beaten

3/4 cup Rice Dream® non-dairy beverage or unsweetened apple juice

1/3 cup unrefined vegetable oil

1 1/2 tsp pure vanilla extract

1 1/4 cups finely grated carrots

1/2 cup organic golden raisins

Sunflower seeds for garnish

1 Preheat oven to 375° F.

2 Combine the dry ingredients in a large bowl and mix.

3 In another bowl, combine the wet ingredients.

4 Add the dry mixture to the bowl with the wet mixture and stir only until the flour is all moistened.

5 Spoon the dough into 12 greased muffin tins, sprinkle with sunflower seeds and bake for 20 minutes.

6 Remove the muffin tin from the oven and let the muffins sit for about 5 minutes before taking them from the tins.

————————  ————————

SWEET TREAT VARIATION:

For a more elaborate guilt-free treat to fill a sweet tooth, cut a muffin in half, place under the broiler for a few minutes, then cover with **Sweet Simplicity Ruby-Red Applesauce** (see page 220) or with **Strawberry Ambrosia** (see page 232).

BLUEBERRY - OATMEAL MUFFINS

These muffins are not only a hearty treat, but they also treat your heart kindly, and the luscious little blueberries take care that you have your share of antioxidants. They make a substantial breakfast, if you're running late (for whatever).

Yields 1 dozen

Dry Ingredients:

2 cups organic oatmeal

1 cup whole spelt flour

1/2 tsp aluminium- free baking power

1/4 tsp sea salt

1/2 tsp ground cinnamon

Wet Ingredients:

1/2 cup Rice Dream® non-dairy beverage

1/2 cup unrefined vegetable oil

1 organic egg, beaten

1/2 cup pure maple syrup

3/4 cup fresh or frozen blueberries

1   Preheat oven to 375° F.

2   Combine dry ingredients in a large bowl and mix.

3   In another bowl, combine wet ingredients.

4   Add the dry mixture to the wet mixture, and stir only until all the flour is moistened.

5   Spoon the dough into 12 greased muffin tins, and bake for 15 - 20 minutes.

6   Remove the muffins from the oven and allow to sit for about 5 minutes before removing from tins.

VARIATIONS:

1. If these muffins are too dense for you, you may whizz the dry oats once or twice in the processor for a finer texture, before Step 2.

2. You may substitute your favourite organic raisins for the blueberries, if necessary.

MINI LINZER COOKIES

These easy-to-make, crispy-crunchy, melt-in-your-mouth cookies, with their health-promoting ingredients, have become my signature cookies. I seem to be giving them away almost faster then we bake them. Everyone loves them; even the most die-hard junk foodies.

Yields 40 cookies or more

1 cup ground almonds (3/4 cup whole)

1 cup oat bran

1 cup whole or white spelt flour

1/4 tsp ground cinnamon

Pinch sea salt

1/2 cup pure maple syrup

1/2 cup unrefined vegetable oil

Sugar-free jam for the filling

1 Preheat oven to 350° F.

2 Cover a large cookie sheet with parchment paper and reserve.

3 In a large bowl, combine the dry ingredients.

4 In another bowl, combine maple syrup and oil, and mix well.

5 Add the wet ingredients to the bowl with the dry ingredients, and mix until it forms a soft dough.

6 To make the cookies: roll the dough in your hands into small, walnut-size balls, and place on the cookie sheet.

7 With your middle finger, make a deep indentation in the middle of each cookie, and fill with jam.

8 Bake 20 - 25 minutes.

HELPFUL HINTS:

1. If the dough doesn't hold together at step 5, add a few drops of cold water.

2. If the dough is too oily, add a bit of flour.

3. If you are into whole health, make sure the jam is sweetened with pure fruit juices only and contains no artificial sweeteners. Health food stores may not carry this item with a *hechscher*; however it can be bought in some kosher grocery stores and kosher bakeries. I am particularly fond of raspberry jam for this recipe.

DECADENT-OLD- WORLD VARIATION:

For people who think butter is better: use 1/4 cup oil & 1/4 cup melted butter at step 4.

HEALTHY CHOCOLATE COOKIES

What makes these delicious, yummy cookies healthy? They have none of the damaging-to-our-health and nutrient-depleting ingredients found in "regular" cookies. They keep for ages but never age.

Yields 48-55 cookies

4 cups whole spelt or whole wheat flour

1 tsp baking soda

1/2 tsp ground cinnamon

3/4 cup organic cocoa powder

4 tbsp tahini

1/4 cup Rice Dream® non-dairy beverage or orange juice

3/4 cup unrefined vegetable oil

1 1/2 cups pure maple syrup

3 tsp pure vanilla extract

1 Preheat oven to 350° F.

2 Cover a large cookie sheet with parchment paper and reserve.

3 In a large bowl, combine the flour, baking soda, cinnamon and cocoa, mix well and reserve.

4 In another large bowl, place the tahini, add the Rice Dream® non-dairy beverage or juice and mix well.

5 Add the oil, maple syrup and vanilla and mix well again.

6 Add the dry ingredients to the liquid ones in four batches. If the dough gets too thick to stir continue to mix it with your hands.

7 Roll the dough into small balls, shape into 1 1/2 - inch discs between your fingers, and place on the cookie sheet.

8 Bake about 15 minutes.

9 Allow to cool thoroughly on the cookie sheet before storing in an air-tight container.

SYMPTOMS OF OVEREAT:

From a sliver to a slice-
From a slice to a slab-
From a slab to a slob!

NOT ALL CALORIES ARE BORN EQUAL !

Calorie counting has its functions, but not when used by yo-yo dieters to manipulate their binge cravings. Calories are units of measurements for the energy value of food. So, let's figure this out together (I'm terrible at math). My first choice is a piece of chocolate cake, which may have around 300 calories. My second choice is a large fresh fruit plate, a handful of almonds and a big bowl of salad with a healthful dressing over it. This may have the same amount of calories as my first choice (not counting the plate and the bowl). The crucial difference between my two choices is that when eating the chocolate cake I have eaten only refined ingredients with empty calories, which cannot supply me with the energy I need daily for maintaining sound health. With my second choice, I have used perhaps the same amount of calories, but I chose totally nutrient-dense food, where each calorie eaten contributes to renewing my cells and energizing me for a health-promoting lifestyle; (please read **The Seductive Evils of Processed Foods** on page 16).

YOUR JUST DESSERTS

SWEET TREATS FOR GUILT-FREE PLEASURES

FRUIT - THE CLEANSING FOOD THAT REFRESHES

It's okay to go bananas! Whenever we eat fruit we are house-cleaning and detoxifying in an extremely pleasant way. Fruits are the simple carbohydrates which provide the best source of sugar for our bodies. They furnish the same heat and energy as starches do, but they need almost no digestion. It is much healthier to get our sugar consumption from fruits rather than from refined sugars, syrups or honey. White sugar has no nutritional value, quite the contrary; it is one of the culprits responsible for many diseases and ill symptoms that plague modern society. The violent youth culture, prevalent in the Western world, can also be blamed to a great extent on refined white sugar consumption (see **Bibliography**, page 257).

Fruits will never clog our veins and are vital to help our bodies fight disease. Citrus fruits in particular have cleansing properties for the blood, lymph, liver and kidneys. The white pith, which most of us pare away, is rich in bioflavonoids. These have anti-inflammatory and anti-allergenic stabilizing properties and should not be discarded. Eating citrus fruits regularly can prevent certain types of cancer, particularly pancreatic cancer.

Fresh berries, which supply us with vitamins and antioxidant substances plus fiber prove that small in nature can be as powerful and effective as big when it comes to our health.

As with all other food groups, we need a variety of fruits on a daily basis to get the benefit of the vitamins, minerals and other micro-nutrients which they supply.

Where or when fresh fruit is not available, dried fruits are excellent sources of iron, potassium and magnesium, and we should try to purchase them organic, sun-dried and not sulphured.

Fruits that are not organically grown should be peeled to avoid ingesting chemical sprays.

When we have indulged (pigged out is what I really mean) after holiday weekends, or after a

Shabbos-plus-two-days-Yomtov-overeating-binge, setting aside a fruits-only day can bring our over-loaded systems back into balance. Since fruits are low in proteins and fats, eating only fruits for a while will help our bodies eliminate toxins and fats.

A good time to eat fruits is during the morning. Another good time is anytime we haven't eaten something else for one hour or more. So when should we **not** eat fruit? - **this will shock you!** - not right after a main-course meal, as that will play havoc with our digestive systems, and I will graciously spare you further details.

For anyone with a delicate digestive system, combining fruits with carbohydrates or proteins may be too acidifying at times. Generally speaking, for the same reason, eating fruits before meals rather than after meals is preferable (see **The Food Combining Chart** page 251).

"We are commanded to lead fruitful lives -
how much fruit is there in your life?"

Sweet Simplicity Ruby-Red Applesauce

No need to desert the dessert. This one is basic, light, refreshing and berry, berry good.

Yields 5-6 cups

1 package frozen, organic, unsweetened strawberries

10 large apples (use the best cooking apples available in your area)

Water (see step 3)

Pure maple syrup to taste

1 Defrost frozen berries in their package at room temperature.

2 Peel apples, slice into quarters, remove the core and slice each quarter once more in half through the width.

3 Place apples into a large pot, add water to cover the apples 1/2 - 3/4 way, cover and bring to a boil.

4 Turn down heat and simmer until soft, 10 - 20 minutes.

5 Pour apples through a sieve and reserve the liquid.

6 Purée the apples and strawberries in a processor, adding from the cooking liquid until you have the consistency you like.

7 Add maple syrup to taste and give it a few more turns.

8 Serve chilled.

FOR PESACH:

Substitute fresh strawberries for frozen ones and honey for the maple syrup.

HELPFUL HINT:

Each kind of apple has a different texture, water and sugar content. Some need more or less water than others, and more or less sweetener than others. If you like the result of one kind of apple, remember the name and keep buying it whenever available.

SAUCY TUTTI-FRUTTI SALAD – A DESSERT STORM

This is a most refreshing spin-off from the **Sweet Simplicity Ruby-Red Applesauce** (see page 220); it makes a luscious and light dessert and adds vitamins and fiber for health. I often serve this dessert to balance an elaborate Yomtov (holiday) meal.

Serves 4 (1/2 cup servings)

1 cup chopped fresh fruit (apple, pear, kiwi, orange, grapefruit, mango, papaya, fresh berries, etc.) (1/2 - inch pieces; use at least 4 varieties)

1 cup **Sweet Simplicity Ruby-Red Applesauce** (see page 22)
Unsweetened fruit juice
Pure maple syrup to taste

1 In a medium bowl, add the fruit to the apple sauce, and stir.

2 Add enough juice to make it saucy (apricot juice is particularly tasty for this), and add maple syrup to taste.

3 Serve chilled.

HEALTHFUL HINTS:

1. This tutti-frutti salad will remain fresh in the refrigerator for up to a week; so you can make large quantities to have on hand, if you so desire.

2. For all you guys and dolls who don't eat enough fruit daily, or who won't bite into an apple or peel an orange, this is a delicious way to get your daily vitamin account upgraded.

QUICKIE VARIATION:

If this recipe is too fussy and time-consuming for you, go buy a jar of applesauce so you don't have to make the Sweet Simplicity Ruby-Red Apple Sauce. But please do me a favor; buy unsweetened applesauce!

"We don't catch disease, we eat it."

PINEAPPLE-STRAWBERRY MOUSSE

This is an elegant, delightfully refreshing and light dessert, especially after a "heavy" *Shabbos* (Sabbath) or *Yomtov* (holiday) meal. "YOU MOUSSE TRY IT!" If pressed for time, or if no fresh pineapple is on hand, canned, unsweetened pineapple chunks, drained, can be used.

Serves 6

1 package frozen, unsweetened, organic strawberries

1 medium, ripe pineapple, peeled

2 tbsp pure maple syrup

1/4 - 1/3 cup **Nutty-Edith Crunch** (see page 181)

1   Defrost the frozen strawberries.

2   Slice pineapple into 1 - inch rings, remove the hard core center and cut each ring into 1 - inch pieces.

3   Process pineapple pieces in a food processor, using the knife blade with a pulsing action, until the pineapple forms a thick mousse, and reserve.

4   Process the strawberries with the maple syrup until coarsely puréed.

5   For each serving, fill a dessert bowl (plain, fancy or use crystal stemware) 1/4 of the way up with pineapple mousse.

6   Top with a layer of strawberry sauce and repeat both layers.

7   Garnish with Nutty-Edith Crunch.

8   Serve chilled.

HELPFUL HINT:
This mousse can be prepared a day ahead.

UNHEALTHY HINT:
If you want to be super-practical, you may use plastic or Styrofoam dishes and clutter up the universe.

FOR PESACH:
Substitute fresh strawberries for the frozen ones and honey for the maple syrup.

MINIATURE TRIFLES

Would I trifle with my health?
For is there any better wealth?
Here's a trifle, elegant and wealthy:
And it's also not unhealthy.

How is this trifle different from all other trifles? It is different in as much as it is not a showpiece in a humongous see-through trifle bowl full of artificial, sugary cream and chemically-flavoured bright jello. With its refreshing flavours and only a hint of cake and wine, it is the most elegant finishing touch to any festive meal, and will brand you a gourmet hostess *par excellance*.

Sponge cake (could be elderly)

Sweet wine or liqueur

Unsweetened canned pineapple chunks, drained

Strawberry Ambrosia (see page 232)

Optional Garnishes:

Homemade Chocoalte Sprinkles (see page 240)

30-Second Chocolate Sauce (see page 239)

Nutty-Edith Crunch (see page 181)

1 In a processor, pulse pineapple until coarsely chopped.

2 In your fanciest individual dessert bowls or crystal stemware, arrange a single layer of cubed cake.

3 Generously moisten cake with sweet wine or liqueur.

4 Spoon pineapple over cake 3/4 ways up.

5 Top pineapple with a generous layer of Strawberry Ambrosia, and decorate with your choice of garnishes.

6 Serve chilled.

"Life is peaches 'n' cream, if the peaches are ripe and organic, and the cream is made from tofu."

QUICK APPLE TREAT

This takes much less time than making applesauce, baked apples or apple pie and quickly fills a sweet tooth.

Serves 1

1 medium sweet apple
2 tbsp sugar-free jam or organic apple butter

1 Peel the apple, cut into 8 or more wedges, and remove the core.

2 In a medium skillet, place the jam or apple butter and heat on medium - high heat until it bubbles.

3 Add the apple slices, turn heat to low, cover and simmer for 10 minutes, turning the apples once.

4 Serve hot or at room temperature.

—— ✂ ——

ICY VARIATION:

Serve with vanilla-flavoured Rice Dream® non-dairy frozen dessert on the side.

"Avoid Six White Foods!!!!!
White Sugar, White Flour, White Rice, White Chocolate, Salt and Milk."

FAST GLAZED APPLE DELIGHT

I find this an incredible nosh. Its sweetness is matched only by the tart flavour of fresh lemon juice; its softness will melt on your tongue. You don't even need an especially good apple; probably any apple will yield to this succulent and wholesome glaze in just minutes. To prepare for one person, you will need a small pan measuring about 6" in diameter. I eat this dish hot right out of the pan. (Don't tell Miss Manners, please!)

Serves 1-2

1 Tbsp pure maple syrup

1 Tbsp fresh lemon juice

1 Tbsp water

1 medium-large apple

1 Add maple syrup, lemon juice and water to a small pan, and place on low-medium heat.

2 Meanwhile, peel the apple, cut into four pieces, remove the pips and hard core and cut each slice again two more times. (You'll end up with 12 slices and that's about as much math as I can comfortably do).

3 Place the apple slices into the pan, and turn up the heat so that things will start to bubble, but don't stray away from the stove!

4 After two minutes, turn the slices over with two spoons, cover and lower the heat.

5 Let it glaze over another minute or two, or until you have it the way you like it.

HELPFUL HINTS AND VARIATIONS ON AN APPLE THEME:

1. There are other creative ways you can use this recipe. For a delightfully light dessert after a "heavy" meal, prepare a large portion of apples in a large pan, as per the above recipe, and, when ready, transfer to a 13 x 9 x 2 - inch baking dish. Keep covered in a 200° oven until serving time. This can be fancied up, served individually with a large dollop of vanilla-flavoured Rice Dream® non-dairy frozen dessert. For an added fancy trim, sprinkle with **Homemade Chocolate Sprinkles** (page 239).
2. Make sure there is enough liquid in your apple dish so as to remain succulent until serving time. (I have not made this dish in a large quantity; if it bombs for you, blame it entirely on me!)

"An aphorism a day keeps the doctor away."

SPICY GLAZED PEARS

These divine-tasting pears are wonderfully light and refreshing to end a festive meal and make a classic signature dessert. You may keep the stems on the pears; they are not for eating, but apparently the food-style mavens seem to think that's elegant.

Serves 8

4 large anjou or bosc pears, totally ripe

Freshly squeezed lemon juice to rub on the pears as soon as they are peeled

1 1/2 cups water

1/2 cup white wine

1 1/2 - inch piece ginger

2 sticks cinnamon

5 whole cloves

1/4 cup pure maple syrup

3 tbsp arrowroot powder

1 Peel pears and try to keep the stems on.

2 With your fingers, cover the pears with lemon juice, so they won't turn brown.

3 Halve each pear, carefully remove the core and reserve.

4 In a medium pot, combine the water, wine, ginger, cinnamon sticks, cloves and maple syrup, cover and bring to a boil.

5 Lower the heat, add the pears, cover and simmer for about 25 minutes.

6 With a spatula, transfer the pears to a serving dish that has a 1 - inch rim or more.

7 Strain, reserve the cooking liquid and discard the spices.

8 Return liquid to the pot and bring back to a boil.

9 Mix the arrowroot with a bit of water and pour into the pot, stirring continuously until liquid has thickened.

10 Pour the sauce over the pears, cool and refrigerate to set.

———————— ❧ ————————

TO PREPARE INDIVIDUAL DESSERT PLATES:

Place one pear half, cut-side down, on each plate and make sure it is amply covered with the sauce. Add a dollop of chocolate-flavoured Rice Dream® non-dairy frozen dessert on the side, sprinkle with **Homemade Chocolate Sprinkles** (see page 240) or dribble **30-Second Chocolate Sauce** (see page 239) over same. For extra elegance and crunch, sprinkle **Nutty-Edith Crunch** (see page 181) over the chocolate sauce.

INSTANT BANANA ICE CREAM

Don't get excited! This is not velvety ice-cream-parlour-stuff; but it's sugar-free, won't clog your arteries and contains no anti-freeze. It is a quick and simple version of the **Berry Good Banana Sorbet** (see page 228), but cannot be used on *Shabbos* (Sabbath) or *Yomtov* (holidays). You can eat it plain, or fancy it up in various ways (see variations below).

1 Peel 1 medium banana per serving, wrap each one in wax paper, and freeze.

2 When ready to prepare the ice cream, remove bananas from freezer, unwrap, slice into 1/2 - inch pieces and process in your processor until just creamy-thick. Do not overbeat!

3 Eat immediately and enjoy this cool and smooth potassium treat.

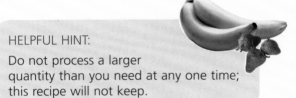

HELPFUL HINT:
Do not process a larger quantity than you need at any one time; this recipe will not keep.

———————— ✥ ————————

BERRY GOOD VARIATION:
Adding some amazing blueberries to the bananas will raise your anti-oxidant account even further.

ELEGANT VARIATION:
Top with **Strawberry Ambrosia** (see page 232).

CHOCOHOLIC VARIATION:
Top with **30-Second Chocolate Sauce** (see page 239).

CRUNCHY VARIATION:
Top with **Nutty-Edith Crunch** (see page 181).

"I love blueberries and I love blackberries but I'm not much into a BlackBerry."

BERRY GOOD BANANA SORBET

The bananas allow for a quick potassium lift, and the flax seeds and oil provide the much-needed OMEGA 3 essential fatty acids that are lacking so sadly in the SAD (Standard American Diet).

Yields 2-1/2 cups

3 ripe bananas, sliced

1/4 cup orange juice

2 tbsp freshly squeezed lemon juice

1 tbsp flaxseed oil

1 - 1-1/2 cups organic unsweetened frozen strawberries or raspberries

2 tbsp pure maple syrup, or to taste

3 tbsp ground flax seeds

1 In a processor, with the knife-blade running, process the bananas until just mashed.

2 Add the orange juice, lemon juice, flaxseed oil, the berries (no need to defrost them), maple syrup and ground flax seeds and process until just blended.

3 Place the mixture into a deep bowl and freeze lightly.

HELPFUL HINT:

This most refreshing and nutritious treat becomes more "icy" than creamy when frozen, and in order to serve it needs to be partially defrosted in the fridge or on the counter about a 1/2 hour before being served.

"To be creative needs not to be time-consuming - all it takes is an instant divine spark of fancy"

CHILLY FROZEN BANANA DELIGHTS

This is a quadruple treat. It fills a sweet tooth, satisfies a chocolate craving, gives a potassium lift and takes only minutes to prepare.

Yields about 15 slices

1 medium banana, semi-ripe, peeled

2 tsp organic cocoa powder

1 tsp Sabra liqueur

2 tsp pure maple syrup, or to taste

Nutty-Edith Crunch (see page 181)

1   Slice bananas into round slices, about 1/2 - inch thick, and reserve.

2   Place Nutty-Edith Crunch on a plate.

3   In a small bowl, mix the cocoa with the maple syrup, add the liqueur and blend well.

4   With two forks, dip each banana slice into the cocoa mixture, hold up to drain off excess chocolate, roll with 2 dry forks in the nut mixture until well-coated, place on a large plate and freeze.

HELPFUL HINT:
Ready to eat 1/2 hour after freezing, but unused portions need to be kept frozen.

VARIATION:

Hot water or any other fruit liqueur of your choice can be substituted for the Sabra liqueur.

BANANA ROLL-UPS

Are you a busy person on the run? Are you health-conscious? Do you like bananas? Do you need an occasional potassium lift? If so, then this recipe is for you! These romaine-banana finger sandwiches are quick and simple to prepare.

For Each Roll-Up:

1/2 - inch slice of banana

1 small romaine lettuce leaf

1 Place banana slice in middle of lettuce leaf.

2 Fold leaf sides in and roll-up.

3 Enjoy and repeat!

HEALTHFUL HINT:

For anyone with hypoglycemic tendencies, this is the best way to eat a banana because the alkaline greens will slow down the sugar absorption into the body and thus avoid the roller coaster effect of an imbalance. The same principle goes for all sweet fruits.

"It's o.k. to go bananas!"

1-2-3 HOMEMADE JAM

This home-made jam which, truth to tell, is not really home-made, takes 5 minutes or less to prepare. It doesn't take days for the sugar to melt down and no sterilized jars and wax on top are needed. And it's free of the devastating sugar monster.

1 jar sugar-free jam

1 jar organic apple butter

1 In a small bowl, place 1/2 cup jam and 1/2 cup apple butter and mix well by hand.

2 Store in the refrigerator in an airtight container.

HELPFUL HINTS:.

1. Apple butter, with a *hechscher* (kosher certification), can not always be found in health food stores. The same goes for sugar-free jam. However, many kosher grocery stores and kosher bakeries do carry them.

2. You may combine any quantity you need together.

3. Keep the leftover jam and apple butter from the store in their original jars in the refrigerator until needed again.

HEALTHFUL HINT:

Read the label on the sugar-free jam carefully; it may contain other chemical sweeteners. I only buy jam that is sweetened with pure fruit purees or pure fruit juices.

STRAWBERRY AMROSIA

Elegance does not need to take a lot of time, or even a full- time maid or in-house cook. This versatile, delectable sauce can be poured over any sweet treat or dessert to upgrade it a notch and put you into the Culinary Hall of Fame; and it takes only minutes to prepare unless you are a turtle.

Yields 2 cups   1 package frozen, unsweetened, organic strawberries

Pure maple syrup to taste

1 Partly defrost one package of frozen, organic strawberries in its package.

2 Place package contents into a food processor or blender and puree until almost smooth, keeping some small bits in it.

3 Add maple syrup.

4 Store in an airtight container in the refrigerator.

HELPFUL HINT:

You can elevate plain applesauce to gourmet status by adding some of this sauce, as in **Sweet Simplicity Ruby Red Appplesauce** (see page 220).

FRUIT SOUP FOR ALL SEASONS

This recipe is not for the 1-2-3 cook with only one foot in the kitchen. But it is definitely for those who would like to switch to healthier eating habits and guilt-free desserts and snacks, without feeling deprived at having to part from the White Sugar Monster. It is an extremely versatile dish that can be turned from a basic soup into a compote, a fruit sauce poured over cake, Rice Dream® non-dairy frozen dessert and many other desserts. Its ingredients can be adjusted to the changing seasons. Its sweetness is genuine and won't send anyone on a trip to the dentist or into outer space. Since it can be a bit time-consuming, try and make large quantities which can be frozen.

Use any combination of the following fruits:

Apples, pears, plums, peaches, apricots, blueberries, strawberries, raspberries, rhubarb, sour cherries and more.

For each serving, use 1 cup chopped fruit to 2 cups of water.

1 Place the fruits into a suitable pot, bring to a boil, cover, reduce heat to low and simmer for 15 minutes or until fruit is almost soft. For the fruits to hold their shape, do not overcook!

2 Remove from heat, let the soup cool completely and add maple syrup and fresh-squeezed lemon juice according to taste, if desired.

3 Ladle into jars or other containers, and refrigerate for up to a week; or freeze for frooty days.

HELPFUL HINTS:

1. Fresh lemon zest to taste may be added when cooking this soup.

2. In winter, replace some of the out-of-season fruits with chopped dried fruits and, when the soup is finished, chopped orange segments can be added for a fresh flavour.

3. If a thicker soup or compote is desired, a tablespoon or 2 of arrowroot powder with a little water can be made into a paste and added to the boiling soup to thicken it at the end.

4. If no fresh berries are on hand, process frozen, organic, unsweetened whole strawberries and add until you have a berry good taste!

5. Freeze fresh sour cherries, blueberries, etc., when in season, and make fruit soups out of season!

"Life's a bowl of cherries if you don't swallow the pits."

DESERT THE DESSERT!

A Sweet Table is an optical illusion; it looks much better than it tastes. Its devious eye appeal masks the white sugar monster and the saturated and homogenized fats lurking within the calorific splendour on display. At the end of a late, gone-cold *simcha*-dinner, the pastry chef's artistic creations seduce the already over-stuffed, sleep-deprived and nutritionally-challenged guests with gooey chocolate tortes, miniature fruit tarts, cream puffs, éclairs, mousses, chocolate and fruit sauces, petits fours, raspberry and mango ices, Crêpes Suzettes flambées, and chocolate-dipped strawberries as big as tangerines.

To partake of these bad goodies is substance abuse of the most devastating kind and a criminal activity, although not considered an offence by law.

My unsolicited advice to you is to lick on the magnificent ice sculptures when no one is looking; they have no calories and can be most refreshing after a catered dinner. If that doesn't work, gravitate towards the fresh fruit platters and train your fingers to pick one grape, one slice of kiwi, and one blueberry. Your fat cells and your stomach will thank you and reward you for it!

Remember Desserts Spelled Backwards Reads "Stressed"!

CHOCOLATE

THE FEEL-GOOD FOOD MOST OF US LOVE

Feeling guilty about eating chocolate? Read on! Research tests conducted in various parts of the world have concluded that chocolate can actually be good for you. So here I am, always ready to jump on the Health Food-For-Whole-Health bandwagon to eagerly share with you my newly found cocoa-choco-wisdom. To make a long story short and sweet, it was found that when rats were fed a cocoa-bean rich diet, it helped to reduce their stress, put off ageing and protected their cells from disease. Now, wouldn't we want to be as healthy as *chutzpah-dicke* (cheeky) rats, minus the *chutzpah* of course.

Polyphenols are a chemical compound present in all fruits and their nutritional benefits are well documented. They are a form of antioxidants, doing combat with all the harmful free radicals that are created in our bodies if we are on the SAD. (Standard American Diet). These polyphenols are also present in a very concentrated form in the cocoa bean, which is the base product of chocolate. Furthermore, they boost the brain's level of serotonin and endorphins, thus being able to enhance our moods. Chocolate also contains 'epicatechin,' a heart-friendly flavonoid that may help to prevent cholesterol from building up in the arteries.

But beware - not all chocolate is created equal. The healthiest choice, if you think you need that stuff in your life, is the kind that contains at least 71% cocoa butter; but I must admit bitterly, it tastes rather bitter.

Read your labels when choco-shopping! Choose chocolate that contains at least 50%-60% cocoa mass, with remaining ingredients being cocoa butter and no preservatives and artificial flavourings.

Milk chocolate is a no-no!! It has too much added fat, sugar and other artificial substances. The poorest choice is white chocolate, as it does not contain any pure cocoa butter at all and is made up mostly of artificial ingredients.

While writing about it, I have developed a new theory about chocolate and shall put it to the test. It is possible that just thinking about it may make us feel good. Wouldn't that be neat!

CHOCOLATE CAKE WITH A DIFFERENCE

Who says you can't have your cake and eat it too? "How is this cake different from all other cakes?" It has only health-promoting ingredients minus all the trans-fats, de-natured flours and the white sugar monster, which all contribute so greatly to the vast array of modern diseases and the ageing process. But that's not all; it tastes great in a sort of melt-in-your-mouth way, and the glaze on top adds the final touch for any closet chocoholic. Since you don't taste the carrots in the cake, you don't need to advertise them for the "I-hate-carrots" crowd. Although the glaze is not the real thing, it's the illusion that counts.

2 organic eggs

1/3 cup unrefined vegetable oil

3/4 cup pure maple syrup

1 cup finely grated carrots

1 cup finely grated apples

1/2 cup Rice Dream® non-dairy beverage

1 1/2 tsp pure vanilla extract

2 cups whole spelt or whole wheat flour

1/3 cup organic cocoa powder

2 tsp aluminum-free baking powder

3/4 tsp baking soda

Glaze:

1 tbsp organic cocoa powder, 1 tbsp pure maple syrup, 1 tsp water or liqueur

1 Preheat oven to 350° F.

2 In the large bowl of an electric mixer, cream the eggs, oil and maple syrup.

3 Add the carrots, apples, Rice Dream® non-dairy beverage and vanilla and mix.

4 In a medium bowl, combine the flour, cocoa, baking powder and baking soda, and mix.

5 On slow speed, gradually add the dry ingredients to the wet ones until well mixed.

6 Pour batter into a greased 10 - inch round spring-form or a 13 x 9 x 2 - inch baking pan, and bake for about 45 minutes or until cake tester comes out clean.

7 Cool thoroughly before unspringing and removing from pan.

8 For the glaze, combine cocoa with maple syrup and water or liqueur, and brush over the cake.

—— 🍃 ——

VARIATION:

If you like dark-brown choco-muffins, you may bake this recipe in 12 muffin tins and bake the remaining batter in a 9 - inch round Pyrex baking dish for an additional little cake; or use all the batter for more muffins.

FOR A SPLENDIFEROUS CHOCOHOLIC DESSERT:

Place a piece of this cake on individual dessert plates, add a dollop of vanilla and/or chocolate flavoured Rice Dream® non-dairy frozen dessert, dribble **30- Second Chocolate Sauce** (see page 239) over the top, and sprinkle with **Nutty-Edith Crunch** (see page 181) or **Homemade Chocolate Sprinkles** (see page 240).

HEALTHY CHOCOLATE COOKIES

What makes these delicious, yummy cookies healthy? They have none of the damaging-to-our-health and nutrient-depleting ingredients found in "regular" cookies. They keep for ages but never age.

Yields 48-55 cookies

4 cups whole spelt or whole wheat flour

1 tsp baking soda

1/2 tsp ground cinnamon

3/4 cup organic cocoa powder

4 tbsp tahini

1/4 cup Rice Dream® non-dairy beverage or orange juice

3/4 cup unrefined vegetable oil

1 1/2 cups pure maple syrup

3 tsp pure vanilla extract

1 Preheat oven to 350° F.

2 Cover a large cookie sheet with parchment paper and reserve.

3 In a large bowl, combine the flour, baking soda, cinnamon and cocoa, mix well and reserve.

4 In another large bowl, place the tahini, add the Rice Dream® non-dairy beverage or juice and mix well.

5 Add the oil, maple syrup and vanilla and mix well again.

6 Add the dry ingredients to the liquid ones in four batches. If the dough gets too thick to stir continue to mix it with your hands.

7 Roll the dough into small balls, shape into 1 1/2 - inch discs between your fingers, and place on the cookie sheet.

8 Bake about 15 minutes.

9 Allow to cool thoroughly on the cookie sheet before storing in an air-tight container.

HOT CHOCOLATE – A CUP OF TRANQUILITY

This is not a super-rich aromatic drink that will quickly raise your adrenalin - it contains hardly any caffeine and no sugar or dairy. If you want a quick, *elegantissimo* and total relaxation experience, this may be for you.

1 cup Rice Dream® non-dairy beverage
2 tsp organic cocoa powder
Pure maple syrup to taste

1 In a small saucepan, bring Rice Dream® non-dairy beverage to a boil.

2 In your favorite mug or cup, place the cocoa powder.

3 Add about 2 tablespoons hot Rice Dream® non-dairy beverage to your mug or cup, and stir to dissolve cocoa powder.

4 Add the rest of the Rice Dream® non-dairy beverage, sweeten with maple syrup, stir and go into seclusion.

Take your Cup of Tranquility to a quiet room that hopefully has a lock on it, but no other human beings or animal in it; no phone, no cell phone, no computer, no V.C.R., no C.D.'s, no D.V.D.'s, no palm pilot, no BlackBerry, or any other E.T.'s (electronic tschatschkes) that may have come on the market since last week, no newspapers or glossy magazines - and get into a comfortable chair.

Now, close your eyes, drop your shoulders, do a few slow, long out-breaths (one of the secrets to sound health), let all thoughts or mental chatter bounce off your brain like feathery-light multi-coloured balloons. BE IN THE MOMENT! Then sip your hot chocolate. No matter how few minutes you have to spare, you will come away de-stressed and re-energized and ready to take on a new batch of **self-imposed stressors**.

Of course, there is an easier way to have Hot Chocolate. Just dump a package of Instant Hot-Chocolate with the following flavour-enhancing delicacies: **sugar, whey powder, dried glucose syrup, artificial flavour, annatto colour, carboxymethyl cellulose, tricalcium phosphate, sodium caseate, monodiglicerides, dipotassium phosphate, diacetyl tartaric acid, esters of mono and dyglycerides** into a cup of hot water, mix and wait a couple of minutes until all the chemicals get comfy with each other and enjoy!

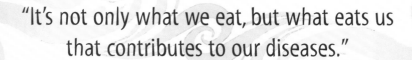

"It's not only what we eat, but what eats us
that contributes to our diseases."

30-SECOND CHOCOLATE SAUCE

This is a great coco-yummy recipe for all those who want to feed their choco-desires without the white sugar monster and his evil designs on our health. Drizzle it on or pour it on to upgrade any or all your desserts!

Yields 1/3 cup
2 tbsp organic cocoa powder
2 tbsp pure maple syrup
1/8 c. boiling water

1 In a small dish, place the cocoa powder and the maple syrup, and stir until smooth.

2 Add the boiling water and stir again until smooth.

3 Keep left-over sauce refrigerated in a small, covered container.

HOMEMADE CHOCOLATE SPRINKLES

This is a homemade version of the pure chocolate sprinkles which decorated so many of the fancy tortes I remember from my childhood, and I can picture my brothers pouring tonnes of the sprinkles on their buttered bread for breakfast every morning. Dutch in origin, we called them: "Hachelschlag".

In a specialty shop, buy a slab of dark, bitter chocolate; the best quality you can get. I try to get chocolate with around 71% cocoa butter in it because it has a low sugar content.

1 On a coarse grater, grate a slab of chocolate until you have the desired amount of sprinkles; you can also try a vegetable peeler.

2 To avoid melting the chocolate, cover your right hand with a plastic bag while you are grating it. (please don't sue me if you're a leftie!)

3 With a spoon, transfer the sprinkles to a container and keep refrigerated.

HELPFUL HINTS:
1. If the above method is too difficult, put 1 1/2-inch cold chocolate pieces in your processor and process with the knife blade running. You will get teeny-tiny chocolate balls which can be used as sprinkles. Keep them refrigerated.
2. These sprinkles are a great little garnish for all desserts, especially Rice Dream® non-dairy frozen dessert, and are meant only as a hint of this incredible dream food.

ICED 'IMAGINE' CHOCO DRINK

This drink is not 'hot' and it's not 'tranquil' (see p.238), but it's nippy in a chocoholic kind of way; and it's chemically-free healthful.

Serves 1

3/4 cup Rice Dream® non-dairy frozen dessert
1/4 cup Rice Dream® non-dairy beverage

1   Measure the Rice Dream® non-dairy frozen dessert into a mug or large cup.

2   Add the Rice Dream® non-dairy beverage and, mix thoroughly until smooth.

3   Treat yourself to a 'cool' Imagine experience!

HOT 'IMAGINE' CHOCO DRINK

In winter, warm yourself with this hot relaxing drink

Serves 1

3/4 cup Rice Dream® non-dairy frozen dessert
1/4 cup Rice Dream® non-dairy beverage

1   Measure the Rice Dream® non-dairy frozen dessert into a small saucepan, add the Rice Dream® non-dairy beverage, stir and heat to desired temperature (do not bring to a boil).

YENTE FAFUFNIK GOES WHOLE HEALTH

(a letter home)

Dear Mendel Shmendel,

You pushed me to come to this here Vegetarian Society Convention in Timbuktu. You don't have nothing to worry with the *kashrus* (dietary laws). All they give you here for breakfast is carrot-apple-parsley juice; for lunch its carrot and celery sticks with sunflower seeds; and for supper its lettuce and celery sticks, eaten with all kinds of sprouts from which I don't know the names, plus a few raw unsalted almonds.

I have a real hard time getting up at five in the morning for the exercise class, which is a "must" here. They tell me I don't know how to breathe properly. Today I asked the instructor how she thinks I survived until now without her. After the first class we do a very slow motion thing from China on the lawn, which they call Tai Chi. They say if we do this every day we will become the healthiest persons in the world.

The evening lectures make me very dizzy. They talk about nothing else but enzymes, proteins, minerals, hormones, vitamins, cholesterol, fibre, metabolism and such stuff. They say if we eat right, our bodies manufacture all these things in the right proportions. Tonight is a lecture by a very big holistic doctor, who came all the way from Australia to talk about: "Cancer, arthritis, heart disease, diabetes, osteoporosis, high blood pressure, hypoglycemia and You". When you read 'you' it doesn't mean you at home; it means 'us' at the convention. I met a woman from North Carolina who said to me: "If you eat a mostly raw food, vegetarian diet, you will lose weight, become healthy, and feel as free and light as a bird".

Well, your bird is flying home on Sunday and there will be some feathers flying in our nest. I am sweeping in a new regime. For starters, you are going to give up coffee, alcohol, donuts and cigarettes. The kids will give up ice cream, pizza, pop, chips and all other junk food. Sunday barbecue picnics will be replaced by large bowls of celery, sprouts, carrot sticks and sunflower seeds.

Could you pick me up on Sunday? Bring the station wagon but leave the kids with your mother because there won't be enough room in the car. I am bringing home a few cases of health books which I bought at special discount prices. I bought two of each because I want each of us to have our own copy, and the rest is for the kids and for birthday gifts for our families and friends. I hope you'll recognize me. I lost ten pounds, but they say I have to lose another 65.

With old love from your new Yente.

P.S. I signed up for next year's convention in Honolulu.

COOKING IN STAGES AND OTHER TIMELESS TIMESAVERS

Plan your work and work your plan,
For if you fail to plan you plan to fail;
If you succeed in planning
You are planning to succeed!

Work with these seven "P"s in your kitchen and you will succeed!
Planning, Preparedness, Patience, Perseverance, Playfulness, Pleasure, Passion!

A whole and natural diet lends itself perfectly to cooking in stages. Many of the foods can be prepared and cooked ahead of time (at least one or two days). However, like any other worthwhile task, it requires planning and organizing and seeing through what was planned so it won't bomb. There are certain kitchen rituals that need to be followed for success and I will be glad to share them with you for whatever they are worth to you. Some of these tricks many experienced home-makers may already know, but I sincerely hope that this book will also fall into the hands of some young 'chicks' who are starting out on their culinary journey of discovery. If it's 5 or 6 pm, and you are tired from whatever your day had to offer, no matter what age or circumstance, or the kids are climbing the walls on a sugar high (because all they had all day was cookies, jelly beans and soft drinks), you are not likely going to start cooking a healthful meal from scratch.

Don't do any kitchen chores that someone else is able and willing to do for you! (You should be so lucky!) This could be any person willing to be recruited and not having two left hands (I'm thinking 'family'). Let your family know that *Chesed* work (doing good and selfless deeds) does extend into the kitchen, which is supposed to be the heart of the home. If you have only boys, call me and we'll discuss it further!

Break up kitchen tasks into manageable time units! Don't work until you drop!

Make a daily list of all the things that need to be done; then prioritize your list! (I make endless lists, and then spend a lot of time looking for them - but that's my problem!)

Have all the ingredients that you will be needing in your house. Don't borrow eggs when you haven't returned the two cups of sugar from two weeks ago. (I never ever borrow; neither from friendly nor unfriendly neighbors - but that's my problem!)

The best time-management tool for a healthful, vegetarian kitchen that I know of is a good, solid steamer. For practicality and efficiency, we need a steamer that we can handle quickly and with ease without running the risk of burning our hands. With this in mind, collapsible metal steamers are not practical for daily use; neither is the oriental bamboo type; that leaves only the stainless steel kind. Having explored the market extensively for steamers, I fully realize it is very difficult to find a good one that has the size and the price that anyone would want to buy. But despite a solid steamer being expensive, I believe it is a most healthful and worthwhile investment in the long run. I was lucky to find a steamer that has only one long black, plastic handle on one side. Nowadays they come mostly with two small round stainless steel handles at each side, which for handling requires two pot holders and great caution not to get burned by the steam.

The rule with steaming is to use the shortest possible time to cook the food. It is better to err on the side of under-cooking. Whatever we steam, particularly vegetables, will have more vitamin and mineral contents preserved with steaming than with any other cooking method. Steaming is a quick, simple and non-messy way of cooking.

When not in use, my steamer is always resting on my back burner, and is only put away for *Shabbos* (Sabbath), when it gets a complete rest just as we do. During the week, while in the kitchen, I always utilize the time there by having my steamer going 'full steam ahead' for food that I will use the next one or two days. Steamed vegetables keep at least as well or better in the refrigerator than raw ones. Or, when I'm finished steaming something, I will usually throw in a few whole carrots that will end up the next few days, sliced or coarse-grated, in soups, salads or a hot grain dish. While busy around the house or schmoozing on the phone (beware of *Loshon Hora*; it's so easy and comes quite naturally to many of us) you can cook or bake potatoes or yams ahead, and cook the pasta you are planning to use in a day or two. The baked potatoes and yams, when you want to serve them, can be cut up into pieces or big slices, sprinkled with a little olive oil and seasoning and broiled.

All manner of grains and beans can be soaked for eight hours, drained and then frozen in baggies so that when you want to cook them they are ready for you. Or better still, cook them and freeze them in the quantities you require, or cook double quantities of whatever, and freeze half of it for next time in portion-sized baggies. I always stock in my freezer cooked chickpeas, adzuki beans, rice and other grains for those frantic, frenetic and frazzled days when the last thing I want to do is have to think: "What am I going to make for supper?" Fortunately or unfortunately, 'ordering in' or 'taking out' is not an option in our house.

There is one other way to short-circuit your cooking preparations - a Significant Other could be recruited in the form of a paid helper. (You should be so lucky, 'poo', 'poo', 'poo'!) Dusting the backs of your pictures and polishing all the *Shabbos* silver every Thursday is not as important as the quality of food you feed your family. Many of the vegetables can be prepared ahead of time so that they are ready when needed. By prepared I mean they can be washed, dried and peeled, and some of them can be cut up. However, they need to be carefully and properly wrapped or placed into air-tight containers, (Ziplocked), before refrigerating. There are further specific instructions on this subject in the introduction to the Vegetables and Salads section.

Here are some other Timeless Timesavers that work for me.

Number One on my list of "must haves" is a simmer ring, also called a heat diffuser. (I know you may not have a clue to what that is). It is a round, doubled-up tin plate with little holes in it and a wooden handle. This is put directly on a low flame, and then you can place any pots with food to be kept warm on it for as long as you want. Nothing will stick and it will remain below boiling. This is sometimes preferable to keeping things in a warming oven, because the food never dries out. (Sometimes I will use two of them together for just the right temperature to keep the food hot). I even use it on *Shabbos* (Sabbath) for one of my water kettles. These heat diffusers are cheap and can be bought in certain hardware stores and kitchen supply stores. They will never wear out, but will get rusty looking; however that doesn't matter as they never touch food.

If you are using bottles or jars that have sticky contents (maple syrup, jam, etc.) place a small plastic baggy over them before replacing the cover.

When you store heavy kitchen equipment on your counter, keep a folded towel under it so that, when needed, it will slide easily towards you, (just in case you missed your weight-lifting session at the gym.)

If and when you have trouble opening a jar, knock it hard a few times against your counter. If it doesn't open, you didn't knock hard enough; I never yet broke a jar that way. Running hot water over the top will also work, but the knocking is better for your psyche; it might get rid of repressed anger, should there be any.

Instead of spinning my salads, I prefer to wrap them in a terry kitchen towel after they've been washed, and keep them rolled up for a while before refrigerating in Ziplock bags or Tupperware.

Before covering a baking sheet with parchment paper, rinse the baking sheet first with cold water, which will make the paper stay in place better.

If you regularly bake a certain cake or cookie recipe, measure all the dry ingredients double and refrigerate the second mixture in a labeled plastic bag, for the next baking session.

Use Ziplock bags for freezing food, even soups, they're so cool!

If you want to defrost soup that has been frozen in a jar, as I always do, place the uncovered jar in a low oven (200°F) for an hour. After a while you can raise the oven temperature to 225°-250°F to speed up the process.

Since I don't use a dishwasher in my kitchen, I am rather paranoid about not cluttering up my sinks with dirty dishes and pots 'n' pans. You may not believe what a neat freak I am; when I juice my breakfast drink, I will wash each part of my juicer and may even assemble the juicer again before I drink my juice.

Back to lists, which seem to be my favourite occupation. Maybe you work in tandem with your computer, or the bio-computer in your head is working full-time; in that case you can ignore my 20th century advice. But I keep a separate writing pad for each of the stores that I frequent. As soon as I am close to running out of a certain product, I mark it down on the respective pad, since I cannot rely on my feather-brained head when compiling a shopping list. But of course, hopefully, there is more to life than only food, and I find hundreds of other thoughts swirling into my head only to be promptly lost to posterity. And since I'm kind of possessive about my thoughts, I devised a system which works great for me. I keep little note pads and pens everywhere in my house and just keep writing notes when something worthwhile, or otherwise, comes into my head. But, here's the rub; those little notes tend to get lost, flying aimlessly all over the place. Therefore, together with the note pads and pens, I keep a container of small plastic laundry hooks handy. Each note gets attached to a hook, which lends it some stability and a certain priority status. It doesn't matter that when I get to read all the notes again some of them have lost their urgency; on the whole it's a great support system for failing memories and senior moments. I realize, of course, that all such gibberish is not intended for 21st century persons who prefer using E.T.s (Electronic *Tchatchkes*) to get through their frantic days. My advice is only for the particular group that gets a 10%-20% discount every last Tuesday or Thursday of the month in their favourite drug and department store.

I will share with you one more kitchen trick which never fails me. Did you ever put a pot on the stove with something in it, or empty, turn on the element to high and depart the kitchen to make a call, or to do any of the many mind-numbing chores waiting to be tackled? (If you are not of that ilk, skip this part and keep on being the perfectionist who never fails in anything!) When we do remember to come back to our hearth, some nasty things may have happened meanwhile. But problem-solving is part of my survival kit. Over my stove, where I have all kinds of hooks for all kinds of *tchachkes*, I keep a blue coiled plastic armband, which is expandable and which is really meant as a keychain. Now, whenever I turn on the stove and have to leave my kitchen, I will slip this armband on my left wrist. Pinching me slightly, it serves as a reminder to keep me kitchen - conscious for the moment. (I have also a pink armband which I use when I run my bath-water).

So let's end how we began:

Plan your work and work your plan,
For if you fail to plan you plan to fail;
If you succeed in planning
You are planning to succeed!

APPETIZERS TO TEASE DISCRIMINATING PALATES

"Edible art makes for happy eaters"

North Americans don't really need appetizers -there seems to be nothing wrong with their appetites. But I am very partial to appetizers. On a whole and natural diet there is definitely a place for them - big time! First and foremost, it fits in with my 20th century - no-waste - policy. Even tiny bits of left-overs can be transformed into colourful and tantalizing appetizers. All you need is a bit of imagination and a sense for colour-schemes. I am a real klutz when it comes to painting with water colours or acrylic, but get a great kick out of painting little miniatures with food (and I don't need to worry about frames).

There is another reason why appetizers are very suitable, specially for a vegetarian diet. Not serving animal food as the main course, there is bound to be more appetite and more room for diversity on menus. The Italians got it right; Antipasti are cold hors d'oevres served before a meal.

Just to whet your appetite - here are some nutrilicious meal starters, combined with my own brand of 'Art Deco' decorating style. I start with a seven-inch bread 'n' butter plate, on which I place a lettuce leaf. Then I arrange bits and pieces of left-over foods on it. This could be a tiny piece of fish, any bit of vegetable (like cauliflower, broccoli or beet), or a miniature bed of spinach with a slice of hard boiled egg perched on top. Or, if I am serving a paté, I might cut a 1/4 - inch thick piece of cucumber on the diagonal and pile the paté on this cucumber barge, adding a decoration. If there's a bit of mushroom sauce or zucchini-tomato sauce left over, I pile it cold onto one or two crackers. Any left-over fish, no matter how it was prepared, can be metamorphosed into a succulent fish salad by adding tofu mayonnaise, fresh parsley or dill. There is really no limit to appetizer possibilities with a bit of creative flair and a new sense of "thrift", which, however, seems mostly trendy among certain billionaires.

Decorating the appetizers is the most fun for me. It's not a cliché to say that we eat also with our eyes, (and some people would do well to eat more with their eyes and less with their mouths). I will use pieces of carrot, tomato wedges, red pepper strips, pickle slices, and/or hard cooked egg wedges. I might add a fancy cracker or a sprinkle of Terra noodles or Terra root chips (colourful crispy, dried vegetable strips and chips) or a tiny cocktail pretzel; and always ending with dabs of Nasoya Nayonaise or **Nayomaise**, (see page 119) and my trademark fresh parsley or dill.

As some of my main course recipes throughout the book can be metamorphosed into appetizers, they will be listed below for easy access.

NUTRILICIOUS MENU SUGGESTIONS

NEW-TRILICIOUS FAMILY MEALTIME TOGETHERNESS

In the long-ago 20th century, some families were called to dinner in the dining room by a uniformed black-clad, white-aproned maid, ringing a crystal bell with a silver handle, while other families would crowd around the Melmac-coated kitchen table to eat unquestionably whatever mother had prepared. In the 21st century, the well-heeled-and-stiletto-heeled mother announces dinner to her Pottery-Barn kids in the following way: "Kids, get in the car, Daddy's waiting at the restaurant!"

But there are other mealtime options for the stay-at-home family: "Kids, come down from the ceiling, your pizza and chips have arrived! Someone get the Coke and the blue ketchup from the fridge and don't forget your *Ritalin*!"

Before I will share with you my own menu suggestions, I want to treat you to a menu that I encountered a while ago at a social function in a fancy hall; and it is verbatim:

APPETIZERS
Herb Crusted Pan Seared Duck Breast resting atop a Grilled Mission Fig
and Drizzled with an Aged Balsamic Syrup

~

Young Baby Greens wrapped in a Cucumber Diaper with Wild Field Mushrooms,
Candied Almonds and a Roasted Garlic Dressing

~

Slow Roasted Butternut Squash Soup topped with Cinnamon, Nutmeg,
Crème Fraiche (*pareve*) and Drizzled with Chive Oil

INTERMEZZO
Mango Sorbet

ENTRÉE
Pecan Crusted Double Lamb Chop served with a Port Wine Reduction
~or~
Cedar Plank Roasted Black Cod served with a Maple Reduction
Accompanied by a Jerusalem Artichoke Mash, Roasted Fingerling Potatoes
and an assortment of Fine French Green and Yellow Beans and Mini Zucchinis

DESSERT
Poached Miniature Forelle Pears with Riesling Ice Wine Syrup and Forest Berry Compote
Coffee and Tea
Sweet Table

If this is the kind of menu you enjoy eating, please skip the next few pages; I have no reductions and no cucumber diapers to offer, or go read one of my stories.

BREAKFAST

1 Beta Bunny-Hopping Cocktail, with Dr. Rosenthal's Nuts 'n' Seeds Mix, stirred in.
Steel Cut Oats-Quinoa Cereal
Coddled Egg

2 Top 'O' the Morn' Cocktail - Rise 'N' Shine
A plate of any sliced fruit of your choice, sprinkled with Nutty-Edith Crunch.
A handful of lettuce leaves

3 Miso Soup for One
Oat Flakes - Millet Breakfast

4 High Octane Punch - Raw Green Power
Blueberry Muffin

SUMMER LUNCH

1 Summer Salad Supreme
Tofony Scrambled Eggs
Whole meal brown rice cakes or whole meal crackers.

2 Chilled Vivaldi Soup
Corny Egg Salad with whole meal bread, whole meal crackers or brown rice cakes.

WINTER LUNCH

1 Dillicious Carrot Salad
Zucchini-Tomato Pizzetta

2 Cleopatra Salad
Basic Winter Veggie Stew on toasted or steamed whole meal bread

SUMMER SUPPER

1 Herbed Soup Carotene, chilled
Beyond the Rainbow Salad
Short-Shrift Risotto
Steamed Broccoli
Pinto Bean Salad

2 Simply Yam Soup
Minced Fish Patties Baked
Steamed Celery
Kale at Its Saucy Best
Baked 'N' Broiled Potatoes

WINTER SUPPER

1
Lentil-Quinoa Soup
Piquant Chickpea Salad
Millet Stew à la Shangri La
Can't Be Beet Roasted Beets

2
Velvety Zucchini Soup
Colour-Me-Purple Salad
Lima Bean Casserole
Steamed and Glazed Greens
Spiced Quinoa

FRIDAY NIGHT MEAL

1
Steamed Asparagus as an Appetizer
Whole Vegetable Soup with Angel Hair Pasta
A Special Occasion Salad
Mashed Potatoes with a Difference
Creamed Mushroom Sauce without the Cream
Fish of your choice
Lightly steamed broccoli and cauliflower florets, served cold on a platter,
garnished with 30 - Second Nayomaise.
Spicy Glazed Pears, topped with Strawberry Ambrosia and Nutty-Edith Crunch
Healthy Chocolate Cookies

2
Piquant Spinach Pâté
Spicy Red Lentil-Yam Soup
A big bowl of green salad
Rice-Shiitake Casserole with Greens
Yam Latkes
Pineapple-Strawberry Mousse
Chocolate Cake with a Difference

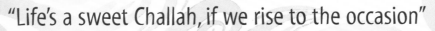

"Life's a sweet Challah, if we rise to the occasion"
- Chani Perman

SHABBOS LUNCH (SUMMER)

1
Savoury Devilled Eggs
Fruit Soup
Celery-Celeriac Salad
Piquant Fish Salad
Rainbow Couscous
Rice Dream Non Dairy Frozen Dessert
Mini Linzer Cookies

SHABBOS LUNCH (WINTER)

1. Chopped Liver but Not Liver
   Barley Bean Cholent Soup
   Beetiful Salad
   Rice 'n' Millet Patties
   Tutti-Frutti Apple Kugel

YOM TOV MEAL

1. Mushroom Pâté
   Simply Pea Soup
   Fresh 'n' Frooty Spinach Salad
   Potato Knishes with a Difference
   Tofu Cacciatore
   Saucy Tutti-Frutti Salad
   Apple-Carrot Cake

2. Zucchini-Tomato Sauce over Challah slices
   Naomi's Hodge-Podge Barley Soup
   Yam-Prune Casserole
   Risotto-Verde with Chickpeas
   Cauliquettes
   A green salad
   European Apple Torte

A SEDER MEAL

1. Piquant Fish Salad
   Whole Vegetable Soup with Floating
   Soup Clouds
   Matzo-Veggie Kugel
   Fried Cauliflower
   Yummy-Baked Yam Cubes
   Sweet Simplicity Ruby-Red Applesauce

A PESACH LUNCHEON

1. Mushroom Pâté
   Whole Vegetable Soup, pureed
   Minced Fish Patties Baked (omit the
   sesame seeds)
   Mystery Latkes
   Steamed Broccoli
   Pineapple-Strawberry Mousse

A SPECIAL OCCASION BUFFET

1. Fresh 'n' Frooty Spinach Salad
   Peasful Hummus
   Herring Salad
   Mini Zucchini Patties
   Suzanne's Noodle Bake
   Piquant Chickpea Salad
   Miniature Trifles
   Chocolate Cake with a Difference
   Mini Linzer Cookies

DESERT THE DESSERT

Try to eat your dessert in between your meals, and find out how much lighter your stomach will feel. Or, putting it another way, try to wait a few hours after a regular meal before partaking of a fruit or sweet goodies. This is the most health-promoting way to avoid what is generally called acid indigestion. And, as I need to explain, acid indigestion leads to fermentation, which leads to putrefaction (literally "rotting"). Such intoxication is the first step in building disease on an internal level. Please see **Food Combining Chart** (page 251).

PESACH WITHOUT PANIC

There is a growing body of evidence that you can have Pesach (the Holiday of Passover) without panic, if you fit into the following categories:

1. You choose to make Pesach at home because you are a work horse and don't need more than 3 hours of sleep at night.
2. You can't wait to have all the family around your table on Seder night, including 3rd cousins and their errant offspring, plus the ones that went "off the Derech" (fell off the wagon) but love matzos and the concept of freedom.
3. Your parents always stayed home so there's nothing to talk about.
4. Nobody invites you to join them to celebrate Pesach together.
5. You like neither hotels nor their humongous dinner portions.
6. You do not like spending every Yomtov meal in a common dining hall with crabby, cranky kids all around you, which are not your own.
7. You are the casual type and do not like to dress up, and you do not have the wardrobe to change 3/7 (three times a day for seven days).
8. You do not like cruises.
9. There is no sugar daddy, father or father-in-law in your family who is willing or able to dish out what is needed to have a Pesach-away-from-home, whether floating on the sea, in the freezing mountains of Switzerland or Hungary or, for the ultimate experience, in a luxury hotel in Jerusalem.

FOR THE STAY - AT - HOME CROWD:

You will find below a list of recipes that you can use on Pesach (Passover). However, there are many more recipes in this book which are not listed here that can easily be adapted to make them Pesach-dick by substituting certain ingredients or even eliminating some; however, I make no claim and take no blame for the end results.

CORRECT FOOD COMBINING FOR MONOTROPHIC MEALS

One Food at a Meal is the Ideal

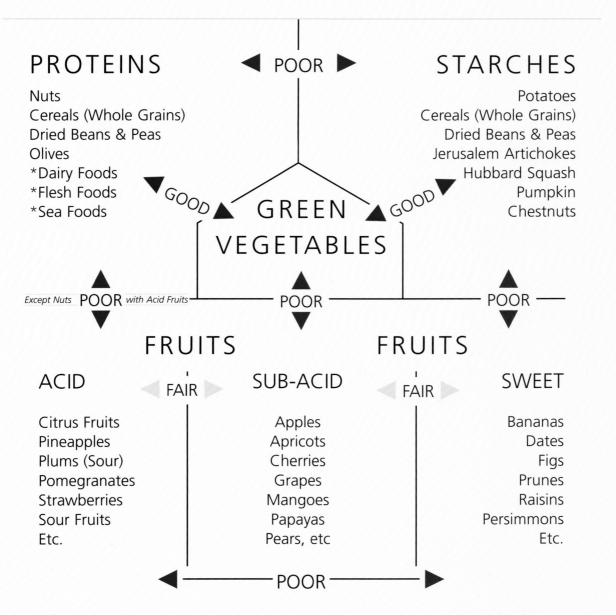

PROTEINS ◀ POOR ▶ STARCHES

PROTEINS
Nuts
Cereals (Whole Grains)
Dried Beans & Peas
Olives
*Dairy Foods
*Flesh Foods
*Sea Foods

STARCHES
Potatoes
Cereals (Whole Grains)
Dried Beans & Peas
Jerusalem Artichokes
Hubbard Squash
Pumpkin
Chestnuts

GOOD ▲ **GREEN VEGETABLES** ▲ GOOD

Except Nuts **POOR** with Acid Fruits — POOR — **POOR**

FRUITS — **FRUITS**

ACID ◀ FAIR ▶ **SUB-ACID** ◀ FAIR ▶ **SWEET**

ACID	SUB-ACID	SWEET
Citrus Fruits	Apples	Bananas
Pineapples	Apricots	Dates
Plums (Sour)	Cherries	Figs
Pomegranates	Grapes	Prunes
Strawberries	Mangoes	Raisins
Sour Fruits	Papayas	Persimmons
Etc.	Pears, etc	Etc.

◀ POOR ▶

AVOCADO - COMBINES WELL WITH ALL FOODS EXCEPT PROTEINS AND MELONS

TOMATOES - MAY BE TAKEN WITH NON-STARCHY VEGETABLES AND PROTEIN

MELONS - EAT THEM ALONE OR LEAVE THEM ALONE

* *THESE SUBSTANCES NOT RECOMMENDED BUT INCLUDED FOR CLARITY*

INDEX

Who's Who in 'NUTRILICIOUS':

BIBLIOGRAPHY

Bach, Edward M.D. *The Bach Flower Remedies including Heal Thyself by Bach; The Twelve Healers by Bach; and The Bach Remedies Repertory* by F.J. Wheeler, M.D. New Canaan, Connecticut: Keats Publishing, Inc. 1979.

Baker, Elizabeth and Dr. Elton. *The UNcook Book, Raw Food Adventures to a New Health High*. Buena Vista, Colorado: Communication Creativity, 1980.

Barnard, Neil M.D. *Turn Off the Fat Genes, The Revolutionary Guide to Losing Weight*. New York, NY: Three Rivers Press, 2001.

Burroughs, Stanley. *The Master Cleanser with Special Needs and Problems.* Burroughs Books, Reno NV; 1973,1993.

Campbell, T. Colin PhD. *The China Study : The Most Comprehensive Study of Nutrition Ever Conducted and the Startling Implications for Diet, Weight Loss and Long-Term Health*. Dallas, TX: BenBella Books, 2004.

Chapman, J.B. M.D, *Dr. Schuessler's BIOCHEMISTRY*, Pomeroy, WA: Health Research Books, 1962.

Chopra, Deepak M.D. *Perfect Health, The Complete Mind/Body Guide*. New York NY: Harmony Books, a division of Crown Publishers, Inc., 1991.

Colbin, Annemarie. *Food and Healing, How what you eat determines your health, your well-being, and the quality of your life*. New York, NY: Ballantine Books, a division of Random House Inc., 1986

Cousins, Norman. *Anatomy of an Illness as Perceived by the Patient*. New York, NY: Bantam Books, 1981.

Diamond, John M.D. *Your Body Doesn't Lie, A New Simple Test measures Impacts Upon Your Life Energy*. New York, NY: Warner Books Edition, 1979.

Dufty, William. *Sugar Blues.* New York, NY: Warner Books, 1975.

Erasumus, Udo. *Fats and Oils, The Complete Guide to Fats and Oils in Health and Nutrition*. Burnaby, Canada: Alive Books, 1986.

Esser, William L. *Dictionary of Man's Foods*. Chicago, IL: Natural Hygiene Press, 1972.

Falk, Rabbi E. *Halachic Guide to the Inspection of Fruits and Vegetables for Insects*. Gateshead, England: 1985.

Furman, Joel MD. *Fasting and Eating for Health, a Medical Doctor's Program for Conquering Disease*. New York, NY: St. Martin's Griffin Press, 1995.

Fuhrman, Joel M.D. *Eat To Live, The Revolutionary Formula for Fast and Sustained Weight Loss*. United States of America: Little, Brown and Company, 2003.

Gagné, Steve. *Energetics of Food, Encounters with your Most Intimate Relationship*. Santa Fe, NM: Spiral Sciences, 1990.

Gibbs Ostmann, Barbara and Baker, Jane L. *The Recipe Writer's Handbook*. New York, NY: John Wiley and Sons, Inc., 2001

Habgood, Jackie. *Get Well With the Hay Diet, Food Combining and Good Health*. London, UK: Souvenir Press Ltd, 1999.

Herbst, Sharon Tyler. *Food Lover's Companion, Comprehensive Definitions of over 4000 Food, Wine and Culinary Terms*. Hauppauge, NY: Barron's Educational Series, Inc., 1995.

Jensen, Dr. Bernard. *Foods That Heal, A Guide to Understanding and Using the Healing Powers of Natural Foods*. New York, NY: Avery Publishing Group, Inc., 1988.

McDougall, John A. M.D. and McDougall, Mary A. *The McDougall Plan*. Piscataway, NJ: New Century Publishers, Inc., 1983.

McDougall, John A. M.D. *A Challenging Second Opinion*. Piscataway, NJ: New Century Publishers, Inc., 1985.

Mendelsohn, Robert S. M.D. *Confessions of a Medical Heretic*. Chicago, IL: Contemporary Books, Inc., 1979.

Miller, Saul and Miller, JoAnne. *Food for Thought, A New Look At Food and Behaviour*. Englewood, NJ: Prentice Hall Press, a division of Simon and Shuster, Inc., 1979.

Mindell, Earl. *Vitamin Bible*. New York, NY: Warner Books, Inc., 1985.

Nussbaum, Elaine. *Recovery from Cancer*. New York, NY: Avery Publishing Group, Inc., 1992.

Reed, Barbara PhD, with Knickelbine, Scott and Knickelbine, Mark. *Food, Teens and Behaviour*. Manitowoc, WI: Natural Press, 1983.

Reed-Stitt, Barbara. *Food and Behaviour, a Natural Connection*. Manitowoc, WI: Natural Press, 1997.

Robbins, John. *Diet for a New America: How Your Food Choices Affect Your Health, Happiness and the Future of Life on Earth*. Tiburon, CA: H J Kramer Inc, 1987.

Sattilaro, Anthony J. M.D. with Monte, Tom. *Recalled By Life*. New York, NY: Avon Books, 1982.

Schneider, Susan. *Eating as Tikun*. Jerusalem, Israel: A Still Small Voice, 1996.

Shelton, Herbert M. *Fasting Can Save Your Life*. Bridgeport, CT: Natural Hygiene Press, 1964.

The OU Guide to Preparing Fruits and Vegetables. New York, NY: The Orthodox Union, 2004.

Tilden, John H. M.D. *Toxemia The Basic Cause of Disease*. Bridgeport, CT: Natural Hygiene Press, 1982.

Trop, Jack Dunn. *You DON'T Have to Be Sick!* New York, NY: Julian Press, 1961.

Turner, Kristina. *The Self-Healing Cookbook*. Grass Valley, CA: Earthtones Press, 1987.

HELPFUL HINTS:
1. Information and books about Dr. Bach's self-healing remedies can be ordered through Alypsis Inc. at 1-800-375-6222, (Peterborough, Ontario) or email to cgalypsis@nexicom.net.
2. If you are interested in purchasing Dr. Chapman's book, "Dr. Schuessler's *BIOCHEMISTRY*", which is a self-help book for self-healing, please call Health Research Books directly at 509-843-2385 or order online at www.healthresearchbooks.com, or write to Health Research Books P.O. Box 850 Pomeroy, WA 99347.

NUTRILICIOUS AFTERTHOUGHTS

My graphic designer just gave me another empty page to fill - how lucky can you get! Just in case you didn't have enough of me yet, here's more stuff and you are welcome to read on. On the other hand, if you've had it with me, don't worry about it; just do your own thing, or read again one of my stories, or eat some bitter chocolate (just a bite not a slab!) or turn to the last page and pray!

Avoid Sugar! (please read or re-read the sugar poem on page…!)

Avoid Salt! (sodium chloride), also known as "The Forgotten Killer". Too much of it can ruin your kidneys and also causes high blood pressure. Instead of iodized table salt, use sea salt sparingly, where the sodium content is balanced with various trace minerals for better absorption into the body. Sea salt has the same consistency as our blood.

Avoid Charred Food! also known as barbequed. The black, burnt part is carcinogenic.

Avoid Heavily and Deep-Fried Food! Most oils when heated become carcinogenic to some degree.

Avoid Cheese! as it may put phlegm on your chest with very unhealthy and unwanted consequences. I mean all cheeses: fresh or aged, soft or hard, plain or processed, sliced or grated, spreadable or full of holes, snow white, yellow or orange, striped, checkered or speckled, grilled, melted and oozing, smoked or lasagnaed, laced with veggies or herbs, smelly or deodorized. Please note the hechsher on your cheese is a kashrus (kosher) certificate; it is not a health certificate!

About Cookware: Acquaint yourselves with the facts about which cookware is best to use and which the least. More and more people nowadays try to consume more health-promoting food. But what is not so commonly known or understood is the damage that can be done when we choose cookware that is cheap in price and inferior in quality. The best cookware to use, as far as I am concerned, is cast iron, coated with enamel. If used properly, the enamel will never chip. It is heavier than other cookware, but the fact that the food cooked in it tastes so much better than cooked in any other cookware makes up for its extra weight. It cleans splendidly, especially when soaking is needed for a while. This cookware is quite expensive, but worth it because of its long-term durability, its ease of use and the fact that at all times it not only preserves the original flavours of the food that is cooked in it but also enhances it (that is, if you can afford to break your piggy bank for it). Cookware made from stainless steel is also good and practical as long as the material is of a heavy steel gauge.

And here is my final message from kitchen-land. The cookware that we should avoid at all costs is inexpensive, plastic-coated, 'non-stick' pots and frying pans. Granted they are light-weight, cheap and easy to use, I believe however they are extremely detrimental to our health in the long run.

It would be ideal if we could make our kitchens the focal point of our homes, and use them to nourish body, mind and soul for our families and/or ourselves. If you wish to embark on a better health journey, I will send you on your way with the ten "C"s and the seven "P"s from this book: Conviction, Commitment, Consistency, Calm, Caring, Cheerfulness, Creativity, Cleanliness and regular Campaigns for anti-Clutter. Planning, Preparedness, Perseverance, Patience, Playfulness, Pleasure, and Passion.

Prayer for Health

Master of the Universe: In Your compassion, grant us the physical strength, health and ability required to function effectively, and may we experience no illness or pain. Enable us to serve You in joy, contentment, and health. Save us from all evil, and prolong our days in goodness and our years in sweetness. Enrich our years and add to our days and years of service to You. Shield us in the shadow of Your wings, and spare us and all our family from any harsh or evil decree. May we be at rest and calm, vigorous, and fresh to serve and revere You.

CHIDA
(Rabbi Chaim Yosef David Azulai, Jerusalem, 1724-1806)

TEACH US TO COUNT OUR DAYS, THEN WE SHALL ACQUIRE A HEART OF WISDOM.

MAY THE PLEASANTNESS OF MY LORD, OUR G-D, BE UPON US - OUR HANDIWORK, ESTABLISH FOR US; OUR HANDIWORK, ESTABLISH IT.

PSALM 90